Praise for
Autism in the Family

"*Autism in the Family* presents a father's perspective on coping with a child who has severe autism. Fathers often have difficulty expressing their feelings and this book should be required reading for all fathers who have a child with a disability."
—Temple Grandin, author, *Thinking in Pictures*

"A comprehensive view of autism across the lifespan . . . Naseef encourages readers to understand and accept those with ASD, and to ultimately connect, adapt, cope, hope, and flourish."
—Emily Iland, M.A., award-winning author, educator, parent, and advocate; President of the Autism Society of Los Angeles

"A powerful exploration of the impact autism has on the entire family . . . Naseef's personal story and pictures are compelling and add depth and honesty to the subject matter. Highly recommended."
—James May, M.A., M.Ed. L.M.H.C., (retired) Director, National Father's Network

"Rarely does a book deliver both breadth and depth. In a single volume, you can explore the breadth of the full family lifespan and the depth of every family relationship—parental, marital, sibling, and extended family. Excellent investment."
—Ann Turnbull, Ed.D., Distinguished Professor, Special Education; Director, Beach Center on Disability, University of Kansas

"Rarely does an author speak to the darkest moments while so eloquently providing hope and reason to celebrate. Dr. Naseef shows us how to connect with our children where they are. He encourages us through his stories and experiences that together we can live an abundantly beautiful new life with our children."
—Kent Potter, founder of AutismSpot.com and father of a son with autism

"I literally laughed and cried . . . This is one of the most honest books I have ever read on the subject. It is direct, warm, compelling, and ever so helpful."
—Paula Kluth, Ph.D., author of *You're Going to Love This Kid!: Teaching Students with Autism in the Inclusive Classroom*

"Every family who receives a diagnosis of autism for their child should be given this book with a hot cup of tea and a warm blanket. *Autism in the Family* is an indispensable read, bound to be read again and again throughout a child's life."
—Shana Nichols, Ph.D., Owner/Director of ASPIRE Centre for Learning and Development and author of *Girls Growing Up on the Autism Spectrum*

"Insightful, accurate and very personal . . . should be helpful to any parent whose journey includes a child with autism. Naseef has provided important information in a caring and compassionate manner."
—Kenneth Thurman, Ph.D., Professor of Special Education, Temple University

D0868909

"Eloquently translate[s] the latest research into terms understandable to all . . . the author walks you through the field of autism spectrum disorders in a way that is unmatched. I highly recommend it!"

—V. Mark Durand, Ph.D., coeditor, *Journal of Positive Behavior Interventions;*
University of South Florida St. Petersburg

"Helps families move beyond grief and into acceptance where the new normal lives. From managing stress and toilet training to adulthood, Dr. Naseef guides you along this complex and difficult journey, shedding guilt and anxiety as you go, until you find yourself in a place where you can celebrate your unique child and all the wonderful things he or she is."

—Nancy Bernotaitis, parent to an adolescent with autism
and moderator for Moms Fighting Autism

"Robert Naseef has the highly valuable ability to combine personal experience with clinical knowledge in a way that creates hope, strength and peace for parents and families of individuals with an autism spectrum disorder."

—Maggi Sullivan, Autism Services Manager, Ontario ARC

"An excellent resource for families and professionals alike. I am moved and inspired by the stories of Naseef and others that are woven in, and will be sharing this [book] with students, families and colleagues!"

—Helen McCabe, Ph.D., Associate Professor, Hobart and William Smith Colleges

"Will enable parents, family members, and professionals to appreciate what they can and cannot do to address the lifelong challenges of loving and caring for a child or adult on the autism spectrum."

—Stanley D. Klein, Ph.D., co-founder and former Editor in Chief,
Exceptional Parent magazine; coeditor, *Reflections from a Different Journey:*
What Adults with Disabilities Wish All Parents Knew

"Beautifully written by Dr. Naseef, both a parent and professional, *Autism in the Family* explores the depths of the experience of autism, with practical guidance for a true holistic approach that is essential reading for family members and professionals."

—Barry M. Prizant, Ph.D., CCC-SLP, Adjunct Professor,
Center for the Study of Human Development, Brown University;
Director, Childhood Communication Services, Cranston, RI

"Dr. Naseef genuinely shares his family's journey with autism. He also provides valuable information for all families with children who have autism to understand that although our situations are as different as our children, we must make this journey together."

—Joe Villalobos, father of a son with autism and
special education teacher of children with autism

"Provides insight and guidance for maintaining a balanced marriage and family when a child with special needs is part of the family. For families just receiving a diagnosis to families beginning the journey through adolescence, Dr. Naseef offers wisdom and hope."

—Bradford Hulcher, Executive Director, Autism Society, Central VA

"Combining the skills of an experienced therapist, the talents of an inspired teacher, and the courage to share the wisdom gained from often painful personal experience, Dr. Naseef is the consummate advocate not only for the child but also for the entire family."

—Lawrence W. Brown, M.D., Associate Professor of Neurology and Pediatrics; Director, Pediatric Neuropsychiatry Program, Children's Hospital of Philadelphia

"A wonderful resource . . . It recognizes the fact that having a child diagnosed with autism is indeed life-changing but it can take you on a powerful journey of discovery about yourself and those around you. I wish I had had this book to read as I was raising my own (now adult) child with autism."

—Judy Swett, Early Childhood Coordinator, PACER Center

"Touching, caring, and compassionate . . . offers readers reasoned and reasonable guidance to negotiate parents' greatest challenges in raising a child with serious disabilities and making very difficult choices as [the child] reaches adulthood."

—Sam Goldstein, Ph.D., coauthor,
Raising Resilient Children with Autism Spectrum Disorder

"This book is one of the best for new parents . . . Dr. Naseef's book reflects his dedication to learn more about his son; teach him; face stress, denial, and anger; and reach acceptance."

—Dr. Samire Al-Saad, Founder & Director of Kuwait Center for Autism, Vice President of World Autism Organisation

"Very comprehensive, yet very readable . . . provides thoughtful ideas both on how to address specific challenges and on the bigger picture of caring for the whole family's emotional health during the journey."

—Lars Perner, Ph.D., University of Southern California

Autism in the Family
Caring and Coping Together

by

Robert A. Naseef, Ph.D.
Alternative Choices
Philadelphia, Pennsylvania

Baltimore • London • Sydney

Paul H. Brookes Publishing Co.
Post Office Box 10624
Baltimore, Maryland 21285–0624
USA

www.brookespublishing.com

Copyright © 2013 by Paul H. Brookes Publishing Co., Inc.
All rights reserved.

"Paul H. Brookes Publishing Co." is a registered trademark of
Paul H. Brookes Publishing Co., Inc.

Typeset by Laserwords Private Limited, Chennai, Tamil Nadu, India.
Manufactured in the United States of America by
Sheridan Books, Inc., Chelsea, Michigan.

The quote on page 110 by Elizabeth McGarry from the Alternative Choices blog is used with permission.

Extracts from Ariel, C. & Naseef, R. (2006). *Voices from the Spectrum: Parents, Grandparents, Siblings, People with Autism, and Professionals Share Their Wisdom,* Jessica Kingsley Publishers, London & Philadelphia. Reprinted by permission.

Library of Congress Cataloging-in-Publication Data

Naseef, Robert A.
  Autism in the family : caring and coping together/by Robert A. Naseef, Ph.D., Philadelphia, Pennsylvania.
    pages   cm.
  Includes bibliographical references and index.
  ISBN 978-1-59857-241-4
  ISBN 1-59857-241-5
  1. Autistic children—Family relationships. 2. Father and child. I. Title.
  RJ506.A9N28 2013
  618.92'85882—dc23

                                        2012036794

British Library Cataloguing in Publication data are available from the British Library.

2016   2015   2014   2013   2012

10   9   8   7   6   5   4   3   2   1

616.85882
Nas

Contents

GERMANTOWN COMMUNITY LIBRARY
GERMANTOWN WI 53022

About the Author

Robert A. Naseef, Ph.D., Alternative Choices, 319 Vine Street, Unit 110, Philadelphia, Pennsylvania 19106

Robert Naseef is a partner in an independent psychology practice with his wife, Cindy N. Ariel, Ph.D., who is also a psychologist. His first book, *Special Children, Challenged Parents: The Struggles and Rewards of Parenting a Child with a Disability,* has received international recognition. He has lectured internationally and appeared on radio and television. He is the coeditor of *Voices from the Spectrum: Parents, Grandparents, Siblings, People with Autism, and Professionals Share Their Wisdom* (2006). *Living Along the Autism Spectrum* (2009) is a DVD which features him along with Stephen Shore and Dan Gottlieb.

Robert is a native of Philadelphia and a graduate of Temple University. He received his doctoral degree from the Department of Psychological Studies in Education. He holds clinical privileges in psychology at Penn Behavioral Health, part of the University of Pennsylvania Healthcare System. Robert also has a broad background of experience in education and has consulted and served on several boards of schools and nonprofit organizations.

As the father of an adult child with autism, Robert's specialty is working with families of children with autism and other special needs. Through his experiences as a parent and as a professional, Robert relates well to both audiences and is a sought after speaker around the country. His works have been published in scholarly journals and other publications. He has a special interest and expertise in the psychology of men and fatherhood.

In 2008, Robert was honored by Variety the Children's Charity for his outstanding contributions over the past 20 years to the autism community. Robert can be contacted at RNaseef@alternativechoices.com or through the web site www.alternativechoices.com, and his blogs can be found on the Alternative Choices Facebook page. He welcomes reactions to this book and is available to make presentations at conferences and in-service trainings.

Foreword

When I was approached to write the foreword for *Autism in the Family: Caring and Coping Together*, I almost deferred as it seemed a daunting prospect. The foreword helps to set the tone and is a window into a book, and I was not sure I was up to writing it. When I started reading the chapters, however, I was entranced and knew my task would be easier than I thought.

I have known Robert Naseef for almost 15 years and met him when we both served on an advisory committee for an early intervention program in Philadelphia County. Meeting Robert was the best reward for the time I subsequently invested on that advisory board. At that time, I had just started to subspecialize in the care of children with autism spectrum disorders. I am a pediatrician with certification in neurodevelopmental disabilities, and over time, I have focused on the care of children with different disabilities—first learning disorders, later attention-deficit/hyperactivity disorders, then developmental delay. By the mid-1990s I found my passion and great interest in the "puzzle" of autism and the complex care of children and families touched by autism. When I joined the advisory board, I had developed expertise in diagnosis and management of children and families affected by autism, but was not as aware of community resources and the profound impact living with an autistic child has on family members. My interactions with Robert have filled in many of those gaps.

Over the years I have had numerous contacts with him. He has spoken at the Children's Hospital of Philadelphia to our group of developmental/behavioral pediatricians and fellows, nurse practitioners, nurses, and social workers about topics affecting families and therapeutic options. I have referred families to his care through Alternative Choices and have uniformly received rave reviews from families about the care he and Dr. Cindy Ariel have provided. I am impressed by his calm demeanor, thoughtful discussions, and the profound impact he has on families with children who have autism spectrum disorders. The best (and true) compliment I have paid to him is when I have described him to others; I tell people I feel calmer just by speaking with him.

This book reads as if you have the privilege and pleasure of spending hours talking to Robert about his life experiences and the profound impact his son Tariq has had and continues to have on his and his family's life. It is written not just for families but for parents, siblings, therapists, teachers, the neighborhood storekeeper, and anyone families may encounter, giving a window into their soul of suffering. This book will be an important tool in my clinical arsenal to support families.

Susan E. Levy, M.D.
Center for Autism Research
Philadelphia, PA

Preface

Cindy Ariel

Robert Naseef and I met on a college campus where we both worked for several years. We were sitting in an office discussing an upcoming presentation when the telephone rang. Robert glanced at the caller ID, looked at me apologetically, and said, "This is one call I have to answer." I heard the brief one-sided conversation as he assured the preschool administrator that he would come to pick up his son and begin looking for new options . . . again. "They just can't deal with him there," he said, annoyed, as he hung up the telephone and started gathering his belongings to leave work early.

Over the next few months, Robert moved out of his house and into a high-rise apartment. We gradually became friends, and he invited me for dinner one weekend when his children were there. What a revelation! His son was in constant motion, and most of it was destructive. He was eating toothpaste, emptying drawers, playing with toilet water, and constantly knocking pictures off the wall. Cheerios were everywhere. His little sister was either crying about the most recent destruction he had just caused to her personal possessions or reporting his latest transgression in the home. "Dad, Tariq's standing on the table pulling down the lights," or "He's tearing the papers in your briefcase again," or "He's pulling down his pants and peeing on the wall."

When I first met Tariq in 1985, he was 5 years old and totally adorable. He was giggly and affectionate and had lots of energy. He also did not talk . . . at all. Robert let me know that Tariq used to have words, and then he lost them. He was sure that if only Tariq would talk, he would be just like the other kids, and Robert was determined to help his son regain his language.

Robert told me how an evaluation of Tariq the previous year concluded that he had a pervasive developmental delay and suggested he had some autistic-like behaviors. The experts recommended that he take Tariq to the Center for Autistic Children (now the Center for Autism) in Philadelphia. When he shared the reports with me and described his subsequent horrifying visit to the school for children with autism his anger was palpable. Furiously, he let me know that those medical professionals could not possibly know his son and his potential; Tariq was just "going through a hard time and was delayed, that's all." We were dating when Robert announced, "If I have to live in the woods alone with my son for the rest of my life, I will do that."

Robert worked constantly to offer Tariq love, encouragement, and new skills. He visited many schools in his quest to find one that could handle his son and help him talk again. For one of his vacations, Robert spent a week and a small fortune with one of Tariq's primary caregivers at the Option Institute to learn to cure him. Tariq was on a strict special diet, took vitamins and more vitamins, and went to all kinds of doctors. He even visited a few alternative professionals who promised healing through head measurements, skin exams, or his aura.

At the time, I had a master's degree and some work experience in the fields of psychology and special education. I volunteered with children, including some with autism, and had spent 5 years working with adults with developmental delays. I was also living with a friend who had much more experience in special education than I did. Together we discussed how much Tariq's behavior looked like autism and we developed behavior plans that I helped Robert implement in his home. "You still have to tell him what this really looks like," my friend implored me. "His boy needs services, and maybe he'll listen to you."

The next weekend, I sat close to Robert on his big comfy chair and told him there was something important we needed to talk about, even though doing so might end our relationship. I had heard him rail enough against the experts who suggested autistic-like behavior to know there was a possibility I may now become the enemy. He braced himself for the bomb I was about to drop: in this case, the A-bomb. "I'm pretty sure Tariq has autism," I began. The room was silent as Robert stared at me through quiet, tearful eyes. I talked and he listened, and sometimes he asked questions. In that moment, he allowed the denial of what he knew all along to break away towards a new understanding and new dreams for his life and child.

Thus began a long journey of autism awareness, discovery, and research. Shortly after our conversation Robert made another appointment with the Center for Autistic Children, and now he had a whole different take on everything about it. He saw that the people there both loved and understood his son. Tariq attended there for many years, and Robert came to love the center's founder and chief psychiatrist. Meanwhile, he continued learning about autism. His research for his doctoral dissertation focused on helping families of children with special needs. He wanted to help others, and in the process he was helping himself. Helping families with special needs became his passion, and he has been doing this as a psychologist for more than 20 years now. There is a lot to be learned from the knowledge and experience that grew out of this father's unconditional love. This book clearly shows how far Robert has come, as both a parent and a professional, in understanding, living with, and treating autism. He is also still my closest friend.

Acknowledgments

I loved reading as a young child. Books were magical to me, but I never dreamed I would write a book—not until years after my son was diagnosed with autism. Then I had a story that I had to tell. I dreamed of my story on the shelves of libraries and bookstores. It touches my heart that it was published and that people read my words and often find comfort and hope.

My story and this book would not have been possible without family. First of all, I am blessed to have my wife Cindy, my best friend and professional partner of over 25 years and Tariq's stepmother, who has weathered the storms of his autism with me and sustained me with her love. She knows what I am trying to say and helps me shape it for others to understand. Likewise, I am filled with awe and inspired by our daughters, Kara and Zoë, who have brought so much light into my daily life. I am also grateful to the family I was born into.

I am particularly indebted to people from the Northwest Child Development Center, the Center for Autism, the Devereux Foundation, KenCrest, Helping Hands, and all the staff from those agencies that have served Tariq and kept him safe and happy. Brookes Publishing became the ideal home for this book after Carol Publishing went into bankruptcy only 2 years after the first edition. In this book, I now have a broader scope of experience through my son's adulthood and decades more knowledge from my professional work, other practitioners, researchers, families, and especially people with autism. The Brookes team has been outstanding in their professionalism and support, including Johanna Cantler, Steve Plocher, Lisa Koepenick, Rebecca Lazo, Heather Shrestha, Melanie Allred, and Beth Ciha. Finally, with gratitude to all the courageous and loving families I have met on this journey, you inform and teach me about what it means to be a family.

Prologue: A Letter to My Son

Dear Tariq,

I will never forget the night you were born. It was magical. After a long labor, when you came out of your mother's belly, you seemed to look all around the delivery room, even before your body was completely out. I jumped from my position behind the delivery table and wound up beside the doctor—my knees wobbling, my heart pounding with excitement. The doctor, an older man who had delivered many babies, commented on how alert you looked.

Right away I could tell that your head was the same shape as mine. The skin on my face tightened as I beamed at you. I counted your fingers and your toes and breathed easier that everything was okay. The nurse cleaned you up while I watched eagerly and wrapped you in a soft flannel blanket. You looked so cute. You were a perfect newborn. I had dreamed of having a boy, and I love reliving these warm memories.

When the nurse put you in my arms, I felt a tingle of electricity through my whole body. You felt so soft and delicate to my fingertips. I cradled you next to my heart. Our eyes met and locked on to each other's for the first time. Your eyes looked so big and round. It was one of the most exciting moments of my life. You made me a father.

Ever since then, I have held a profound respect for every woman's special partnership in the miracle of life. I thought of my mother, who gave birth to eight healthy children. Through you, the wonder of life began to be revealed to me. Now I know what Khalil Gibran meant in

Holding Tariq for the first time in the delivery room.

The Prophet about how inextricably woven together our moments of joy and sorrow are, for sorrow opens our hearts to the experience of joy in everyday life.

You were born in the wee hours of November 29, 1979. Jimmy Carter was the president; American hostages were being held in Tehran. I saved the newspaper for you to read about what was happening in the world on the day you were born at the Medical College of Pennsylvania, formerly Women's Medical College, the first medical school for women in our country. That hospital is now closed, but there is a preschool for children with autism there.

When I left you and your mom in the hospital that night, I looked at the sky with its stars shining brightly. There were a few clouds, and a nearly full moon cast a warm glow over the earth. It was a perfect moment frozen in time, in my memory, and in my heart. The cool night air filled my lungs and refreshed me, and even though it was winter, it reminded me of the words of a poem by Robert Browning that I had learned in grade school:

The year's at the spring,
And day's at the morn;
Morning's at seven;
The hillside's dew-pearled;
The lark's on the wing:
The snail's on the thorn;
God's in his heaven—
All's right with the world.

Announcing your birth was exhilarating. You were the second grandchild and the first grandson my parents had. I remember my dad saying how lucky I was to have been present at your birth. He had never seen any of his children being born, and his reaction brought me closer to him, knowing the excitement he must have felt and his wish to have been more involved.

I wish you could read this someday, Tariq. I wish you could know what you have meant to me. I was crushed for a long time when I found out that you had autism and eventually realized that you would never read, or write, or carry on a conversation. Those feelings have subsided, and I have survived and started over.

I want you to know that you have never lost your place in my heart. I still save that yellowed newspaper from November 29, 1979. Some of my greatest joys and deepest sorrows have been in the moments you and I have shared. Your life is limited in many respects but priceless to me and to the world beyond us.

Pearl Buck had only one biological child, who had an intellectual disability. Buck wrote about her daughter in *The Child Who Never Grew*. The title reminds me of how you will always be a little boy inside. Buck concluded that we can learn as much from illness as from health, that disability can have as much meaning as ability and sometimes even more.

When I began writing *Special Children, Challenged Parents: The Struggles and Rewards of Raising a Child with a Disability* in 1989, I imagined it having quite a different ending. I wanted to change you, so that you could talk and do all of the things that I have dreamed of for you and me. I even hoped that someday you would read it and be grateful to me for my efforts to rescue you from autism. By the end of that writing when the book was published in 1996, I realized in my journaling the simplest and most profound truth—you had changed me. You had helped me become the man I needed to be.

Without speaking a word, you have taught the little boy in me to speak and remember what I once knew. In this way you are always with me. You have a range of emotions. You taught me to see them readily. When you feel good, you show interest and excitement. When you accomplish something you set out to do, you show pride. You have a refreshing sense of humor. When you are upset, you yell. When you are startled, you let me know by raising your eyebrows, opening your eyes wide, and opening your mouth. You flap when excited or upset or just because you feel like it.

I have learned how to tune into the signals I used to miss, living more in the present moment. You don't recognize danger, and you seldom sense fear, so I have to be extra vigilant. When you're in distress, you let people know it, although it's often hard to tell what's bothering you. Because you can't connect with others, we can only guess and use empathy to try to understand you. But what power lies there! Nonverbal people such as you teach us to look inside ourselves and to be patient with others.

Nature blessed me with intelligence and ability, but I was a shy child. Before you came, I did not understand my feelings. When someone would ask me how I felt, I usually went blank. I felt frustrated and inadequate when I could not answer.

I was unable to connect my thoughts and feelings. Now I know really well the shades and colors of my inner life—both positive and negative. You and your sisters have all revealed different treasures that have helped me be a better man and a better father. You have helped me translate our experiences together in a way that has made me more articulate and able to help others as a psychologist.

This new book includes what I have learned about family life and from my professional experiences with children and families—especially those with autism. I am continuing to share what you have meant to me—an unconditional love on the other side of sorrow. Life can be so full and rich amid all the difficulties.

You still hold my hand like a little boy. It is beyond words—a matter of heart and soul.

I love you,

Dad

References

Browning, R. (1896). Pippa passes, and other poetic dramas. Ann Arbor: University of Michigan Library.

Buck, P.S. (1992). *The child who never grew.* Bethesda, MD: Woodbine House.

Gibran, K. (1923). *The Prophet.* New York, NY: Alfred A. Knopf.

Naseef, R. (1996). *Special Children, Challenged Parents: The Struggles and Rewards of Raising a Child with a Disability.* Baltimore, MD: Paul H. Brookes Publishing Co.

To differently - abled, differently - minded,
and unique people of all ages and their families

My Story

> Everybody is a story . . . It is the way the
> wisdom gets passed along.
>
> RACHEL NAOMI REMEN, *KITCHEN TABLE*
> *WISDOM*

MORE THAN 30 YEARS AGO TARIQ SEEMED PERFECT. He was all that I had imagined him to be, with something new to discover every day. At 4 months old, for example, he began to lift up his head and look around. I took a picture that I still prize because it bears an amazing resemblance to an old picture of me.

A month or so later he began to crawl. It was so much fun to see and feel his excitement. There was a gleam in his eye as he motored at will around the house. Now it was necessary to keep him safe, such as by steering him away from the steps or the fireplace.

By his eighth month he could pull himself up to a standing position, beaming with pride. He would glance around smiling and planning his route to whatever looked like fun. A few weeks later he began to cruise, holding onto furniture and getting around upright whenever he could. I had fun holding his hands above his head and walking behind him.

Before long it was his first birthday, and his first baby steps came on that big day. I recall the look of apprehension and then the thrill of achievement on his face as he took those first awkward, wobbly steps. I was so proud of him. What an amazing accomplishment! I was cheering him on. I enjoy showing this photo of him at many of my public lectures.

Tariq raises his head for the first time.

Tariq takes his first steps on his birthday.

By 18 months he was just beginning to speak and had a small vocabulary. He had been meeting all of the developmental milestones. I imagined that before long he would play Little League baseball. I would beam with pride and cheer as he fielded a ball or swiftly ran the bases—a better version of me, who had played in right field from Little League through adult softball with limited skills. I would watch Tariq as my father had watched me. I imagined discussing social justice and sports with him as a young man. Our relationship would be close and warm. I would be patient when he needed or wanted it—a better version of my father.

At 18 months, in May 1981, Tariq was treated for an ear infection. By coincidence he was never the same again. He became frustrated and withdrawn. He cried a lot and did not sleep well at night. I worried, especially at night, when I was awake with him. My oldest daughter, who prefers privacy and does not want to be mentioned by name, had been born that same month. At first the pediatrician thought that Tariq could be having an emotional response to her birth. I hoped that the doctor was right, but I was scared.

Tariq stopped talking and stopped playing with the toys he had received for his birthday—such as the little workbench with its nuts and bolts and tools. My parents had given it to him because it was just like one I had had as a little boy. He began playing with a transparent rattle with brightly colored beads inside. He seemed fascinated by this toy and played with it for hours while ignoring virtually everything else around him, including his newborn sister. *This was the beginning of his falling in love with things and falling out of love with people.* It would not be until years later at the 2011 Autism Society of America Conference, that I would finally come to learn how

Tariq plays with the workbench from my parents.

this process had been documented through the research of Ami Klin, Ph.D., and his team at the Yale Child Study Center (Klin, Warren, Schultz, Volkmar, & Cohen, 2002). Children later diagnosed with autism begin life focusing their gaze on people and gradually shift from faces to things during the early months of life.

Meanwhile, when our daughter was born, I was thrilled. Life seemed complete, but that feeling did not last. I became tense and anxious, wondering if his mother or I had done anything to cause Tariq's condition. I kept telling myself that everything would be okay.

A rude awakening was imminent. The excitement from new accomplishments was gone. My sweet toddler was gone. He became very agitated and upset if the rattle was taken away. His life, which had been a great joy, became a worry that preoccupied me. I was glad to see him when I got home from work, but the fun was gone. He still liked being touched and cuddled, but he turned his face away. He preferred the rattle. I longed for Tariq to look into my eyes and speak.

When he was 2, I spent the summer with Tariq while on vacation from my teaching job. The pediatrician had said that he might just need time. I worked to get his attention and establish eye contact. I would put him on the swing and stand in front of him as I pushed him. I tried to catch his gaze for a second. He would turn eyes to the side. He was a master at avoiding all sorts of connection including eye contact.

It felt like a personal rejection. The situation was especially frustrating because I expected to be able to help him. At work, teaching remedial reading and writing in a support program, I could help college students with learning differences, but my efforts with my own son were fruitless. Eventually I learned to back off and make contact in different ways, but not until he was diagnosed with autism a few years later.

As his third birthday approached, it was clear that Tariq could not attend a typical preschool. His lack of speech indicated that he was far behind other children his age, but that fact was hard to face. His mom and I took him to a preschool that included children with special needs, but he did not even fit there because he could not sit still for more than a few seconds. The preschool's consulting psychologist thought he might be hearing impaired, because he was not responding to his name. On his advice I toured a school for children with hearing impairments. My insides shook as I worried that my boy would be walking around with two hearing aids.

I wondered what his life would be like. He would just be different, I told myself—just different. There were trips to numerous specialists and special schools and many sleepless nights waiting for test results and no answers to the mystery of why Tariq had stopped speaking.

A specialist found fluid in his ears that was blocking his hearing, and he was treated with medication. There was hope for a simple solution. Tests of his brainstem indicated that his ears worked, but it was impossible to tell whether he comprehended words. The fluid cleared up, but he still expressed himself by grunting, babbling, and crying. He constantly twisted and turned to get away. At night, I dreamed that the babbling would turn into words again.

Tariq was in an early intervention program by his third birthday. In the early 1980s, early intervention began at age 3 as opposed to at birth. He was the most difficult child in the school to manage. He required one-to-one attention at all times. He could not stay in his seat for more than a few seconds if left unattended. Whenever possible, I spent the day with him, helping his teacher. I kept asking his speech therapist why she was just playing with him and why he was not talking. She gave me a pamphlet from the Autism Society of America with stick figures illustrating the signs and symptoms of autism. The words and illustrations were a blur that I could not read.

Eventually Tariq was diagnosed with a pervasive developmental disorder. In 1984 autism was diagnosed in 12 out of every 10,000 children (Gillberg, Steffenberg, & Schaumann, 1991). The team of professionals that evaluated him at the hospital where he had been born used the words *autistic like* and *retarded* in their diagnosis. I was first numb and then livid. They seemed to have no hope for my son. How could I give up? Their words sliced through me like a knife. My head throbbed, and I thought it was going to explode.

The social worker broke the news with, "Hasn't anyone told you that your son is autistic?" What a way to tell a parent about autism!

I withdrew. It was painful to read that autism was a severely incapacitating and lifelong disability. It was hard to comprehend that my child's brain was so impaired. I was told that communicating with others or the outside world would be extremely difficult for Tariq.

I couldn't talk about it. I wanted to, but the words just stuck in my throat, especially the A word: *autism*. I couldn't get it out. Once in a while I would blurt out my worry that my son still was not talking, even though he was older than age 3. At night I cried and cried. There was no comfort. Professionals, relatives, and friends rarely knew what to say.

Like many other parents, I spared no expense in the quest to find a cure. We tried alternative therapies, megavitamins, and a wheat-free diet. The burden of the debts from these and other treatments was a reminder of my dreams for Tariq's recovery. My dreams died a slow death as I ran out of treatments to try. As I faced reality, I began to grasp that Tariq's condition was permanent.

Unfortunately I felt the most alone at home. To put it simply and kindly, the strain of Tariq's disability added to other stresses, which led to a divorce. After years of trying to go through it together, it was easier to try alone. As a single parent with joint custody, I faced a life that had changed permanently and profoundly—something I had not planned or allowed myself to imagine.

Vigilance was required every waking minute. Because Tariq rarely slept through the night, I was constantly exhausted. The sleep deprivation lasted for more than 7 years, and the feeling stayed in my body even longer. I never knew what would happen next. My son was in perpetual motion, and it was hard to know what you would find as you followed or chased him. The entire house had to be child-proofed. Even the refrigerator, drawers, and toilets had to be locked.

Because he knew no danger, there was a constant threat that Tariq would run into traffic, burn his hand, or step over the edge of the pool into the deep water. The only part of my dream for Tariq that came true was that he became a fast runner, but unfortunately this made for few relaxing moments for me.

Once he got out of my apartment in the middle of the night. I was terrified as I ran looking for him; my heart pounded so hard that I thought my chest would burst. I found him playing happily in the playground a few blocks and busy streets away, but my heart kept beating quickly. His death was the only thing that I could imagine being more difficult than his life with this diagnosis.

I decided to begin psychotherapy, and this helped me keep going. It was the best thing I could have done for myself. I came from a family that did not often express feelings, but this was a skill I needed now. My therapist helped me to express my feelings, but it was hard to make sense of them. I was being flooded and overwhelmed with emotion, and it felt crazy at times.

Why couldn't I calm down? Professionals constantly emphasized doing more for Tariq, but this was not helping me ease my guilt or find acceptance. It felt like a defect in me was keeping me from accepting my son as he was. Was I a bad person? Why wasn't love enough?

At that point, more than 25 years ago, my colleague and close friend Cindy showed me an article called "Handicapped Children and Their Families" in the then-current issue of the *Journal of Counseling & Development*. This article talked about the grief experienced by the parents of children with disabilities. It was written by Milton Seligman, Ph.D., of the University of Pittsburgh and also the parent of an adult child with a disability. As I read slowly, his article spoke to me.

Many disconnected feelings and thoughts began to make sense. When I completed the article, I leaned back in my desk chair; took a few slow, deep breaths; and realized, "So that is what Tariq's life is all about for me: I am a bereaved parent." *I diagnosed myself with grief.*

From that day onward, my life began to change for the better. I had a new lens through which to analyze my experience. This helped me learn to cope with the many problems that come with autism. It took time and help. I understood my thoughts and feelings better. In retrospect, I believe that at that time there was a general lack of support for parents of children with disabilities or understanding about the grief they experience. That lack still exists and motivates my professional work as a practicing psychologist, presenter, and author.

I struggled through some horribly dark moments, but I began to reclaim my life. The friend who showed me that article helped me by encouraging me to talk and by listening without judgment or expectation to everything I had to say. Cindy eventually became my girlfriend, and several years later we married. Life did indeed go on with new dreams.

I had entered a doctoral program in the Department of Psychological Studies in Education at Temple University before fully understanding that my son would have this disability for life. Because I was doing everything possible for Tariq, I knew in my heart that he would want me to pursue my own development. It was trying at times, but my professors and my boss at work were very supportive. There were things to look forward to once again—personally and professionally.

When my daughter learned to read, I was very thankful. Every time she learned a new word it let me know that her brain was normal. I cried tears of joy while observing her breaking the code and learning to read. It was unbelievably exciting to live through this period—not to mention a great relief that she could learn in the typical way.

I literally could breathe easier. Typical human development seemed like a miracle. My oldest daughter has a special talent in art and writing, and I was filled with pride and gratitude when she gave me a drawing or painting or showed me something she had written. I had learned that life is very fragile at times, and you never know when something might break your heart.

For my doctoral dissertation, I researched how families coped successfully with having a child with a disability. It was a way of focusing on resilience and finding balance. Besides my interest in knowing as much as possible for myself, I hoped that what I learned might be of use to others. I hoped to foster understanding and partnership between families and professionals.

This began happening after Tariq's ninth birthday as I spoke to groups of parents and professionals. I became effective at helping people connect and collaborate. By this time, Tariq's disability was so severe that he needed around-the-clock care and had to be placed in a residential program. This was the hardest decision I ever had to make, and one I explain in more depth in Chapter 13. In 1990, I was asked to help develop a training package for the New Jersey Department of Education to foster parent–professional collaboration.

Subsequently I became a full-time trainer for the New Jersey Department of Education. I got a lot of practice focusing on professional issues while drawing on my own life experience. I spoke to thousands of parents and professionals in preschool programs and at professional conferences. It was a way that I kept Tariq with me and derived meaning.

In 1991, the *Journal of Counseling & Development* published my article "Lost Dreams, New Hopes," about my life experiences and their impact on my professional life. I got letters and telephone calls from people who read the article. It was extremely rewarding to hear from college professors who used it as a handout in counseling and special education classes.

That same year Cindy and I had our first child, Kara. A little more than 2 years later, in 1993, our daughter Zoë was born. Kara and Zoë's development was a testament to the vitality of our relationship. In 1992, Cindy and I founded Alternative Choices, an independent psychology practice. Our practice grew to the point that I was able to leave my full-time position with the New Jersey

Department of Education. I now specialize in working with the parents of children with autism and other special needs. Cindy and I have always been able to work our schedules around our family. It is a life that we enjoy together.

In addition, I have served as a consultant to schools and parent groups, including having been the consulting psychologist to a special 3-year Head Start project to increase the involvement of fathers and male role models in the lives of young children. Currently I work with families and lecture nationally and sometimes internationally. I make a living doing what I enjoy. It is a special treat, and one that I am proud of.

I have come a long way. My son's disability helped me to develop more than I had ever imagined. He gave me the opportunity to do something special. The knowledge and wisdom that I acquired is still helping me to be all that I can.

Tariq has made me aware of the value of life. He is so innocent and generally happy. Tariq is such a gentle soul that he has always been a staff favorite wherever he has been. These thoughts alone bring me a calming stillness and a smile.

I now live a rewarding but different life. I keep learning as I help other families who are living with autism. Sometimes I'm not sure if I deserve such a full life. When I walk into an early intervention program or a consultation with the parent of a newly diagnosed child, I revisit my own experiences. As I look inside myself, the survivor's guilt softens. I am reminded by their story that I deserve to feel good—for I have paid my dues.

My focus in this book is this lifelong process of taking care of everyone in the family after a diagnosis of autism. My goal is to integrate my personal experiences, clinical expertise, and knowledge of research and practice to speak to families in similar circumstances to mine. My work feels like a success every time I can empower parents by helping them understand their thoughts and feelings, find humor in their situation, and go forward loving their child and helping him or her grow.

2

The Emotional Journey

From Lost Dreams and
Chronic Stress to Acceptance

*The soul would have no rainbow if the eyes
had no tears.*

NATIVE AMERICAN PROVERB

"WHEN YOUR PARENT DIES YOU HAVE LOST YOUR PAST. When your child dies you have lost your future," according to Dr. Elliott Lube in *The Bereaved Parent* (Schiff, 1978, p. 23). Certainly the dream of a perfect child can die a painful death. If you have a child with autism, you just want the autism to go away, and it won't. Your child is quite alive and often lively, but your future is unimaginable.

Japanese writer Kenzaburo Oe eloquently described this very intense and exceptionally personal loss. In 1964, his first child was born with brain damage. He named his boy Pooh and described their very close bond in a story called "Teach Us to Outgrow Our Madness." Oe was convinced that he himself directly felt the physical manifestations of his child's pain and perceived his child's impact on his dreams like a nuclear explosion—a personal holocaust. This metaphor came from growing up in Japan in the aftermath of the Hiroshima and Nagasaki bombings. Oe wrote of his connection to his child in a series of novels whose central character was the young father of a child with brain damage. He won the Nobel Prize for literature in 1994.

It is common to dream of having a perfect child, but starting with pregnancy, parents worry that something could go wrong. There is a wide range of typical development, and when a child's development is slower than expected, doctors often wisely urge parents to be patient. But patience is not always rewarded. According to the Centers for Disease Control and Prevention, 1 in every 88 children is diagnosed with an autism spectrum disorder (ASD): 1 in 54 boys compared to 1 in 252 girls. The autism spectrum ranges from severe to mild—from classic autism to Asperger syndrome. Whether a child is low or high functioning, when he or she is diagnosed with autism, life changes dramatically. The odds don't really matter when it happens to you. The father in the movie *Lorenzo's Oil* highlighted this fact when he said that he had taken one of life's biggest gambles and lost.

Expectant parents have a lot of dreams. Will the child be a boy or a girl? Who will he look like? What kind of personality will he have? What will she be when she grows up? What kinds of things will you enjoy doing together? What exciting places will you go to? Most couples look forward to children as the fulfillment of their marriage and their legacy for the future. So autism has a profound impact on the expectations that parents have for their child. Dreams for a typical child evaporate, because the real child cannot fulfill all of these possibilities. Positive feelings are deflated, as pride and hope slip away and become difficult to recover. There may be a sense of failure for bringing an "imperfect" child into the world along with shame and guilt for feeling disappointed in your child.

As a child I was very shy, so I hoped for my son to be confident and articulate. Like many parents I wanted to recreate myself and come out better. I gave my son the middle name *Donato*, my Italian grandfather's first name, which means *gift*. His first name, Tariq, is the name of a star and a famous Arab general from the 10th century. The Rock of Gibraltar is literally "Tariq's rock," where that general crossed from Morocco to Spain. I had big dreams for my son—I wanted him to do things that I had not, to be the man I had not yet become. These dreams set the scene for Tariq's birth.

At times Tariq's diagnosis hurt so much that I wanted to block out my pain. This is natural, because people are hardwired to decrease pain and increase pleasure. Sometimes they have to block out pain in order to function from day to day. But if people never face their painful feelings and thoughts, they do not go away and instead tend to increase. Pop psychology urges people to replace negative thoughts with positive thoughts as a way to feel better. This strategy often helps them feel better, but it sometimes discredits the feelings of people who are struggling with their difficult emotions.

The Chinese Finger Trap

In recent years, I have begun to use concepts from acceptance and commitment therapy (ACT) in my work with parents. To explain accepting a difficult experience, psychologist Stephen Hayes used the metaphor of the Chinese finger trap, which most people have played with as children. You put your index fingers into a tube woven out of straw. When you pull to get them out, the tube gets smaller and tightens around your fingers. The harder you pull, the tighter it gets. It can even start to cut off your blood flow. Conversely, if you push into the tube, it loosens and you can move your fingers around.

If you think of life as a Chinese finger trap, it's a question of how to get room to move around. The more you struggle with life's problems, the more constricting they may seem. When you quit struggling, push in, and examine them closely, you have room to move. This translates into having the freedom to make choices to deal with your problems instead of feeling trapped or stuck. The pain begins to lessen only when you look into it. Although it sounds counterintuitive, accepting your child starts with looking into—as opposed to away from—the pain.

It can be difficult to look into these upsetting feelings. It is necessary to develop a vocabulary. Asking people the simple question "Are you angry?" might not get an honest answer because it is hard to admit and not socially acceptable to be so upset about your child. Intense feelings can also occur at other times, such as when you experience

- The death of someone close

- The end of a relationship

- A limiting injury

- The loss of a job

- Moving from a community

- A miscarriage

- Disappointment in a child

- The chronic illness of a friend, family member, or yourself

What Did You Feel When
You Held Your Child for the First Time?

I have developed activities to help parents explore their responses to their child's birth, diagnosis, and life after diagnosis. When I speak at conferences or when I initially consult with parents, I ask them what it felt like when they held their infant for the first time. At first people are hesitant to respond, and then I ask them whether they have photos like I have of holding Tariq as a newborn.

Check out the eye contact at 1 day old.

They always have a lot to say about this life-altering and defining experience and what they felt:

- Awe

- Fear

- Love (in an unconditional way never felt before)

- Pride

- Relief

- Shakiness

- Tenderness

- Worry (if their infant was taken to the neonatal intensive care unit)

- Pressure

- Excitement

- Adoration

- Thankfulness

I ask them to tell me about their child's birth and early development. Unless their infant was premature or had medical issues at birth, they remember thinking everything was going well. These memories of their initial experiences with their child help them reach an understanding of the meaning of autism and how their family has been affected. Next I ask about how they experienced the developmental problems that culminated in the diagnosis. This time there is a range of upsetting reactions:

- Shock

- Disbelief

- Anger

- Worry

- Numbness

- Guilt

- Relief

Anxiety

The most common feeling that parents have on learning that their child has been diagnosed on the autism spectrum is anxiety. When a mother is upset, others want to calm her down. She is difficult to be around, so her uneasiness is treated as a problem. But anxiety by itself is not a problem—it is a feeling that serves an important purpose. It does not help when someone says, "Calm down—things are not as bad as you think." People cannot calm down just because someone wants them to or they themselves would like to. The psychological system is mobilizing energy for the tasks ahead. The feeling of anxiety can range from a sense of insecurity to a panic attack. A mother who has worried that something was wrong might now be relieved to know the diagnosis.

Although extreme anxiety can be debilitating and requires treatment with psychotherapy and sometimes medication, a moderate amount is necessary for everyday functioning. When your child is not developing in a typical way, it is necessary to mobilize energy to cope. During Tariq's childhood, I was constantly on edge and concerned about his safety, and my anxiety helped me to anticipate problems he might have and solve them *before* Tariq faced certain dangers. This process required an enormous amount of energy.

In addition, parents who have a child with autism are often afraid to have another child. Because autism has a genetic component, some parents cannot even discuss the possibility of trying again. Recent research by Ozonoff and colleagues (2011), in the largest such study to date, has documented that 18.7% of 664 infants with an older biological sibling with ASD who were followed from early in life to 36 months and evaluated by experienced professionals developed ASD. According to this study, the risk for male infants to develop ASD is 25.9% versus 9.6% for female infants. Some couples are deeply divided about whether to try again and are never on the same page on the issue. Clearly counseling would be helpful for parents struggling to decide whether to try to have a typically developing child.

Years after Tariq's diagnosis, when Cindy and I were expecting Kara, I felt more nervous than the average parent. We had been told that our daughter was fine, but there is no prenatal test for autism. I remembered the discussions about birth defects in the childbirth classes. There were no questions or discussion, and the instructor simply moved on to the next topic. I did not blame the other parents-to-be, because I had not had questions before Tariq's birth either. Yet this time around I knew that my worries would not go away until I was sure that this child did not have autism.

Cindy and I faced our fears together, and fortunately we had a typically developing child. Kara has been a source of great joy for more than 20 years now. Her development helped to reassure me that I am a vibrant person who can survive tragedy and maybe even come out better for it. I did not worry so much when we were expecting Zoë, and her development has also delighted us.

In 1995, when I was writing my first book, I heard a news report that a 6-year-old boy with autism had gotten out of his family's apartment and been run over and killed by an early morning commuter train. I got an especially queasy feeling in my stomach when I heard that the accident had taken place near the train station only a block from our house. I trembled, remembering how I had lived with the fear that Tariq might get out and wander onto those same tracks, and my heart filled with grief for the boy's family and with relief that my son had the round-the-clock supervision that he needed. A few years later at a conference, I met the emergency care physician who had been first on the scene after hearing the train screech to a halt. This doctor was also the father of a child with Angelman syndrome. Experiences such as this are part of the shared bond in the community of people with special needs.

Guilt

It is not unusual for parents to blame themselves for something they did or did not do that caused their child's autism. The very process of diagnosis often exacerbates these feelings of guilt. Every time they take their child for help somewhere, they hear a line of questions something like this:

- When did you first notice something was wrong?

- What was your pregnancy like?

- What was your mental state during the pregnancy?

- If you were working, when did you stop?

- Are there any similar problems in your family?

These questions can be particularly painful for mothers who wonder what they might have done wrong during pregnancy. Fathers may doubt that they took good care of their spouses. No matter what their religious background, somewhere in the back of many parents' minds is the question, "Is this a punishment for something I have done or even thought?"

Because it is commonly believed that good things happen to good people, it follows logically that bad things happen to bad people. Why do some people have children with impairments, whereas others have typically developing children? This is a gut-wrenching question. Parents feel terrible if they believe they have caused this condition. I recall how I blamed myself and wondered whether the conflicts between Tariq's mother and me had caused or contributed to his condition.

When Bad Things Happen to Good People by Harold Kushner is the book I recommend to parents dealing with feelings of guilt. There is a common belief that God is just. When people feel guilty, they often come to the conclusion that they deserve what they got and think it is punishment for sins. As a rabbi and the parent of a chronically ill child who died, Kushner speaks to the unfair and uncontrollable distribution of suffering.

The world is not as orderly and understandable as people might like. The resolution of guilt is an individual matter. Guilt is about responsibility. Naturally, parents wish that they could have done something to avoid autism. They are able to let go of their guilt only after settling for themselves what their responsibilities are toward their child. For example, learning that autism is neurologically based helped me realize that marital conflict and divorce could not cause it. What a relief to no longer believe that I had caused Tariq's autism! But marital conflict does not help children, so parents do bear responsibility for dealing with differences constructively.

Guilt is part of a normal and unlearned response to the experience of loss. It is as natural as the loss of a seed to form a sprout, or the transformation of a bud to a flower. Every loss sets the stage for future growth. As Naomi Remen, a doctor who lives with Crohn's disease, wrote, "The way we deal with loss shapes our ability to be present for the rest of life" (1996, p. 51).

My Journey to Acceptance

At the time of his diagnosis and for years afterward, I swore I would never accept my son's autism. I thought I would never smile or laugh again if Tariq did not start speaking again. Yet like many folks, I continued to hope for a cure. For a long time I believed that the best medical care I could find along with love and my own efforts to participate in his therapies would bring him back. After 3 decades there are still moments when I wonder who my son might have been, and who I might have been as well.

These years have taught me that life is not about making war or peace with autism. Neither seems sustainable. The feelings come and go, and any peaceful moment can be shattered by a meltdown or behavioral challenge. I have learned that accepting is about opening up and being in the present moment as one is experiencing it.

So what does it mean to accept your child's autism? Let's start with the grief. Sigmund Freud said that mourning is a kind of work that you have to do in order to move on, and that those who do not do the work will stay in a state of melancholy. It is human nature to ponder our experiences and try to make sense out of our thoughts and feelings.

My grief unfolded through my dreams, which evolved over the years. At first, when I knew something was wrong, I could not accept the severity of the problem. At night I would dream of my daily interactions with Tariq doing things that the speech therapist had showed me and things I had read about. For example, I would try to take turns stacking blocks with him. He was not interested, so I would try to do it hand over hand, but he would just knock them over. Then I tried imitating his movements; I would flap my arms when he flapped. When I would do this during the day, Tariq would usually notice me and stop what he was doing for a few moments. He would give me a little smile and then go back to what he was doing.

By night, in my frequently recurring dream, Tariq would look at me intently, making eye contact, and then slowly form a word or two. My heart beat faster. The sound of his voice thrilled me. I would hug my son and hold him next to my chest. In the morning I would awaken full of hope, believing that he *would* talk, and I kept working with him—taking turns with simple puzzles, stacking, and mirroring his flapping. By day the dream fueled my efforts. I recorded his grunts and groans and babblings and listened to them, searching for progress.

At times I thought I heard some. But no words came back after years of effort and the same dream over and over.

Over time I began to wake up exhausted. It was hard to go on. My hopes were fading. While writing *Special Children, Challenged Parents: The Struggles and Rewards of Raising a Child with a Disability*, I retrieved one of the tapes from a dusty box in our basement. Listening for just a few moments brought back the feeling as if it had all happened yesterday. I heard myself patiently trying to coax meaningful sounds out of my son. Soon I could not listen any longer. I realized that Tariq still makes the same vocalizations; the only difference is that his voice is deeper now that he has undergone the adolescent transformation.

When a child is not speaking by age 5, hopes fade that typical speech can develop. Time was running out. Still, I continued to hope and be very disappointed. All my life, whenever I worked hard at something, I had gotten results—things had worked out. U.S. culture teaches that with hard work people have the opportunity to achieve anything. I remembered many examples of things that I had achieved, including developing from a physically awkward child to a competitive athlete in high school.

Early in my relationship with Cindy, I had a daydream that our love could heal Tariq. I would see us sitting in a grassy spot under the willow trees in the park near my apartment. Tariq would come running to us with a daisy in his hand, saying, "Look at the flower!" I would hug Cindy, and we would both hug Tariq. It was so hard to admit that this was not to be.

Fortunately, I got some help from my dreams. Around Tariq's eighth birthday, I had a new dream: He spoke to me in sentences. I ran to share the news with Cindy. But when I woke up from this dream within a dream, I knew that Tariq had not spoken. I felt a deep relief that I could just live with things the way they were. *Not that I liked it.* I did not have to keep pushing. If a miracle came, I would accept it, but Tariq just could not talk. In my sleep, my mind had helped me to let go of having a typical son.

That dream repeated for a few years, and then another dream came. Tariq talked, looking me in the eye, and told me that he loved me, felt my love, and knew I had done everything possible for him. He told me that he was happy and wanted me to be happy. Then he went back to being his autistic self—playing with his tongue, making unintelligible noises, flicking his fingers, and being unaware of me unless he wanted something. I still longed for what might have been. On awakening, I found that I had moved on a little further. Tariq was still a part of me, but I had not drowned in my grief. By inviting the feelings in, accepting the lost dream, and living with it, I had grown.

Understanding the Stages of Grief: Working Through It

Elisabeth Kübler-Ross, M.D., brought death and dying out of the closet in 1969 in *On Death and Dying,* based on her work with people dying of cancer. She did for death what Freud had done for sexuality. It has since become far easier to talk about loss, and in this respect alone her work is monumental. Kübler-Ross (1969) conceptualized five stages that people pass through with impending death:

1. Denial

2. Anger

3. Bargaining

4. Depression

5. Acceptance

It is now commonplace to hear people casually talking about these stages. This model has even been adapted to the experiences of families of children with special needs. A diagnosis of autism can feel like the death of your hopes for having a typically developing child. When I ask parents which stages they have been through, they usually identify stages similar to Kübler-Ross's theory. Not everyone goes through the same stages in the same order, and they may overlap or repeat. Let's see how a parent might work through his or her heartaches without considering the Kübler-Ross model too rigidly.

Denial: I Cannot Wrap My Head Around It

There is little disagreement that denial comes first. Denial creates a necessary buffer zone, because it takes time to deal with a new reality. The thought "Not me, it cannot be true" is a virtually universal response to loss. Although people may say, "Face reality," the initial reaction of disbelief is perfectly normal and healthy. Because there is no blood test or neurological test for autism, it can only be diagnosed by observing behavior. Most children with autism look typical in every other way. Its effects are invisible, so it is easy to deny or misunderstand its severity; some parents may even resist or delay implementing professional recommendations.

Some people do not understand why parents might deny that their child has autism. This denial can seem cold and impatient. It might even seem that these parents are being irrational. However, grief is not simply a cognitive phenomenon. Although some parents get stuck in denial, most move on—when they are ready. Denial serves an important role in human nature. If you think constantly about all of the terrible things that could ever happen, how could you live? How could you manage to go out the door? Why have children if you think about everything that could possibly go wrong?

Before his diagnosis and for years afterward, I constantly told myself that my son Tariq would be okay. He would talk again and catch up. In his audio tape, *Not me! Not my child! Dealing with parental denial and anxiety,* psychologist Ken Moses explains that denial buys time to discover the inner strength to handle a problem. He based this on his own experience as the child of Holocaust survivors and as the parent of a child with a disability. In addition, external support is necessary. Which relatives and friends can be relied on? Denial makes the pain bearable until parents find the inner strength and the supports they need.

Parents may look for a cure or refuse to believe the disability is severe. At the time of the diagnosis it is impossible to predict how far a child can develop. Many parents, through hard work, hope, and love, have helped their child develop far beyond the expected potential. In the Academy Award–winning film *My Left Foot,* which is based on a true story, Christy Brown has cerebral palsy and is unable to walk or speak. Everyone but his mother thinks he is severely cognitively disabled. Eventually he learns to express himself by writing on the floor with chalk held between the toes of his left foot. Christy understands his surroundings while being locked inside his body. Once he begins to communicate, his mother finds a special education program for him. He learns to talk and become proficient in art and writing. His autobiography is a gift.

Many parents share the attitude of Christy's mother. She saw her child's potential, and she did not let the negative assessments of others blind her to his potential. Despite her child's obvious impairments, she developed a strong bond with him, as recommended by renowned pediatrician T. Berry Brazelton, who enthusiastically helped parents focus on the strengths of what their child can do. Such parents help some children to eventually astound the experts. What resembles denial may instead be unconditional love that results in tremendous progress.

In *Voices from the Spectrum: Parents, Grandparents, Siblings, People with Autism, and Professionals Share Their Wisdom,* Stephen Shore relates that he was hit with the "autism bomb" at 18 months. He went from being a social and talkative toddler to a child who withdrew, throwing tantrums, losing speech, and engaging in self-abusive behaviors. In the early 1960s, his parents were at a loss as to what to do. At age 2½, he was diagnosed with "atypical development, strong autistic tendencies, and psychotic behaviors" (Shore, 2003, p. 21). Institutionalization was strongly recommended, but his parents refused. Because it was 1964, they were left to provide what is now called *early intervention* on their own. Stephen was still nonverbal at age 4. He relates that he was always accepted in his home as a full and complete human being. Today Stephen has his doctorate and is Assistant Professor of Special Education at Adelphi University on Long Island, New York.

Stephen is a sought-after presenter at conferences around the world and an inspiration to children and adults with autism and their families. Stephen and I have presented together frequently, and we have recorded a DVD. Of course, I had hoped that my son would turn out like Stephen, but hard work does not solve every problem. Autism is considered a spectrum, and individuals with autism vary in terms of their symptoms and their severity. Stephen and Tariq are at opposite ends of this spectrum but share some core symptoms.

Some disabilities are detected at birth and are traumatic, but parents of children with such disabilities have told me that they experienced very little denial of the reality. "Invisible" disabilities, such as autism, learning disabilities, attention-deficit/hyperactivity disorder (ADHD), and emotional disorders diagnosed well after birth, can be much more difficult to accept. *When a child looks normal, our eyes deceive us.* With time, as the reality settles in, feelings begin to naturally rumble.

When Stephen Shore is in Philadelphia, he likes to visit Tariq with me. Photograph by Zoë Naseef.

Anger: This Is Not Fair

Because the loss of a dream cannot be openly acknowledged and publicly mourned, the grief that results is disenfranchised. Some people deny the pain even though they may accept the reality. They often feel pressured to move on. They want the anguish to end. The words of Leo Tolstoy can be comforting: "Only people who are capable of loving strongly can also suffer great sorrow; but this same necessity of loving serves to counteract their grief and heals them" (2012, p. 109).

As the parent's denial fades, anger arises that his or her child's condition may not improve significantly. This is the first expression of pain and resentment at the apparent unfairness. I remember resenting the injustice that healthy children are born to parents who abuse or neglect them. This reaction can lead to becoming bitter and chronically angry. To find peace, one needs to find a new sense of fairness. Kushner (1981) spoke to this age-old question about justice. He stated, "Anguish and heartbreak may not be distributed evenly throughout the world, but they are distributed very widely" (p. 124). It is just hard to accept.

However, great energy and vitality can come from this anger, and the resultant activity can be rewarding. It gave me the drive, for example, to work with my son every day. Passive acceptance of his condition would not have done this. Many parents want to work personally with their children because they know that this kind of homework can make a difference. Wanting to prove the experts wrong spawned the ambition in me to make more money to pay for my son's therapies. Many parents have told me that they did not know what they would do, who they would be, or how they would function without the anger.

In this stage, people look for where to point the finger. Many people even experience a spiritual crisis because the God they thought to be just now seems unjust. Sylvester Stallone said that when his son was diagnosed with autism, he went out into his backyard, looked up at the sky, and cursed God. A mother told me that she no longer believed in hell since finding out that her only child had autism—she said she was living it here and now. Other parents have shared that they might not have been praying properly or their child would have been healed.

The feelings of anger may be spewed out and displaced in all directions, making it difficult to cope for all who are involved—including professionals who are trying to help. Sometimes anger leads to isolation because it may seem that no one can possibly understand. You might also feel guilty for being angry. If you blame your child for putting you through such intense challenges, you will probably feel guilty for blaming such an innocent soul.

In my case, Tariq was 5 before I was able to admit to myself that I was angry at him. He was simply not who I wanted him to be. Even now it is uncomfortable to admit—a flaw that I would rather hide. Isn't a parent's love for a child supposed to be unconditional? I met my anger face to face one of those many nights when he woke up and I heard him making noises and playing in his room. It took me a few minutes to wake myself and try to rock him back to sleep. I was quick, but not quick enough. As he had on other occasions at home and in school, he had a bowel movement and started playing with it and smearing it all over himself and the walls and furniture. I have since heard other parents in groups that I have led call this "diaper art."

I was so furious at him for doing this to *me*—for making me go through this when most other 5-year-olds knew better—I wanted to throw him out the window of his room. I really did. I did not touch him, however, except to lead him to the bathtub and start cleaning him up with warm soapy water and a washcloth. I felt the rage within me boiling, ready to erupt, and I was terrified of what that might lead to. Remember the television show *The Incredible Hulk?* In each episode, David Banner would warn an adversary not to upset him or he would explode. If he did get angry, the mild-mannered Banner turned into an out-of-control monster. I took a few slow, deep breaths. As I washed Tariq and put clean pajamas on him, I thought once again about those abusive parents with healthy kids.

Now that I owned my own anger, I was not mad at those parents anymore. I hugged my child. This experience is an example of what William Faulkner, in his Nobel Prize acceptance speech, called the human heart in conflict with itself. It is the agony and sweat of the human spirit—not that I did not still long for that dream of pure untainted love for my child. I was able to realize from understanding my own passionate anger that I was capable of controlling it. I now had empathy for people who lose control—they need help to learn it. What a fine line divides us!

I met Jaclyn at a workshop on the stresses of raising a child with autism. She shared, "Once I let go of my anger, I had a whole new life." She told her story. Several weeks before her child was due, she was rear-ended in her car and taken to the hospital. When she went into labor a few days later, she thought it had been caused by the driver of the car that struck her. Later when her child was diagnosed with autism, she blamed that driver. She said that she needed someone to blame. This went on for years.

She related that when she let go of her anger, she started to really enjoy her child and her life. She had been miserable staying angry. Anger is often about a perceived sense of injustice. Next time you feel your anger brewing, check your thoughts. See if you are thinking that you have been wronged, or slighted, or mistreated in some way. Remember that just because you think something does not make it true. But the more you think about it, the truer it may seem.

Anger is complicated. It comes and goes in the normal emotional flow of peoples' lives. Often, if people look deeper, they discover that they are feeling tender or hurt. Losing something precious hurts and may evoke anger; parents want and even temporarily need someone or something to blame. It might be themselves, each other, the doctor, vaccines, and so forth. Anger may energize them to fight for justice, for what is fair and human, such as the services their child desperately needs. It can inspire change that needs to happen, or it can eat people up inside.

The journey of letting go involves coming to grips with the issue of what you can and must change and what you cannot change and therefore must be willing to live peacefully with. This can take years to come to grips with. Handling anger well is a skill that involves emotional intelligence, which is the ability to monitor emotions, differentiate among them, and use this information to guide thinking and choices for taking action. Goleman (1995) quoted the philosopher Aristotle: "Anyone can become angry—that is easy. But to be angry with the right person, to the right degree, at the right time, for the right purpose, and in the right way—this is not easy" (p. xix).

Although it is crucial for people to be open and honest about their feelings and to have a life story that makes sense, they can get stuck in that story. When that happens, they just rehearse the anger and suffer because things are different from what they expected and wanted. When she was able to let go of her anger, Jaclyn began enjoying the progress her son was making and her daily life with him and the family she loved.

Bargaining: Let's Make a Deal

Fantasy may help to fight off the overwhelming feelings of anger and sadness that are often buried just below the surface. Parents may imagine a miracle cure. Perhaps if they work extra hard, the child's condition will improve. They were unable to face the sad facts in the first stage of grief and angry at people and God in the second stage, but perhaps now some kind of deal can postpone the inevitable.

Several themes emerge as parents travel the road to acceptance. Initially they struggle with the symptoms of autism. Time stops as parents initially become very upset with their child's difficulties; they begin the protracted journey of putting together the appropriate interventions. Through the heartache, in the passage to acceptance, they love their children passionately. They learn everything they can about their children and about autism and a few things about themselves in the process.

The professional literature often refers to this phase as "shopping" for a diagnosis, or hoping that there is a way out. If the right program or treatment will make this problem go away, then life can go back to the way it was before. To the outside observer, it may seem that the parent is grasping at straws. Parents frequently complain that their pediatricians are impatient with them when they want alternative treatments. I advise them to ask their child's physician for an extended consultation. The physician may respond differently when approached this way and when the parents come prepared with questions and information. Given more time to discuss things, the physician may be more supportive of an alternative treatment and more understanding of the parents' wish to try another approach. If not, the family might choose to change doctors.

Bargaining can also be another way of buying some time. Usually the bargain is with God or another higher power. Tariq graduated from early intervention at 5 years of age and was due to start public school. He wore a little cap and gown like his classmates and squirmed through the ceremony in my arms. I could not accept a special education class such as the ones being recommended. At the time, the choices were a self-contained classroom for children with multiple disabilities or a specialized program for children with autism. I thought these places would make him worse because he would have no typically developing peers as role models.

I could not believe that his condition was permanent, and I could not find a nursery school that would take him for an extra year to help him catch up. So I found a Montessori school that accepted him and gave him extra

Tariq graduated from early intervention at age 5.

help for an increased fee. I took on extra teaching and therapy cases to make the money. After trying hard for more than a year, it was clear to me that Tariq was not improving. The teachers could not manage him and give enough attention to the other children at the same time. The parents of the other children, who at first had been patient, were now complaining.

I took Tariq to the Center for Autistic Children (now the Center for Autism) in Philadelphia, a specialized program that I had visited a year before. At first it had looked cold and pessimistic—therapists working one to one with children who could not benefit from group activities. I had sworn to myself at the time that I would keep my son out of such a place at all costs. But now I had spent more than a third of my gross salary on private school and therapies with no visible results. My parents, grandparents, and siblings had lent me money, hoping along with me to find a cure.

This time the Center looked different: It appeared that one-to-one therapy was a realistic place to begin with my son. The social worker, the therapists, and the psychiatrist were warm, caring people who loved children such as Tariq, knew how to work with them, and helped me feel comfortable with my decision to accept their help, which I had previously refused. What a difference a year made!

Depression: Redefining Who You Are

When reality can no longer be denied, when angry energy does not change a child's condition, and when there are no more deals to be made, a sense of depression may set in. Sadness grips the heart as reality must be dealt with. The truth is extremely painful and often overwhelming. During this period, parents may question the meaning of life and their value as human beings. Because of the intense grief and shame, they may avoid others with typically developing children.

The depression that accompanies loss varies from person to person. It can be deep and compelling, as described by William Styron in the account of his own depression, *Darkness Visible.* It is a pain that can be unimaginable to those who have not suffered it, and as Styron recounted, it can "frighten the soul to its marrow" (p. 21). If your child's diagnosis is made a relatively long time after his or her birth, your grief reaction may be more intense because your hope for having a typically developing child lived longer. But your bond with your child is stronger, and that can be an advantage. Whatever its intensity, sorrow is the natural response that has been waiting in the wings.

It is hard to feel like a good parent when your child is just not an average kid. Energy and hope are in short supply. Many people report a feeling of hollowness, headaches, disturbed sleep, eating problems, and other physical symptoms. Self-confidence may be shot. The parent may feel physically or mentally drained and be unable or unwilling to perform even routine tasks. There may be little interest in activities that previously brought pleasure; there may be aches, pains, fatigue, poor digestion, or too much or too little sleep. When these symptoms are severe or prolonged, the parent may be experiencing clinical depression—a mood disorder that calls for professional help in the form of intensive psychotherapy and quite possibly medication.

Adjusting requires adapting to the everyday demands of autism. There is no cure or fix, so new coping skills must be developed. In U.S. culture people tend to minimize reality. Often one hears clichés such as "Cheer up, things will work out." These are not comforting words when life is telling us otherwise. Things don't always work out, and it hurts when they don't. For instance, when a relationship fails, it can be very hard to fall in love anew. People may fear being hurt again and think that if they refuse to dream and love again, then they can't be hurt again.

Beth told me about periodic bouts with overwhelming sadness. She would burst into tears after her son Darren got on the bus to go to kindergarten. It was very painful for her to watch him standing on the edge of the playground not knowing how to join in. There was guilt along with her pain because she was still blaming herself for her son's lack of progress. In therapy, she learned to acknowledge those feelings instead of trying to push them away. By being kind to herself about how low she felt and just letting it wash over her, she was able to gradually feel refreshed.

Chronic Stress: Cannot Catch a Break

When I speak at conferences to parents about the stages of mourning, people find the ideas helpful. It never fails, however, that someone asks, "When do you get over this? It happens to me over and over." In fact, this is true for most parents who have children with autism. Very intense feelings are triggered over and over again by the events of daily life. There is no solution or resolution. It is just there. So how can we understand this? When parents get more comfortable talking about how life really is, they often reveal signs and symptoms of clinical depression, anxiety, traumatic stress, anger management issues, sexual dysfunction, and so forth. People come to Alternative Choices struggling to deal with the stresses of autism:

- A mother sobs as she remembers the time her son said, "I wish my imaginary friends were real so that someone would play with me."

- Middle school boys and girls with autism learn how to control their tempers, especially when they are being teased.

- Another mother recounts how her life seems like "one long day" because her 8-year-old son rarely sleeps through the night.

- A father sobs about his son's seizures, which have been difficult to control. He and his wife live in a heightened state of anxiety about when the next seizure will come.

- A 12-year-old boy tries to understand why other students are tired of hearing him talk about insects, one of his special interests.

- In a group of fathers, a dad reiterates how his own father had been "the commander-in-chief" but that this does not work with his son with autism.

- Another man weeps as he recalls when his oldest son stopped talking.

- Couples come looking for help because they fear that their marriage will break under the strain.

Cecelia, the mother of an 8-year-old boy with autism, put it this way: "Every time I think I have accepted my child's disability, something happens that sets me back. We're enjoying him and celebrating his accomplishments, and then he has a bad day, kicking and screaming, and I just freak out. I feel traumatized, but I don't know whether I should compare myself to people who have been abused. I need help." Having a severely developmentally delayed child was referred to as a trauma by prominent child psychiatrists Daniel Stern and Nadia Bruschweiler-Stern (1998). This emotionally staggering crisis can stop time in its tracks.

Trauma is an emotional shock that can cause lasting and substantial damage to a person's psychological development. According to the American Psychiatric Association (2000), *trauma* is the personal experience of an event that involves a threat to one's physical integrity. Trauma can also be caused by witnessing such an event or by learning about such an event happening to a family member. Since 2000, reports of traumatic stress related to autism and other developmental disabilities have begun to appear in the professional literature. This can provide a lens for seeing the effects of autism on families, as I mentioned in an article I coauthored, "Technologies to Lessen the Distress of Autism," listed in the resources at the end of this book.

Traumatic stress is an overwhelming experience that affects both mind and body and affects people's ability to think and make sense out of their experiences (van der Kolk, McFarlane, & Weisaeth, 1996). These experiences often overwhelm temporarily and often chronically people's capacity to cope. The trauma of autism can be severe because it is chronic and affects the family over the entire life span of the child. Just as the child and family overcome one crisis, another crisis may take its place; this can intensify as the child grows older and compound the ongoing trauma. For example, a child may be making steady progress and then develop seizures in adolescence.

Challenging behaviors can add to the trauma. Many children with autism will cry and have frequent tantrums, break things, injure themselves, and shriek. In many cases, they cannot communicate the pain caused by medical problems or their environment. Some children engage in dangerous behaviors, such as running out into traffic, into pools or lakes, or even up high-tension towers. They may break windows or dart into a neighbor's house to search for items they are obsessed with, such as video players, remote controls, and so forth. Just to ensure that the child will not escape, many families have to lock themselves in their own homes, putting the whole family at risk in the case of a fire.

One of the most draining problems families deal with is hyperactivity and the lack of sleep a child with autism may experience. After only 2 hours' sleep, such children may be up and on the move again. People with autism may be among those most seriously affected by sleep problems, and research suggests that most individuals with autism experience sleep difficulties at some point in their lives (Durand, 1998). This lack of sleep puts weary parents at high risk for depression or for an anxiety disorder.

Parents must stay vigilant because the crisis may never end. The family's constant and evolving struggles with sleep problems, unusual behaviors, and communication can trigger the symptoms of posttraumatic stress disorder. This reaction to trauma includes fear and hopelessness. There is also persistent reexperiencing of the traumatic event, be it the diagnosis or a particular crisis. There may be avoidance of circumstances reminiscent of the original trauma and numbness in general responsiveness. The trauma may also cause increased arousal, which results in parents being irritable and on edge indefinitely. These symptoms may cause clinically significant problems in daily social and occupational functioning. Families are often preoccupied with wondering whether their children are happy, whether they love their families, and whether they themselves are doing the right thing.

Another cause of stress for the family is dealing with the general public. The child with autism has no physical characteristics to indicate the problems that may occur. When the family attempts to go out in public, both parents and siblings may be embarrassed if the child exhibits odd behaviors. Many uninformed people tend to blame the child's parents for these unusual behaviors. Feeling judged and rejected and embarrassed in this way may cause the parents to isolate themselves (Miller & Sammons, 1999).

Traumatic stress is a normal response to an abnormal event. Families of children with autism may experience this response repeatedly throughout the life cycle. They are often confused by the symptoms of trauma and may fear going crazy. Likewise, their extended families, friends, and colleagues may be equally confused and may withdraw in the face of anger, fear, and anxiety. Understanding and making sense out of their reactions, which affect every aspect of human functioning, is central to the recovery process (Herman, 1992).

Acceptance: Learning to Live Day by Day

Despite all of the stresses encountered by parents of children with autism, love makes giving up unthinkable. Many people question how the acceptance stage can apply to autism. I did for years. The very term *acceptance* seems to imply that some type of closure has occurred. Instead, because the child continues to live, the grieving and coping experienced by parents is more complex. The goal in acceptance for parents is regaining balance and taking care of everybody's needs in the family. This involves having endurance, having courage, and learning to live with and accepting whatever remains unchangeable.

Although it takes time, feelings of depression and anger eventually subside. Kübler-Ross (1969) stressed that this is not a "happy" stage. For a dying person, the pain is gone and the struggle is over. For parents of children with autism, the pain and suffering may have lessened but the hard work is ongoing. According to Jon Kabat-Zinn, (2005) who is known for his work bringing mindfulness into the mainstream of medicine and society, acceptance can take monumental fortitude and commitment to finding a way to relate wisely while accepting the responsibility to do everything you can about the problem which in this case is the struggle due to autism. In some respects, acceptance is not just a stage but a way of living mindfully. There may be fear that new dreams and goals will only be crushed once again. No one wants to be hurt again. Learning to love your actual child involves making new goals and hoping to achieve them. Coming to understand acceptance in this way can actually lessen the burden of suffering.

One thing that remained difficult for me was passing a Little League baseball game on a summer's night. Until Tariq was too old to be playing Little League, whenever I heard the crack of the bat I wanted to stop and watch and see my son there. I wanted to cheer him on, and then I would get a tear in the corner of my eye or a lump in my throat. That feeling did eventually pass as I was able to live in the present moment, and I deeply enjoyed watching Kara and Zoë play softball.

Whether one considers thoughts, feelings, sensations, or stages, the family's process of adapting to the evolving challenges and accepting autism is life long. Many factors affect how each individual and family responds to a diagnosis of autism. The individual nature and severity of the autism are major factors. After working through their initial upset, parents can collaborate with professionals and stop blaming them for not curing their child.

When the child is making progress developmentally and challenging behaviors are minimal, families most commonly retain a sense of hope and reassurance. But a bad day is often lurking in the shadows. For example, if a child has a tantrum in the supermarket that disrupts the atmosphere and attracts attention, or if the child bolts across the street without looking, a parent or sibling may experience terror—terror that may trigger palpitations, shortness of breath, dizziness, and even flashbacks to life-threatening incidents. Family members may experience nightmares and disturbed sleep as well as a sense of despair. They may spend long periods of time on edge and behave irritably with one another as a result.

But families are resilient, and with support and effective intervention, some sense of order and predictability can be restored to their lives and the overpowering sense of helplessness and powerlessness alleviated. Families go on to find meaning in their struggle and love for their child and life itself. Families of children with autism need the awareness and support of the rest of society—as well as good services that are increasingly harder for many to come by.

In my work with parents, I try to help them really look at their grief. It does not help to pretend to be positive when underneath you may be lonely, afraid, or sad. I learned that you do not have to lie to yourself. You can grieve. You can complain. You can mourn. This helps you to go on, make the best of the situation, and enjoy life. The life force is resilient, but the longing for a healthy child or a typical existence may endure.

You have to learn to live with that yearning, but you do not have to lie to yourself about how hard this can be. As Winnicott said, "Mothers are helped by being able to voice their agonies at the time they are experiencing them. Bottled up resentment spoils the loving which is at the back of it all" (1993, p. 75). Feeling your experience is the first step in handling it wisely.

I also try to help people accept themselves just as they are. This is key to accepting your children with an open, kind, and loving heart. A perfectly lovely child or adult on the spectrum can be very hard to be with because of their behavioral, social, or communication issues. But when you love someone, you expect yourself to love to be with them. When you do not feel that and think you should, the guilt can be unbearable, and your heart aches. This is a conflict many parents have, but when a child has autism, it can happen much more frequently.

You cannot accept yourself or any experience without seeing it clearly in a tender, compassionate way. What Tariq has taught me besides accepting him is accepting myself. The challenges in children radiate inward and underscore their parents' own imperfections. So I had to begin accepting my own flaws, warts, and blemishes—things I could change and things I could not.

Finally, accepting your pain and yourself leads to enjoying your child, and that awareness is the gateway to love and wholeness. People on the autism spectrum bear witness to the diversity and resilience of the human condition. Awareness keeps the heart open and the mind clear. Yearning for what you do not have blocks your knowing and loving the child you do have. Seeing your child for who he or she is and giving what he or she needs to whatever extent is possible is the path of acceptance for families. You do not have control over autism, but you do have a lot to offer in your relationship with your child or loved one who is living with this condition.

Each individual person brings his or her own thoughts and beliefs to the process of acceptance. For example, some say that "God gives special children to special people" or "God wouldn't give you more than you could handle." Although I respect the beliefs of others, I myself do not find comfort in these sayings. I do believe that my experiences have transformed me and made me somewhat special. Philosopher Friedrich Nietzsche believed that life does indeed break people at times, but when they heal, they heal stronger where the break occurred.

According to Groopman,

> Hope can arrive only when you recognize that there are real options and that you have genuine choices. Hope can flourish only when you believe that what you do can make a difference, that your actions can bring a future different than the present. (2005, p. 24)

Thus, parents need a balance between their distress about the problems that autism presents and the possibilities for the future of the family.

I have been fortunate—I have survived, and time and people have been kind to me. I have gotten over isolating myself from people with typically developing children. I cannot describe how good it is to enjoy hearing and sharing the joys that a father experiences when he beams with pride about his child. It is a normal part of my life now.

I have come to know that Tariq's life makes a difference in the world. He is still my little boy. He still puts his head on my shoulder, and I have never stopped wanting to hear the sound of his voice. Yet I love him no less because of that, and perhaps more in ways I could have never imagined. His greatest gift to me is a glimpse into the human heart in which it is not who you know or what you know or what you have, but who you are. My son has only ever spoken aloud to me once in a while—in my dreams—but this reflection on his silence and communication without words is how his autism speaks to me every day.

3

Understanding Autism

> *I am different. Not less.*
> Temple Grandin

COULD IT BE AUTISM? When is a child just different or quirky? With autism awareness in the major media almost daily, these are the questions that parents struggle with and agonize over with their doctors. According to the Autism Society of America, each day 60 families in the United States find out their child has autism.

The early warning signs or red flags include the following:

- Lack of or delay in speech

- Odd use of language

- Little or no eye contact

- Difficulty with social interactions

- Repetitive mannerisms, such as flapping, spinning, or twirling objects

- Lack of spontaneous or imaginative play

- Preoccupations with objects

- Inflexible routines or rituals

Whether they are shocked or relieved to find their worries confirmed, the first response of many families is to jump in head first to find out what they can do. When my son was diagnosed in 1984, very little information about autism was available for families or even the professional community. Today there is the opposite problem. Googling "autism" yields 159,000,000 results. Amazon lists 6,800 books.

A sign of the times in Montgomery County, PA

The Beginnings of Autism

In 1943, Dr. Leo Kanner first described autism, a condition whose name derived from the Greek for "self-absorption." Kanner was the first physician in the world to be identified as a child psychiatrist. His landmark paper "Autistic Disturbances of Affective Contact" (Kanner, 1943) and Hans Asperger's (1991) "Autistic Psychopathy in Childhood" together form the basis of the present-day study of the autism spectrum. Although they were contemporaries, Asperger's paper was not translated into English until 1991.

Kanner (1943) suggested that the 11 children he had observed did not have the usual motivation for social interaction. He observed these children to be rigid and inflexible. They had severe communication problems and a need for sameness that caused them to react negatively to changes in routine or surroundings. Kanner also suggested that although the condition was congenital, it could be influenced by parenting. In other words, the symptoms were a combination of nature and nurture—a nuanced view ahead of that of the professional community.

Until the 1960s most psychiatrists considered autism to be caused by poor mothering. Some thought it was a form of childhood schizophrenia. In retrospect, I believe that they were confused to see mothers with depression bringing children with autism into their offices. Which came first, the chicken or the egg? Experts now know that depression is a common reaction in parents of children with autism who do not bond in the typical manner with their mothers and fathers, an issue that is discussed more fully in Chapter 4.

Dr. Bernard Rimland was a research psychologist whose son Mark, born in 1956, was diagnosed with autism. Not yet familiar with the word *autism,* after his son's diagnosis Rimland went on a mission to understand autism and bring attention to the disorder. In 1964, he published *Infantile Autism: The Syndrome and Its Implications for a Neural Theory of Behavior.* Its foreword, by Leo Kanner, gave the book credibility among professionals in the field.

At the time Rimland's book was published, and for many years afterward, the standard theory was that autism was caused by unloving *refrigerator mothers.* The term *refrigerator mother* was coined around 1950 and blamed mothers for their children's unusual behaviors. This label was based on the assumption that autism was caused by the emotional frigidity of the children's mothers. As a result, mothers suffered from excessive blame, guilt, and self-doubt. This unproven but widely accepted idea was advocated by University of Chicago professor Bruno Bettelheim in *The Empty Fortress: Infantile Autism and the Birth of the Self* (1967). Bettelheim claimed that the traumatized unloved child retreated into autism.

As a professional research psychologist, Rimland was well positioned to launch the first major attack on Bettelheim's theory. Rimland's was the first authoritative voice to dispute Bettelheim's research and question his conclusions. Parents from all over the United States were excited that for the first time a professional in the field was not accusing them of maltreating their child with autism, and they began to write to Rimland.

Rimland called a meeting in Teaneck, New Jersey, at the home of one of the families that had written to him, and this small group of parents, including Ruth C. Sullivan, became the nucleus that founded the Autism Society of America. Sullivan herself became the first president of the Society. Also involved in the founding of the Autism Society of America was Dr. Bertram Ruttenberg, my son's first child psychiatrist, who had founded one of the first outpatient facilities in the country for children with autism. Drs. Rimland and Ruttenberg both endorsed my earlier book.

Components of the Diagnosis

Several diagnoses under the umbrella of pervasive developmental disorder are considered to be ASDs. These include autistic disorder, Asperger syndrome, pervasive developmental disorder-not otherwise specified (PDD-NOS), childhood disintegrative disorder, and Rett syndrome. These diagnoses appear in the *Diagnostic and Statistical Manual of Mental Disorders (DSM)*, which is the standard for classifying mental and behavior disorders into categories used by healthcare providers as well as researchers in the United States. It is a necessary tool for collecting data and communicating. For each disorder there is a set of criteria which indicates what symptoms must be present or not present to qualify for a particular diagnosis. Because there is no biological test for autism, the diagnosis is made according to behavioral criteria that are reported by parents and observed by evaluators.

Currently, there are three neurologically based core domains of symptoms:

- *Impaired social interaction:* including eye contact, facial expressions, gestures, and body postures. These differences make it difficult to read and understand the feelings and experiences of others as well as their points of view.

- *Impaired communication:* a delay or absence of spoken language with no effort to compensate through gestures; an inability to initiate or sustain a conversation despite having speech; a repetitive or stereotyped use of language; and a lack of spontaneous imaginative or make-believe play.

At the beach in Atlantic City, NJ, Tariq was only interested in the sand running through his fingers.

- *Repetitive and stereotypical patterns of behavior:* a preoccupation with patterns of behavior; compulsive nonfunctional routines or rituals; repetitive mannerisms or self-stimulatory behavior; and/or a persistent preoccupation with parts of objects.

According to *Diagnostic and Statistical Manual of Mental Disorders, Fourth Edition, Text Revision* (American Psychiatric Association, 2000), autistic disorder is defined by at least six symptoms across all three of these domains. Asperger syndrome, in contrast, is distinguished by three symptoms—two related to social interaction and one to habitual or repetitive behaviors. Individuals with Asperger syndrome generally have intelligence in the average range or higher. Language development must be within normal limits, but pragmatic language impairments are common. Asperger syndrome is often not diagnosed until a child reaches school age, when social problems become more apparent. PDD-NOS is used as the diagnosis for children who do not have clear symptoms for another diagnosis within the autism spectrum.

Is it a little confusing as to where your child actually fits? This is no surprise, for in practice, even at leading medical centers, these labels are often not consistently and accurately applied. For the first time, in the *Diagnostic and Statistical Manual of Mental Disorders, Fifth Edition* (American Psychiatric Association, In press), pervasive developmental disorders fall under one large category of ASDs. There will be two core domains with social interaction and communication combined into one with the other being repetitive behaviors with three levels of the diagnosis being proposed.

The impairments associated with ASDs range from total impairment to near reasonable functioning, with a great deal of variability in each individual. There is a wide range of sensory differences, such as sensitivities to noises, textures, tastes, or the way certain things look. Some children may not like to be hugged or touched, whereas others seek out this kind of contact and enjoy it. Some are completely nonverbal, others have very limited speech and may repeat things over and over (*echolalia*), and some may speak very fluently but have narrow interests and have difficulty holding a two-way conversation.

Although the degree of impairment is highly variable, the impact on individual children and their families is life altering. Research has consistently shown that understanding the core symptoms and intervening early and vigorously with educational, communication, and behavioral treatment positively affects the outcome of children with ASDs.

Causes of Autism Spectrum Disorders

There is no single cause of ASDs. The evidence now points to a genetic predisposition with environmental interactions. The data to support this conclusion come from family and twin studies. The risk of having a second child with an ASD is now reported as high as 18.7%, and if the second child is a boy, the risk is 25.9% versus 9.6% for girls (Ozonoff et al., 2011). The identical twin of a child with ASD has a 65% chance of having autism (Folstein & Rutter, 1977). Fraternal twins, in contrast, have no greater rate of autism than other siblings. These various rates suggest an interaction of multiple genes with as yet unknown environmental factors. There is also an increased risk for autism among premature infants. Researchers have also reported a heightened risk in women who became pregnant within 12 months of having their first child (Cheslack-Postava, Kayuet, & Bearman, 2011).

In approximately 10% of children with autism, specific genetic, neurologic, or metabolic disorders are causal factors. These include tuberous sclerosis, fragile X syndrome, Prader-Willi syndrome, Williams syndrome, and Angelman syndrome. In addition, some children with Down syndrome and other genetic syndromes may also have autism. Many medical symptoms are commonly reported in children who have autism. For example, epilepsy is reported in about 25% of children with ASDs. Up to 9% of children with ASDs also have tics or brief involuntary motor movements. Moreover, 50%–70% of children with autism have sleep disturbance with night walking, difficulty getting to sleep, or difficulty staying asleep. Abdominal pain, reflux, diarrhea, constipation, and bloating are also common among children with ASDs. Abdominal discomfort may be a trigger for behavior changes and needs to be assessed and treated as mentioned by Buie and colleagues (2010).

Is There an Epidemic?

The incidence of autism has increased dramatically from 5 in 10,000 in the 1980s (Yeargin-Allsopp et al., 2003) to 1 in 88 in 2012 (Baio, 2012) with boys affected more frequently than girls at a ratio of nearly 5 to 1. Autism was considered rare in the 1980s, whereas today it is a household word. In the 1980s, few pediatricians had been exposed to the symptoms of autism in their training. Most parents had never heard of the term. In contrast, today parents who have concerns about their child's development routinely ask, "Could it be autism?"

Despite the increase in the numbers of children being diagnosed, autism did not become a special education classification in the United States until 1994. The question of whether the total increase in the number of autism diagnoses can be accounted for by increased awareness about the disorder, changes in the criteria for diagnosis, or the establishment of the special education classification is still open to debate and scientific inquiry. The professional consensus is that these trends explain much of the increase. Although a link between environmental exposures and ASD is plausible, there is little specific evidence on this front to explain the huge increase in the number of reported cases of autism.

When Tariq was diagnosed in 1984, only children with severe symptoms were classified as having autism. Children diagnosed today with milder ASDs such as PDD-NOS or Asperger syndrome would not have been diagnosed like this at that time. In fact, only 2 of the 12 children in my son's early intervention preschool class were diagnosed with autism. Yet looking at the pictures I took in his classroom, and reminiscing about how these children interacted and behaved, my guess is that 9 or 10 would probably meet today's criteria for such a diagnosis.

When Tariq started public school, he was placed in a class for socially emotionally disturbed children. The only other option for him was a class for children with intellectual disabilities (IDs). Children with milder ASDs were placed in classes for children with learning disabilities, other health impairments, multiple disabilities, neurological impairments, and so forth. Although there had always been children with the symptoms of ASDs in special education classes, their rising numbers led to fears of an autism epidemic in the media and among parents.

In 2007 a landmark study in the United Kingdom showed

Tariq plays at his early intervention program.

that 1 in every 100 adults has an ASD, either diagnosed or undiagnosed. This report suggested that rates of autism are not increasing because the prevalence of the disorder in adults is in line with the number of children being diagnosed (Brugha et al., 2007). Those adults were no more likely to be using services for mental and emotional problems than members of the general adult population.

Psychologist and grandparent of a child on the spectrum Thompson (2008) traced the history of the epidemic controversy. The term *epidemic* usually describes a rapidly spreading and contagious disease. If there were an outbreak of autism, it stood to reason that there must be a cause. Many parents noticed that their child's symptoms began around the same time as childhood vaccinations were given, particularly the measles–mumps–rubella (MMR) vaccination. Occasionally the MMR vaccination can cause high fever and convulsions within 2 days.

Tariq had received the MMR vaccination in the second year of life, around the same time he lost his speech and started flapping. Like many parents, I wondered about a connection but was not convinced. I was an agnostic on the issue. Our daughters had had their vaccinations with no such symptoms. From my scientific training, I knew that the timing did not prove causation. In 1998, Dr. Andrew Wakefield and colleagues published a study in the prestigious British medical journal *The Lancet* that proposed a causal link between the MMR vaccination and autism. Even though most of Wakefield's coauthors wrote a retraction stating that they did not agree with the conclusion, parent activists in the autism community were especially alarmed about the idea that the MMR vaccine caused autism. What Thompson (2008) described as a "cultural wild-fire" took on a life of its own.

Do Vaccines Cause Autism?

Parents were terrified their children could in effect be infected with autism through vaccinations. Some parents felt certain that immunization caused their child's autism and signed onto litigation against the pharmaceutical companies that had made the vaccine.

A landmark study in Denmark compared 400,000 children who received the MMR vaccine with about 100,000 children who did not get the vaccine (Madsen et al., 2002). There was no difference in the rates of ASDs among the children. Klein and Diehl (2004) reviewed 10 well-conducted studies in the MEDLINE database that had found no evidence of a relationship between the MMR vaccination and autism. Wakefield's (1998) original paper had proposed an association between the MMR vaccination and the onset of gastrointestinal symptoms and ASD. In 2010, *The Lancet* retracted the article because it was based on fraudulent data. Wakefield's medical license has been revoked in the United Kingdom.

Another hypothesized cause of ASDs is the ethyl mercury–based preservative thimerosal, which was used as a preservative in childhood vaccines prior to 2001. Thimerosal was removed from vaccines because it contained potentially toxic levels of mercury that some believed might affect genetically susceptible children and cause ASDs. Yet the rate of ASDs actually increased after the removal of thimerosal from vaccines in Denmark (Madsen et al., 2002). Researchers attributed this increase to broadened diagnostic criteria and increased awareness.

Despite evidence to the contrary, many parents continue to believe that vaccines caused their child's autism. Some pursue chelation therapy to bind and remove heavy metals. Although there is no cure for autism, their hope is to find one and bring a sense of normalcy to their child and themselves. Although I disagree with this point of view and with their deep mistrust of pharmaceutical companies, hospitals, medical professionals, and the U.S. Food and Drug Administration and feel responsible to say so, I certainly respect their passion for their children. I have not been beyond my own paranoia and conspiracy theories regarding help to cure my son. Yet to date there is no scientific evidence of a direct causal link between vaccines and autism.

Associated Conditions

ID (formerly mental retardation) was historically associated with 70%–75% of children with autism. Current estimates are approximately 40% (Chakrabarti & Fombonne, 2001) because of the changes in the diagnostic criteria to include Asperger syndrome and heightened awareness of the core features. Because autism is increasingly understood as a social learning disorder, the number of individuals with autism who have average intellectual capacities has increased. Behavior difficulties may be caused by the core features, such as perseveration and obsessiveness. These lead to symptoms such as aggression, hyperactivity, and self-injury. Problems with mood, including various manifestations of anxiety and depression, may also be related to the impact of the core symptoms.

Overlapping conditions occur very frequently with autism. By the teenage years more than half of all children with ASDs have different forms of anxiety. As Tony Attwood has stated in his lectures, "Autism is anxiety looking for a target." A struggle with social issues is at the root of much of the anxiety experienced by individuals with ASD. Depression, obsessive–compulsive disorder (OCD), bipolar disorder, ADHD, oppositional defiant disorder (ODD), and other conditions may also be diagnosed. Long lists of labels, however, do not help people understand autism. Yet they do help to get services.

An in-depth discussion of these associated conditions is beyond the scope of this book, but you can learn more from the works listed in the Resources section. For example, Tony Attwood's *Asperger Syndrome: A Guide for Parents and Professionals,* James Coplan's *Making Sense of Autistic Spectrum Disorders,* Bryna Siegel's *The World of the Autistic Child,* and Stephen Shore and Linda Rastelli's *Understanding Autism for Dummies* are excellent resources. These conditions require special attention in a child's individualized education program (IEP) as well as treatment outside of school or the symptoms may worsen. At times, medication may be helpful and should be considered.

The Natural History and Trajectory of Autism

For several centuries before the term *autism* was coined by Leo Kanner, the symptoms of autism were described in fictional and historical characters, such as Victor, the wild boy of Aveyron who was apparently abandoned in the forest before being found in the 18th century. However, as recently as the 1980s, ASDs were presumed to be rare. Today they are a public health issue, second only to ID as a developmental disorder. The natural history of ASD demonstrates that most children with autism show improvement over time naturally or spontaneously regardless of intervention. The best known predictors of functional outcome are cognitive ability (IQ), language development, and age at diagnosis. Changes in screening and diagnosis plus the availability of early intervention show promise for altering the course or development of autism. Wherever your son or daughter begins on the spectrum at the time of diagnosis, chances are good that he or she will become less impaired over time.

Kanner was actually the first observer of the phenomenon that some children with ASD show remarkable improvement during the middle childhood years. He summarized his observations in "Follow-Up Study of Eleven Autistic Children Originally Reported in 1943" (Kanner, 1971). He reported observing five of the children between 5 and 6 years of age and finding:

- Varying degrees of emergence from solitude

- Gradual fading of echolalia

- Correct use of personal pronouns

- More spontaneous language

- Acceptance of more food choices

- Better toleration of noises

- Decreased frequency of tantrums and meltdowns

Socially speaking, the children he followed began to relate to a limited number of people to get their needs met, answer questions, learn skills such as reading, and so forth. They tended to deal with people using as few words as possible, preferring to spend their time alone. Between ages 6 and 8, they began to play on the periphery of a playgroup in parallel but not directly with the other children. In school, they learned to read but could not comprehend the overall meaning.

Kanner (1971) concluded, that despite their children being different from their same-aged peers, families were encouraged by progress and improvement. More than 40 years later, many parents, clinicians, and educators make very similar observations. What is remarkable about Kanner's conclusion is that this improvement occurred without any recommended forms of intervention such as ABA, TEACCH, the Picture Exchange System, or Floortime. Kanner reported that several of the original 11 children had done reasonably well as adults, and one had even attended college. Kanner's papers make for very interesting reading and are available at www.neurodiversity.com.

Neurodevelopmental pediatrician James Coplan has proposed a diagnostic model with a possible trajectory for development along three dimensions of the autism spectrum. Coplan (2010) suggested that Kanner's observations as well as those of other scholars indicate that a considerable portion of the progress of children with ASDs is due to the "natural history" of the condition—the course or process of the disorder over time. By having a sense of what would have happened without treatment, experts may be better able to assess the effects of various treatments and plan interventions more effectively.

Coplan (2010) proposed a developmental model that takes into account the fact that not all children with ASD show the same degree of improvement over time with maturation. Atypicality is the first building block of the model and includes social relatedness, language development, repetitive behaviors, and sensory differences. The second building block is intelligence (IQ), based on language, self-care skills, and problem-solving ability. Among children with

ASD, intelligence should not be based on language, as language is affected by autism and can cause others to underestimate the child's intelligence. Time is the third building block in this useful model of motion along the autism spectrum, because children change naturally over time, and with intervention this improvement can be facilitated.

Understanding the Dimensions

A three-dimensional model of autism is congruent with contemporary research that suggests two components of the disorder: 1) social and communication symptoms and 2) repetitive behaviors. In fact, social skills and communication are combined in the Autism Diagnostic Observation Schedule (ADOS), which is the gold standard for diagnosing autism. The ADOS is a semistructured instrument used by a trained professional to evaluate whether individuals—from toddlers to adults, from children with little or no speech to adults with fluent speech—may have autism (Lord, Rutter, & Le Couteur, 1994). The activities that are used in the ADOS provide for interesting and engaging situations in which interaction can occur related to the possible diagnosis of autism.

The National Research Council Report

In 2001, the National Research Council released a report by a blue ribbon panel of experts who had reviewed the evidence from studies of early interventions for children with ASDs. They concluded that ASDs could be reliably diagnosed as early as 2 years of age. They proposed that all preschool-age children with ASDs receive a minimum of 25 hours per week of structured intensive early intervention.

The main goals of autism treatment were spelled out as follows:

1. Fostering development

2. Promoting learning

3. Reducing rigidity and repetitive behaviors

4. Eliminating maladaptive behaviors

5. Alleviating family distress

A comprehensive approach to treatment is recommended, including an IEP, behavioral supports, development of pragmatic language for use in social situations, and family support. These issues are discussed in later chapters of this book.

Public Health and Social Justice

Autism is an equal opportunity challenge. It occurs in equal rates in every social class and culture. Yet access to services to meet the challenge of living with autism is far from equitable, and this fact represents a disgraceful commentary on the state of public health in the United States.

Mandell, Wiggins, Carpenter, DiGuiseppi, Durkin, and colleagues (2009) reported significant racial/ethnic disparities in the diagnosis of children with autism—African American children are identified on the average 2 years later than Euro-American children. These findings are similar to research that documents disparities in the diagnosis and treatment of many health conditions. Significant disparities with the age of diagnosis were also found for Hispanic and Asian children.

The delay, according to researchers, may be caused by inadequate screening, slow response from professionals to parental concerns, or misdiagnosis due to the similarity of some symptoms of ASD with other childhood conditions. For example, hyperactivity and behavior difficulties can lead to a diagnosis of ADHD. Repetitive behaviors may lead to a diagnosis of OCD. Noncompliance and resistance to change may lead to a diagnosis of ODD as opposed to ASD. Mandell, Ittenbach, Levy, and Pinto-Martin (2007) found that African American children who were ultimately diagnosed with autism were 3 times more likely than Euro-American children to receive another diagnosis first. They were also much more likely to receive a diagnosis of conduct disorder or adjustment disorder. These researchers also found that evaluators may be more likely to diagnose autism in Euro-American children and to overdiagnose ID in racial and ethnic minorities.

Parents with more education and information may be more aware of the symptoms of ASD and may be able to observe these symptoms and advocate more effectively for their child's needs. Despite the increasing ability to diagnose autism accurately in very young children, it seems that interaction between parents and professionals lies at the heart of these disparities, which reflects the inequities in U.S. society.

There is an urgent need for state-of-the-art services for all children and families who have been affected by autism. It is alarming that in most parts of the United States a 2-year-old just diagnosed with autism receives only a few hours of home-based services per week, although experts recommend 25 hours of programming per week. Parents should not have to beg and scream for services. Part of the problem is that many schools are poorly funded, especially those in inner cities and rural areas. Staff members are often inadequately trained, and there are too few opportunities for children with autism to develop social skills with their same-age peers.

Interventions and Treatment Strategies

There are still no medications available to treat the core symptoms of ASDs. Medications are routinely prescribed to address challenging behaviors such as hyperactivity, impulsivity, short attention span, sleep problems, repetitive behaviors, anxiety, agitation, aggression, disruption, and self-injurious behaviors. Oswald and Sonenklar (2007) found that 70% of children with autism spectrum disorders from ages 8 and up were receiving some form of psychotropic medication in a given year. These psychopharmacological interventions often help behavioral and educational strategies to work more effectively.

Although medication may alter to some extent the behavior of children with autism, it does not solve the problem of what to pay attention to. Although medication may reduce the occurrence of repetitive behavior, it does not promote social skills. These are skills to be systematically developed and nurtured. Treatment focuses on improving core deficits as well as addressing challenging behaviors and providing help for other difficulties associated with autism, such as anxiety, attention, and sensory difficulties. Behavioral interventions are drawn from the principles of applied behavior analysis (ABA). Social skills interventions focus on facilitating social interactions. Play- or relationship-based interventions use interactions between children and parents or therapists with the goal of improving imitation, joint attention skills, or children's ability to engage in symbolic play. Cognitive-behavioral therapy is used to relieve symptoms such as anxiety. A detailed discussion of these approaches is beyond the scope of this book, but the following web sites are good places to start learning about these treatments:

Organization	Web site
Association for Behavior Analysis International	www.ABAinternational.org
Early Start Denver Model	www.ucdmc.ucdavis.edu/mindinstitute/research/esdm/
Floortime/Developmental, Individual-Difference, Relationship-Based (DIR) Model	www.icdl.com
Picture Exchange Communication System (PECS)	www.pecs.com
Pivotal Response Treatment	www.education.ucsb.edu/autism
Relationship Development Intervention (RDI)	www.rdiconnect.com
Social Communication/Emotional Regulation/Transactional Support (SCERTS®)	www.scerts.com
Training and Education of Autistic and Related Communication Handicapped Children (TEACCH)	www.teacch.com
Verbal behavior	www.behavior.org

Complementary and Alternative Medical Therapy

There is no cure for autism, there is controversy about the best treatment approaches, and many children have poor access to effective treatment. Thus, it is not surprising that many families turn to complementary and alternative medicine (CAM). In fact, a study at the Children's Hospital of Philadelphia found that more than 30% of recently diagnosed children were using some form of CAM (Levy, Mandell, Merhar, Ittenbach, & Pinto-Martin, 2003). Sleep disorders and gastrointestinal problems are very common among individuals with ASDs and not addressed by the standard treatments. Therefore, these novel treatments can be very appealing to families because they claim to address the underlying causes of autism. Although there is extensive literature of case studies and anecdotal evidence, there have been very few systematic controlled studies of alternative treatments.

The gluten-free/casein-free diet is one of the most commonly used alternative treatments. Its advocates usually describe the likelihood of rapid response and provide anecdotal evidence of children who have recovered from autism as a result of following this diet. The diet is based on the theory that children with autism may have an allergy to certain foods, specifically those that contain gluten and casein. This allergy is believed to cause or exacerbate the symptoms of autism. The purpose of the diet is to reduce symptoms and improve social skills, cognitive functioning, and speech. One of the most well-known advocates of this approach is the celebrity Jenny McCarthy. There can be considerable cost and stress to maintain this diet, and the scientific literature does not support the results reported in the popular press.

Marshall (2006) wrote about her experiences using this diet for her daughter Hannah. Hannah also attended an inclusive preschool and received ABA and speech, occupational, and developmental movement therapy. The family was also involved in a form of relationship therapy called RDI. Marshall wondered how much of Hannah's progress was due to the diet and how much was due to the other interventions Hannah received.

Some nonbiological interventions, including auditory integration training, optometric exercises, craniosacral manipulation, massage, yoga, and meditation show promise in helping with self-regulation. As Levy and Hyman (2005) concluded, families of young children with ASD often feel pressure to act immediately. They urged the creation of well-designed studies to assist families in choosing the therapies that are right for them. Scientific evidence, not marketing copy, should be the primary source of treatment information for families and professionals.

Differences Between Boys and Girls

Girls with autism often present themselves somewhat differently than boys, and therefore they tend to be underdiagnosed. Their strengths often mask their challenges. Because boys are frequently mentioned in the mass media, it is often overlooked that girls are also on the spectrum. Although 80% of children with ASDs are boys, 20% are girls, which is a significant number and probably a conservative estimate. Psychologist Tony Attwood has identified common characteristics of girls and women with ASD from his clinical experience. Girls with autism

- Play with dolls to replay and understand social situations

- Often have imaginary friends

- Often have a single friend who provides guidance

- Often observe and try to understand a situation and may mimic the characteristics of others

- Read or watch television and movies to help learn about inner thoughts, feelings, and motivations

- May be categorized as tomboys

- Tend to be more interested in the traditionally masculine areas of mathematics and engineering

- Often show no interest in fashion

- Learn more social skills than boys but may still need to be directly taught certain social skills

- Tend to have a special interest that is unusual in terms of its intensity rather than its focus

- May be more successful at "pretending" to be normal

In general, boys with ASDs are more likely to get noticed because they have bigger challenges with social skills and more of a tendency to exhibit disruptive or aggressive behavior when stressed. Perhaps because girls have better verbal and communication skills than boys, girls are more able to compensate for their autism; therefore, their symptoms do not seem as severe, and they are not diagnosed.

There is relatively little research on gender differences and autism. However, Matson, Dempsey, LoVullo, and Wilkins (2008) did find that in a sample of toddlers, there were gender differences only for the restricted interests and repetitive behavior domain, such that girls had significantly fewer restrictive and repetitive behaviors than boys. The girls were more likely to have obsessional interests centered on people and relationships (whereas the boys tended to have obsessional interests centered on objects); however, the girls' interests were more likely to be acceptable to their parents and therefore tended not to be reported. Despite the differences in presentation between the genders, a treatment strategy should be based on the child's needs, not his or her gender.

Recovery

The idea of recovering from autism is extremely divisive in the autism community. As psychologist Ami Klin has pointed out in his lectures, "In the absence of a definitive cure there are a thousand treatments." Families struggle to get past the shock and turmoil of the initial diagnosis and get the needed services for their children. With dedicated, loving parents, children and their families progress—some by leaps and bounds, some slowly, and some barely if at all. Such is the mystery of the spectrum known as autism. Such is the process of coming to terms with what is changeable and what is not, which varies for each individual.

I have not seen children outgrowing autism, but I have seen how early diagnosis and intensive intervention can lead to developmental progress. I have seen children, teenagers, and adults with autism learning and developing language, academic skills, and social skills and sometimes seeming to be dramatically different from how they were as young children. Fein (2011) reported that most children with ASD still show signs of autism and do not move off the spectrum. It is unknown what percentage of individuals can move off the spectrum or how to predict this outcome. Even those who do move off the spectrum show residual signs of problems with attention, anxiety, and social awkwardness. Prizant (2008) pointed out how promises of recovery often come from professionals with a vested interest in promoting their brand of treatment, whether behavioral, educational, or biomedical. Parents may invest themselves emotionally as well as financially in the idea of recovery, which is supposed to happen by the early elementary school years, according to the professionals with vested interests in advocating these approaches.

There can be profound despair when this recovery does not occur. I am not an impartial observer, as I too lived through the promises of false prophets. Trying things that seemed to make some sense at the time, such as a wheat-free, casein-free diet and other alternative treatments, helped me to live without guilt and regret for not trying hard enough. When parents wonder whether they should try some of the alternative treatments, I counsel them to answer this for themselves by looking carefully at the scientific evidence as well as possible side effects before making up their minds. This prevents one from having to live with regrets later.

Tariq did not recover from his autism; he never spoke another word. Although I sometimes still wonder what might have been, I recovered from my depression when I learned to love my son as he is by understanding what his autism means for him and for me.

4

Starting Over and Falling in Love Again

> *Children learn to smile from their parents.*
> SHINICHI SUZUKI

IT IS HARD FOR PARENTS TO ACCEPT THEIR POWERLESSNESS OVER AUTISM. Yet they do have an influence over their relationship with their children, and they can still have happy children after the diagnosis. Acceptance is a new beginning for parents. When I went for a second opinion because I could not believe the diagnosis, I met Dr. Bertram Ruttenberg, Tariq's psychiatrist at the Center for Autistic Children in Philadelphia. At first I did not like him. He told me that my son's autism could not be cured but only treated, beginning with what he called relationship therapy.

I was really upset and asked him question after question. I asked whether a child could be partially autistic. He looked me in the eye and spoke so slowly and so calmly that I got impatient and thought he had missed the question. But his tone reassured me; he had heard exactly what I had said, and he gave a thoughtful answer. He said it was like asking whether a woman could be partially pregnant. He did not say or imply that I should not be upset. At that point, I was determined that Tariq would recover. It took me another year to understand what he meant.

Observing Dr. Ruttenberg playing with children helped me to appreciate his wisdom. One day he was playing catch with a child, and it was like he was grooming the next Hank Aaron. Another treat was seeing him with the children at Christmastime—my favorite Jewish Santa Claus sitting each child on his knee and giving out presents. From the special way he was treating them, you could get the sense that these kids could be future astronauts or scientists.

Children on the autism spectrum may initially have limited horizons, but their possibilities expand through maturity and treatment. The value that Dr. Ruttenberg placed on the lives of children with autism was a testimony to humanity—people's fundamental relatedness to one another. As I experienced through Dr. Ruttenberg, placing a value on your children places a value on you as a parent, and I could feel it. The essential lesson was to make contact with each

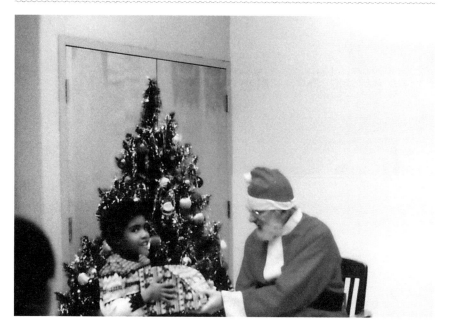

Dr. Bert Ruttenberg with Tariq

child wherever he or she was and grow from there. The approach for dealing with families was to support their journey.

This is not an easy lesson. For parents of children with autism, grief and disappointment can cloud every day. The therapists who worked with Tariq celebrated all of the little things he could do, such as hanging up his jacket or throwing away his trash. I just couldn't get it. He was not talking. He was not becoming more normal. I thought something was wrong with them. I thought, What do they know? They don't go home with him at night!

Eventually I considered the possibility and the growing probability that Tariq, now around 6, might never have typical speech. *Then I began thinking that something was wrong with me.* His therapists loved him as he was. My suffering and my depression came from my own longing for things to be different from what they really were. Now I got it. The tension in my chest lessened. Instead of wishing and pushing him to be normal, I began to make contact with Tariq, the real boy I loved as much as life itself.

Dr. Ruttenberg helped me to see that my efforts, far from being fruitless, contributed to making Tariq more of a pleasant, happy person and more likeable to others. Tariq's personality engages people's interest and their wish to understand and help. He certainly needs a lot of help, and it is to his lifelong advantage that people like giving it to him.

It is comforting to know that Tariq's lovable personality is my legacy to him even after I am gone, and it will help him get what he needs for the rest of his life. Giving everything and expecting nothing in return—no ballet recitals, no homeruns, no As on the report card—this is one of the lessons that a child with autism teaches and perhaps forces a family to learn. This means loving your child unconditionally, not for what he or she will achieve or acquire in life. Learning this has made me a better father for my daughters than I otherwise would have been.

Becoming Parents

It can be extremely helpful to see autism through the wide-angle lens of the parenting experience. Through love and biology, an ordinary man and woman procreate a child. What is less obvious but no less profound is how a child gives birth to two parents. For at the moment of birth a woman becomes a mother, a man becomes a father, and a family is born. Typically there is a powerful drive and near boundless energy to protect and nurture the newborn infant.

The Birth of a Mother, by psychiatrist Daniel N. Stern, pediatrician and child psychiatrist Nadia Bruschweiler-Stern, and Alison Freeland, is an important contribution to understanding parenthood. How rare and wonderful that a book about mothering (and fathering) also embraces the challenges of bonding with and raising a child with special needs. Through interviews and decades of experience, the authors demonstrate how a woman's mental life changes fundamentally with the arrival of an infant. The change in perspective includes shifting from being a daughter to being a mother, becoming a part of the broad community of mothers, seeing one's husband become a father, and forming a mother–father–child triangle. The mother gains awareness of every sight, sound, and smell of the new infant. In modern society, the new mother balances infant and career as she also finds a new role in her family of origin. The new mother counts time with her infant's age and developmental milestones.

A three-part process is suggested (Stern et al., 1998). In the first phase, "Preparing to Be a Mother," while the mother's body forms the fetus, her mind paves the way for her new identity. Hopes, dreams, fears, and fantasies abound about who her infant will be, what motherhood will be like, and how her husband will respond as a father. The physical birth of the infant spawns the psychological birth of motherhood as the real infant comes into focus. The mother looks at the real infant through the lens of her hopes, dreams, and fears. Understandably, a mother may want to repair or redo her own past through her child, but ballet classes or science fairs, for example, are not necessarily the child's wish. It is necessary to put aside these self-fulfilling prophesies and see the infant as a unique individual.

The second phase, "A Mother Is Born," includes feeding, nurturing, and caring for the infant. The intimate relationship with the infant, unlike other relationships, is nonverbal in the beginning. Fundamental questions about loving and being loved are enacted as the mother and infant learn to respond to each other and grow the relationship. Mistakes are inevitably made and need to be corrected. The mother's unfinished business with her own mother may show up and need to be addressed. Ultimately each new mother decides how much of her own relationship with her mother she wants to repeat or reject with her infant—no small dilemma.

The third phase, "A Mother Adapts," deals with career issues and the possibility of having an infant prematurely or with special needs. There are also new dimensions of partnership with the husband. Stern and colleagues embrace the staggering obstacles faced by a new mother learning that her infant is not completely healthy. Faced with such a dramatic loss, a mother cannot anticipate what the future will be for her infant, herself, and her family—there is no clear picture of her infant as a preschooler, adolescent, or adult.

> The birth of a severely developmentally delayed baby is a trauma that virtually stops time in its tracks . . . suddenly your future is unpredictable, and emotionally unimaginable. At the same moment, your past, full of hopes and fantasies of pregnancy, is obliterated and becomes too painful to remember. Parents are held prisoner in an enduring present. (Stern et al., 1998, p. 183)

The Agonizing Process of Acceptance

There is a predictable path through this emotional trauma to an uncertain future. It involves learning about your child's differences in intimate detail and learning to see past the autism disability and repair the bond with the infant you fell in love with when you held him or her for the first time. Whereas the birth of a healthy infant empowers a woman as a mother, the slipping away of an infant with autism can wound her to her core. It can be an agonizing process. The full nature of the problem is not clear at first, and even top experts cannot predict how the child will turn out. Autism becomes a condition of the whole family— not being able to predict the future and feeling isolated and bewildered. Parents need to explore these painful experiences, share with others, and seek counseling when necessary in order to move away from the pain and go on living. Parents can and do learn to grow and love their child in wonderful ways that can seem unimaginable at the time of the diagnosis.

Parents of children with autism live within the spectrum of the parenting experience. No child is perfect, and it is the bond that connects the parent and the child that will sustain families over the long haul. There are similarities and differences in how this bond develops among parents with typically developing children and among parents of children with autism. In all cases, the infant cradled in the parent's arms is different to some degree, small or large, from the child fantasized in the mind. The reconciliation of these images is central in the daily work of all parents. In this sense, parents of children with autism are far from an isolated minority.

Most women and men have some fear of giving birth to a child with special needs. The barrage of information about the impact of food, drugs, alcohol, tobacco, and pollution on the developing fetus serves to heighten the fears that universally haunt expectant parents. Brazelton and Cramer (1990) explained that parents counteract these fears by visualizing the infant as perfect. Positive wishes for the infant and wishes to be perfect parents increase throughout the pregnancy. This is normal and blocks out the worries.

Men's and women's experiences during pregnancy differ. Because their bodies do not change, men are usually able to put aside their worries. However, morning sickness, fatigue, emotional lability, and the growth of the fetus inside are constant reminders to women that their pregnancy is real.

Some parents even imagine what they will do if they have an infant with cognitive disability, cerebral palsy, or even autism if these conditions are present in their families. These scary thoughts explain why most expectant parents want reassurance from their obstetrician that the fetus is developing in the typical manner. When the infant is finally born, they want reassurances from the pediatrician. Even experienced parents may find themselves getting up in the middle of the night to check on the new infant's breathing.

The Six Stages of Parenthood by Ellen Galinsky focuses on how parents develop as their children grow. The major adjustment to a newborn involves the parents' need to feel better about themselves through bonding to the actual infant. In order to do this, they must mourn the perfect yet imaginary infant that got them through the pregnancy. According to Galinsky (1987), this imaginary infant is created in a process called *image-making.* Parents have mental pictures or dreams of how they imagine things will go. Parents remember themselves as children and imagine how they would have liked to have been treated by their parents. Myriad images filter in and out of their minds. Parenthood can be experienced as a journey of images failed and achieved in response to their children's growth.

After *image-making,* which occurs during pregnancy, comes *nurturing,* which extends from birth through the first couple years of the child's life. The *authority stage* comes next, as small children begin to show independence and assert their wills and parents have to learn to set limits. Then the *interpretive stage* follows, when children reach the age of reason and parents explain the world and their values. The *interdependent* stage follows, when teenagers challenge authority, and finally *departure* occurs when parents let go and their children move out into the world. Parents of children with autism wonder and worry whether this will ever happen.

Children do not come with a user's manual, and more often than not, parenthood seems like a land with no clear roadmap. There are countless articles and books about the stages children go through in their development, but they provide little insight into how parents develop after creating or adopting a child and accepting the challenges of family life.

Is this just a stage my child is going through? Or is something seriously wrong? For parents of a child with the warning signs of autism, these haunting questions can come back over and over. Simply put, kids go through stages, parents go through stages, and kids and parents go through stages together. When a child has a disability or special health care needs, these stages are both similar and different to those of typically developing children. The goal of this book is to provide a context for understanding how to sort this out while taking care of the needs of the whole family.

The initial stage of bonding with the actual child and letting go of the image of the perfect child can be far more difficult than usual when the infant has autism or a related disorder. The gap between the real and the imaginary is much wider and harder to accept.

In and Out of Tune

From the first moments of their newborns' lives, parents hunger for responses from them. Infants begin their social interaction by making soothing body contact, by making eye contact, and then later by smiling and making sounds. What expecting parent doesn't dream of a smiling infant who snuggles in their arms?

Infants come into the world "wired" to elicit responses from parents and need this feedback loop. The infant's responses fuel the endless work of parenthood, encouraging a strong attachment and reassuring parents that their love is helping. The parents' enthusiasm in turn encourages and nurtures the child stage after stage. The child is also fueled from within as anticipation generates energy and a sense of mastery begins to develop. This propels the infant toward the next achievement along with the responses in the environment.

When a newborn breaks into the tiniest of smiles, the adoring parent enjoys this and will smile back and often talk to the infant. The infant may coo or gurgle and wriggle in response. This in turn causes the parent to continue the interaction. As child psychiatrist Daniel Stern observed, the face of the mother and the face of the infant have a dialogue with each other. The infant is prewired to look at the parent's face, because this is where the affective bridge first occurs. Thus, the infant is interactive from birth and an active partner in the relationship.

Stern's book *The Interpersonal World of the Child* has a painting by artist Mary Cassatt on its jacket. An infant is focused on the mother's face and reaching a hand up to it, demonstrating how the initial bond between the faces is built. The French sculptor Auguste Rodin conceptualized the face as the mirror of the soul based on the premise that it is in the face that love is found. How common it is to see a new parent making silly faces in order to get an infant to smile and then smiling back in the quest for this pleasant interaction.

As the infant gets older, the capacity increases for verbal interplay—and it *is* play, genuine fun for both parents and child. If an infant says "ooh," for example, parents may say, "That's good!" or say "ooh" back in an encouraging way. Infants like to look at faces and can understand facial expressions and tone of voice, so the parents' natural response offers reinforcement for the infant, who is then fueled to do more and develop further.

It used to be thought that parents had the primary influence in the parent–child interaction. More recent research, however, has shown how vital the child's response is to parents. In this early type of dialogue, each partner influences the other and sets up a response to the reaction of the other. Difficulties experienced by either partner can profoundly affect the relationship.

When the infant's ability to respond to parental nurturing is impaired by the biology of autism, parents' expectations for the relationship are slowly crushed. Their dreams are deflated, which reduces their interest, excitement, and energy level. Quite naturally, this unpleasant feeling results in parents playing and talking less with an infant who does not respond, so the positive flow of affect is interrupted. The impact on attachment is monumental. It is hard to describe the experience when your child stops being interested in you.

The infant, in turn, receives less of a response from the parent and thus loses some of this source of motivating energy, making interactions even less rewarding. This may lead quickly to a withdrawn infant who slumps away from the parent instead of reaching toward the face. Brazelton (1992) explained how the parent then becomes withdrawn or even frightened and slumps away from the infant, feeling helpless and ineffectual.

The infant who has trouble interacting and responding needs more help, not less, from his parents. He needs them to talk and play even more than if he were ideally responsive. Because infants with developmental disabilities have many challenging behaviors, such as frequent and loud crying, difficulty being comforted, and infrequent eye contact, these infants discourage their caregivers from responding. Thus, the parental bond is ruptured and the infant may become even more withdrawn.

Autism Speaks, First Signs, and the FIRST WORDS Project have collaborated to develop the ASD Video Glossary. This web-based collection of videos illustrates the early signs of autism, screening and diagnosis considerations, and common interventions for families and professionals. Videos contrast typically developing children with children of the same age with ASD. Even more helpful and inspiring is seeing the progress that children make with intervention. Readers can access this resource from the web sites of any of these organizations (see the Resources section).

Mothers' Early Experiences

The early mother–child relationship has been likened to a dance in which both partners experience connection, intimacy, and love with each other. Development is an interactive cycle in which relationship is vital. Autism ruptures this cycle. Mothers often experience intense feelings of rejection, disappointment, guilt, and confusion as they become increasingly out of sync with their infant. However, there is hope whenever a new milestone is reached.

It is especially important for mothers to be able to voice these experiences. Referring to typical infants, Winnicott (1993) described maternal preoccupation as a normal stage from which most mothers recover. Yet it is normal for this phase to linger among mothers of children with autism. After the diagnosis and beyond, repairing the ruptured bond is essential. All too often, parents and professionals become too focused on fixing the problems and do not pay enough attention to the key relationships that help everything—including the therapies—to work. The way to turn this around is to make a game out of whatever the child is doing. Just as in the first days of life, the parent–child bond will inspire and fuel both mother and child.

Tariq smiles and shares his joy.

Joint attention occurs when one person alerts another person to something interesting or exciting by means of eye gazing, finger pointing, or another verbal or nonverbal indicator. "Look! Do you see what I see?" is the nonverbal message. For example, one person may gaze at another person, then point to an object, and then return his or her gaze to the person. In this case, the pointing person is initiating joint attention by trying to get the other to look at the object. The person who looks is responding to joint attention. Joint attention involves two people and an object or event outside of them. It is the precursor to more advanced social and communication skills.

A problem with joint attention, which develops between 6 and 9 months of age, is one of the first signs of autism. Some infants develop this skill, then lose it, and may subsequently be diagnosed with ASD. Without the skill of joint attention, children struggle with learning how to speak or how to get their parents' attention when they want something. This leads to them using challenging behaviors as a way to communicate. The parent–child activities described in the next section can help you rebuild joint attention and help your child continue relating and learning throughout the life span.

Getting Back in Sync

Getting in tune with your actual child and letting go of your lost dream for the perfect child starts with coming to an accurate understanding of who your child really is. Brazelton and Cramer (1990) stressed looking at what your child can do and how it can promote bonding and help you understand your child's challenges. The child with an ASD is first of all a child.

When I talk to parents individually or in groups, I always ask them to share the following:

- What new things has your child done lately?

- What do you enjoy doing with your child?

- What are you looking forward to next?

- What are you learning from your child?

These questions bring out the highs as well as the lows of everyday life. In the overall scheme of life, parents are children's primary teachers. It is through everyday routine activities that children learn and develop. Just being there and learning to enjoy your child again is the starting point for getting back in sync.

This starts with taking turns, an essential relationship skill. If your child has autism and might not respond to others, try the following:

- Start with imitating or mirroring your child's actions or vocalizations.

- Follow your child's lead.

- Use facial expressions, gestures, and expressive vocalizations to signal that it is time to take turns.

- Increase the number of turns that keeps your child engaged.

- Decrease whatever leads to less engagement.

The interactive match is fundamental, according to the High/Scope Educational Research Foundation (Wiltshire, 2011). Adults are encouraged to match their child's behavioral style, interests, and developmental level. This means that adults are responsive and interactive rather than directive and controlling. This is the basis of a give-and-take relationship with leading and following as well as speaking and listening.

Strategies include the following:

- Observe your child's behavior.

- Be aware of your child's current developmental skills.

- Adopt your child's pace.

- Respond to your child's cues.

- Follow your child's interests.

- Imitate your child's actions and verbalizations.

- Play with toys in the same way your child does.

- Do and say things equal in length and complexity to those of your child.

- Expand on your child's activity within his or her abilities.

- Return to your child's activity if expansion does not keep him or her engaged.

This developmental app-roach to early intervention is the core of child psychiatrist Stanley Greenspan's Floortime technique. Floortime is basi-cally unstructured time when a parent follows the child's lead and the child's interests—the child is the director. With little children, you might get down on the floor on their level. With older children, you might be sitting, walk-ing, playing a board game, or engaged in a sporting activity.

Playing with Tariq at Sesame Place

The main idea is to build a warm, trusting relationship. A parent can't always just join a child at that child's level, but the more the better. This joining with a child establishes a communication loop on the child's level in which feelings can be passed back and forth. The warmth and trust provides the foundation or platform from which to grow and develop.

Using this approach can transform a seemingly solitary and meaningless activity. For example, at 4 years of age Timmy, who had very little language, just loved to bang LEGO blocks together. His parents tried to hide them from him, but he either found them or cried until they gave them back. Together we sat on the floor in my office while I coached his parents to imitate their son. He looked at them and smiled. They smiled back and felt a connection.

By their next session, they expanded into sticking two blocks together and then pulling them apart and banging them together. Gradually they were able to expand into towers and then buildings. When I heard from them a few years later, Timmy was building shopping malls from LEGOs and having a great time taking turns doing this with his parents.

In my own life, I enjoy walking with my son. One day in the mall Tariq stopped to enjoy the fountain; he sat on a bench, giving us some rare time to be still together. I knew he would be itching to walk again as soon as he finished his soft pretzel. I put my hand on his shoulder and squeezed tightly for a moment—he likes deep touch. My thoughts drifted to other peaceful moments, such as sitting by the ocean listening to the sound of the waves.

Just then Tariq got up and yanked my arm. It was back to the present. He had had enough sitting, and he wanted to walk. That ended our stillness for a while. Now all I could do was just follow his impulses. If the whole family had been together, I might have had to hold him back. He would have protested—stomping his feet and uttering sounds of frustration. That tension breaks my heart.

Whenever possible, I try to go at Tariq's pace. This makes our time pleas-ant. Dealing with the trouble spots that come up is part of the learning curve for parents. This time for me it meant walking at a brisk pace. People must have been noticing—a tall, young man smiling broadly, babbling like a toddler, holding his father by the hand, leading him through the mall twice as fast as everyone else. Occasionally Tariq would twirl his free hand near his head, making an unusual sound, or stick out his tongue, seeming to enjoy the sensation.

I wondered what people thought, and I imagined that most people probably preferred not to think about it. I thought that they must have realized that it was hard being his dad. I imagined that they knew how much I loved him. It had taken me years to stop being angry at the world and to understand Tariq as he is.

Kabat-Zinn and Kabat-Zinn described the deep connection that is "available to us virtually in any moment, even in the more difficult ones, if we stay attuned both to our children and to this moment" (1997, p. 2). There can be moments of pure bliss, such as a child's first steps or first words, or moments of intense frustration and pain, such as during a meltdown or an episode of aggressive behavior. These difficult moments have the possibility of opening parents' minds and hearts to new learning and growth. This inner experience is missing in much of what has been written about parenting in general and about parenting children with autism in particular. Now let's take a closer look at how to get back in sync.

Julie and David, Her Busy Child

Several years ago Julie sought my counsel to help her relationship with her very active 4-year-old son. "He's my only child," she told me, with tears in her eyes and her voice trembling. "He was born when I was thirty-eight. I waited for him my whole life, and this is the way he is. You see it, everyone sees it—he isn't normal. That hurts to say; I'm not sure a good mother would say such a thing or would feel so very, very disappointed in her own child."

David was a bright-eyed, attractive child, but it was obvious that he was different. The new environment of my office excited him. He fidgeted; he went from toy to toy, and he did not seem to listen to his mother. At home he was never still for long, and he got into everything. In preschool he would not sit in the circle. In public, Julie always felt like people were looking at her critically. David's difference made her feel different—at times even ashamed.

"Their eyes seem to say that I'm the mom of a bad kid," she blurted out. She told me how overwhelmed she felt just trying to keep up with David and keep him safe. He was very impulsive. If Julie was not vigilant, he would get out of the house and wander through the neighborhood. She cried as she related to me how he would never just sit and cuddle with her as other children his age did with their mothers. She never got the quiet time she longed for.

At the playgroup she brought her son to, the daughter of one of her friends sat on Julie's lap for a breather. It felt so good to her. As she soaked it in, Julie wanted those moments to last and last. Then she felt guilty for wishing for another child. She wondered why she couldn't just love David as he was at that moment, playing actively and happily with one toy after another. That was the real David. There was something special in this boy's zest for life.

What a bind for a parent to be in! Yet understanding these complicated feelings is essential. It is the dilemma of every parent whose child is not typically developing—working to help the child and yet simultaneously loving and accepting the child as he or she is at that moment. It helps to remember that children are not static but rather dynamic individuals with potential for growth.

Julie worried about her parenting because she sensed that her interaction with her son was not helping him. Intuitively she knew that a change in her could help her son. From birth David had had a generally positive mood, and he was easy to comfort when upset. This quality had kept her going even when she was discouraged by his dislike for physical contact. Now he was becoming moody and disgruntled. Julie thought that this was because she had to supervise and correct him so much of the time.

Julie experienced this tension as a maternal failure. She had expected everything to come naturally and blamed herself that it had not. She needed professional guidance to help her be more comfortable with her son and to encourage his development despite his overactive nature and social difficulties. Many parents in this situation experience similar challenges.

Julie felt some harmony with her son when she was able to match her rhythms and behaviors to his own. I saw this happen while observing them at the playground near my office for one of their sessions. The first step to helping Julie was observing her child in action. I noticed David's agility in climbing and the sparkle in his eye as he took pride in his prowess.

This was the same behavior that often exhausted, stressed, and even angered Julie at home when it was more than she could handle. In the environment of the playground, however, climbing could be embraced almost unconditionally. The only limits or rules were that he couldn't break things or hurt anyone. Julie was then able to breathe easier. It was a relief not to have to correct David, and he was able to play freely.

Next I encouraged Julie to respond to David by joining him while acknowledging his excited emotional tone. Showing interest in what the child wants to do helps him feel valued for who he is. In this case it was climbing.

"Wow! Look at my boy. You're really good at this," she remarked. In enjoying him and staying nearby in the playground, she entered his world. This gave David the support to build his own drama and simultaneously offered an incentive to reach for his mother's slower pace. He paused for a moment and smiled back. Then he quickly moved on to his next challenge. His mother's support encouraged him.

"Look at this!" he exclaimed as he slid down a pole. Continuing to express approval, Julie had encouraged her son's play. Julie took pride in her son, as David took pride in himself. It seemed contagious—what a boost to the sagging self-esteem of both parent and child! Finding the opportunity to respond to her son in this way helped Julie feel like a good mother.

After about 20 minutes of play, David came over to the bench, where Julie and I were watching, and sat on his mother's lap. The drama reached its conclusion. David's high-energy play had received approving expressions, gestures, and words, and now David was reaching out to his mother in a tender moment. Julie began to feel more fulfilled as a mother. David's basic nature would not change, but their relationship could change.

In the moments of mutual comfort and acceptance there is warmth and tenderness. This kind of reciprocal relationship sustains the development of the child and bolsters and heals the injured self-esteem of the parent as well. Julie had entered David's world as a partner and facilitator, a rare role in everyday life, in which she was forced to struggle to contain and control his extremely active behavior. David was able to feel his mother's love, and their relationship helped to facilitate effective behavioral strategies during the rest of the day.

This relationship-based philosophy can also be a guide for engaging infants or young children at the other end of the activity spectrum. Young children who are slow to respond or whose development is delayed also crave mutually pleasurable interactions. Holding or gently touching such a child; talking or singing in a quiet, soothing voice; or rocking or swaying can be quite pleasant and stimulating. When a parent joins in at a faster pace, it can motivate the child to join him or her at a somewhat slower pace. It may not always be reciprocal like this. David might not like to sit and cuddle when his mom wants to, but he may do it on his own terms. If this is the case, then Julie will have to adjust and enjoy this as best she can.

These activities can be built into the daily routine when feeding, dressing, bathing, and diapering or toileting. Siblings, relatives, and friends who are comfortable with the child can all learn to participate in this way—making for a more cohesive family life and facilitating an interlocking web of relationships that can be beneficial for everyone. Every child is constantly maturing, evolving, and dynamic.

There is an unfolding of temperamental qualities and behaviors that is not apparent at birth, especially in the seemingly typical beginnings of children later diagnosed as having autism. Knowing and accepting your child's unique developmental skills is fundamental to relating to him or her in a mutually satisfying way. Expectations that are too high will frustrate when they are not reached. However, expectations that are too low can be a self-fulfilling prophecy. There is a constant process of assessing your child's skills, joining in, and then readjusting the bar for more growth.

Finding Connections

It is normal to wonder and worry when you are a parent of a child with autism. The best antidote to the worry is to find connection in the here and now. Lisa Rudy writes about this in *Get Out, Explore, and Have Fun: How Families of Children with Autism or Asperger Syndrome Can Get the Most out of Community Activities.* There can be life after diagnosis for families and children. Families of children with autism as well as other special needs struggle to arrive at a place that comes naturally to most typical families.

Parents usually jump into learning about a disorder and its therapies and doing all they can to help their child. But the family can risk becoming trapped in a lifestyle that is often devoid of the fun and engagement that is so vital for healing the hearts broken by the diagnosis and fueling the growth that is to come.

Although therapies are vital, lives that revolve almost exclusively around therapy can

Tariq self stimulating while happy and enjoying his Snoopy toy.

become virtual prisons. Parents who imagined becoming soccer or softball or ballet moms and dads become therapy moms and dads. In contrast, shared interests are fertile ground for real engagement, interaction, and learning. Sometimes the simplest principles can be profound, for engagement is central to all of the behavioral, developmental, and educational therapies and approaches to autism and other developmental disorders. Regardless of whether a child is verbal, there are numerous strategies to get any family started.

In this same vein, *The Out-of-Sync Child Has Fun: Activities for Kids with Sensory Processing Disorder* by Carol Stock Kranowitz presents 100 activities that are both fun and therapeutic. Sensory challenges with touch, balance, movement, body position, vision, hearing, smell, taste, and motor planning are all covered in lively and engaging ways that address the underlying issues that so many children with ASDs have.

My years of personal and professional experience have taught me that finding mutually enjoyable activities helps to promote the relationships that families crave and deserve. Although parents might feel powerless in the face of conditions on the autism spectrum, they have numerous possibilities for meaningful lives and family relationships. In *"Just Give Him the Whale!" 20 Ways to Use Fascinations, Areas of Expertise, and Strengths to Support Students with Autism,* Paula Kluth and Patrick Schwarz help teachers and parents understand that the deep interests and fixations that come along with autism can be used as potential tools. Take, for example, Max of the television show *Parenthood,* who seems fixated on bugs. This interest could possibly be expanded into the study of other species and gradually expanded to the study of biology or other aspects of the environment.

Kabat-Zinn and Kabat-Zinn suggested that children can be

> Perpetually challenging live-in teachers, who provide us with ceaseless opportunities to do the inner work of understanding who we are and who they are, so that we can best stay in touch with what is truly important and give them what they need most in order to grow and flourish. (1997, p. 22)

Being the parent of any child demands a lot. Children constantly hold mirrors up for parents to see their best and worst images.

People's lives are fundamentally interdependent. Perhaps this is even more true for children with autism. If their children are not doing well, parents feel it and suffer; parents cannot avoid being affected. This implies that regardless of whether their child has autism, mothers and fathers have to be continuously aware of their own needs as well as those of their child.

How does everyone in the family get what they most need? From my perspective, this occurs in the moment-to-moment interactions in families. Can parents love and accept their children for who they are? When children need it the most—during emotional upsets or challenging behavioral outbursts—love is usually the hardest to give. It is in these moments that parents need the clarity to choose how to be and to see their options. This is the constantly shifting and evolving process of acceptance.

As Pulitzer Prize-winning journalist Gaul poetically observed,

> Life isn't made up of exclamations so much as a succession of small moments strung together like beads on a necklace. Where we go wrong is by expecting too much. Then disappointed and empty we have to find someone to blame. (1993, p. 71)

The resentment pales as parents learn to live moment by moment and find those beads to string on their necklaces.

5

Understanding and Guiding
Your Child's Behavior

> The consequences of an act affect the prob-
> ability of its occurring again.
>
> B.F. SKINNER

"SIMPLY IMAGINE HE'S NOT YOUR CHILD. EVERYBODY KNOWS HOW TO RAISE OTHER PEOPLE'S CHILDREN." Whenever I talk to groups about handling the challenging behavior of children with autism, this statement evokes hearty laughter. Autism is diagnosed by observable activity, and sometimes that activity, otherwise known as behavior, presents problems. The balance between accepting who your child is and handling challenging behaviors is one of the toughest encounters for parents of children with autism.

It is difficult but vital to learn how—in the heat of the moment—to back off, take a breath, and look at the situation, including your own reaction, calmly and objectively. It is important to seek support and insight from another adult—a spouse, a friend, or a professional with experience in the behavioral issues faced by parents of children with autism.

This chapter provides a framework for addressing challenging behaviors: First, get in touch with the deep inner feelings evoked by your child; second, understand the meaning or function communicated through behaviors; and third, learn to flexibly yet firmly apply behavioral strategies. Numerous helpful books, articles, and web sites are available, but professional guidance is often necessary. If you are spending more time correcting your child than guiding and enjoying him or her, then that may be the signal that it is time to seek help.

Getting in Touch with Yourself

The mass media often associate high-functioning autism with bright, quirky kids. In reality, even a mild case of autism or Asperger syndrome results in a child being very different from the average child. A parent may be sad or anxious thinking about a toddler's diagnosis, but by the time that child is in preschool his or her challenging behaviors may arouse frustration or anger. This reaction may produce guilt for not being more accepting; this is a cycle that is not easy to break.

Several years ago I met with George, who was very troubled by his feelings about his son. His eyes glazed over as he described how he had looked forward to the birth of his son as the fulfillment of everything he had wanted in life. Yet his frustration was becoming unbearable. After George was diagnosed with colitis, his physician had recommended that he seek psychological help. He was irritated with his 4-year-old Billy, short-tempered with his wife, and grumpy with their 2-year-old daughter.

George's son had Down syndrome and autism. Billy was not yet toilet trained, and his speech was limited to a handful of words. George had been thinking that he should have been able to handle things by himself. There was no one in his everyday life he could turn to. He had started crying unexpectedly whenever alone in the car—something a lot of men confide to me but usually do not tell their wives because they are trying to be strong.

George and his wife were best friends who had always been able to talk about their problems. But when the subject of George's difficulties with Billy came up, they usually had to stop talking before it got too tense. George told me that his wife felt that he was blaming her for giving birth to a child with Down syndrome and blaming Billy for having the extra chromosome, short forehead, and slanting eyes. He did not want his wife or his children to be the target of his grumpy moods. Even more, he was worried that his frequent crying meant that he was weak.

"Sometimes I feel that my life is over, that I have no future; Maureen is afraid to try again for a normal son. Maybe this is all there is for us. When I'm thinking like that lately during the day in the office, then I don't want to go home. It's so disappointing that Billy can't run up and hug me and sit on my lap and tell me what he has been doing all day. That's what should be happening. Other people are so excited talking about their children. I'm not even enthused about my daughter, and that's not fair. I find myself avoiding them and feeling guilty . . . . I've read up on this stuff, gone to workshops and support groups, and gone through what I've recognized as stages of grief, but I'm stuck. Other people think I have it together—that I'm a good father. I know it's not true, but I wouldn't want anyone to know."

Where was he stuck?

"It's like I've got a chip on my shoulder. I'd love to be a bad dad of a typical son. At least he'd play sports and do other things that I could brag about. And most of all, he'd bring grandchildren with my last name to see me even if I was a jerk. It feels like a contagious disease infecting my family."

Typically Billy woke up around three or four in the morning, usually wanting to play. George and Maureen took turns getting him back to sleep. Lately George had been getting more agitated, which seemed to make his son stay awake longer. Then George might start yelling. That woke up Maureen, and she would get mad at him. George felt like a real jerk, because she did not wake him up when it was her turn. As a result he started his day in a grumpy mood.

As we discussed the rest of a typical day, it was clear that George had a good feel for how to manage many situations. He was a knowledgeable parent who might have done well with a typically developing son. By the end of the session, George commented that he felt relieved from unloading his heavy feelings. I asked him to reflect on his interactions with Billy in the middle of the night so that we could understand and perhaps modify how he dealt with this flashpoint.

George told me about his family history and why he had wanted a son so badly. His dad had spent a lot of time playing baseball with him and his older brother and taking them to Phillies games. He wanted to do the same with his son and pass on the tradition. He related how he had begun sobbing lately every time he passed a Little League baseball field with a game going on. He wondered if that was "normal" in his situation, and I assured him that it was.

"You know, I feel guilty at times like that. It's not Billy's fault. It feels wrong of me to be upset about baseball. He's such a peaceful child. Everyone who works with him tells us how well he is doing. He likes playing a little rough with me, and I feel really good then."

What was he thinking and feeling the last time he was up in the middle of the night?

George's voice started to shake. His face got pale, and his eyes widened. He leaned slightly toward me. "When I got angry the other night, I wished that Billy and Maureen would die. Then I would be free of this horrible, ugly burden. Then I could go on with my own life...right now I'm stuck with the two of them."

Then the tears started. George took a few deep breaths before wiping them away.

"I feel such a sense of relief that I told someone. I've been having these thoughts for a while. How can you tell the woman you love that sometimes you wish she was dead? I'm not sure what you think of me. . . . I wonder if any of the other people in my support group have thoughts like these. Has anybody else ever told you something like this? Can you tell me that?"

Now that George was strong enough to admit to having these scary thoughts, he would soon have the courage to ask others what they were really thinking. It is relieving to hear from others. As for me, I have heard similar things many times and usually with tears. The tears do not come easily, especially for men, even though they are often on the inside. Admitting and embracing your sorrow is part of the healing process.

The pressures of everyday life can push any parent to the edge, but having a child with autism only magnifies this stress. Feelings of inadequacy often arise around basic daily activities, such as eating and sleeping. These feelings can be frequent and intense because of the high stress levels of parents of children with autism who have difficulty regulating themselves physically and emotionally. Being angry with one's child can exacerbate these feelings. Yet it is necessary for parents to admit to having these feelings in order to reconstruct an image of themselves as good people just trying to do their best in trying circumstances. George was a good man who was acting badly. Being able see himself in a friendly and compassionate way made it possible for him to think clearly and find different ways of handling a practical situation.

George had to learn how to regulate his own feelings in order to learn how to manage Billy's behavior better. *Coregulation* refers to the process by which relationship partners, in this case a father and son, form an emotional system that can oscillate between arousal and calm. In the middle of the night, when his defenses were down, George had discovered the darker side of his personality, and times such as these presented opportunity for growth. Having been there myself in the middle of many nights with Tariq, I remember all too clearly how horrible George could have felt. *Acknowledging such dark, frightening thoughts was the first step in breaking free of the shame of having them and learning to regulate them.*

The following week George told me that he felt 20 pounds lighter and less angry. He was still short on sleep, and life was still the same. When it was his turn to be up with Billy, he was better at getting him back to sleep. He was able to rock him and play lullabies and do what worked without getting caught up in his anger, which had been making things more difficult. Sometimes when we can change the way we are relating to a situation, it leads to a change in our child.

Once he started handling things better, George was able to confide in his wife the dark feelings he had been experiencing. Maureen said that she had been feeling like he wanted to get rid of her and Billy. She said that some days she felt as if life were not worth living. Now George felt closer to Maureen, and they became able to comfort each other and work out problems. Their marriage could once again provide the emotional support both spouses needed.

In this case, George had to get in touch with his anger in order to understand himself and begin thinking clearly about how to handle his problem. Another situation could involve embarrassment about a child's behavior in public, guilt over a strict punishment, or inadequacy in understanding a child's needs. Whatever the case, understanding and embracing your inner reaction and discussing it with others is the key to accepting your anger and figuring out solutions.

I always wondered what he was trying to tell me.

Understanding What Your Child's Behavior Means

Once a child becomes mobile and develops the ability to communicate his or her needs and wants, questions of authority become increasingly important. Parents are faced with a set of questions that will remain with them for many years, such as

- When do I say yes?

- When do I say no?

- How do I enforce the rules?

- How do I know when I'm right?

- What is safe for my child?

From the moment of the child's birth, child and parent learn to understand each other through smiles, eye contact, crying, and cooing. As a child's mobility increases through rolling, creeping, crawling, cruising, walking, and climbing, parents will have more and more decisions to make about what to allow and how to enforce it. Near the end of the child's first year of life and on into the second, what has been complex and subtle becomes more direct and verbal. Included in the parent–child repertoire is the concept of "no," which can be conveyed verbally or physically. The emergence of autism, usually not yet diagnosed, complicates this stage for parents.

The challenges faced by parents of a child with autism can be overwhelming. It can be extremely difficult to remain objective. Individuals vary in terms of their behavior and how they express it. Some children exhibit intense expressions of emotion, biting, kicking, or other physically forceful behaviors. They may have extreme difficulty making the transition from one activity to another or separating from their parents. A parent's inevitable frustration can escalate into anger at the child, which is very uncomfortable. An angry parent can make a child feel unloved, humiliated, and abandoned, feelings the parent may remember from his or her own childhood. As Galinsky (1987) mentioned, an unmet expectation is usually at the core of a parent's anger. This upset is compounded by guilt when the parent regrets his or her reactions.

A child's behavior also draws attention to the parent. When a child is having a tantrum in a supermarket, for example, other customers may wonder why the parent cannot control that child. The parent is likely to be embarrassed and may feel inadequate. The frustration and anger generated can be very toxic. It is common to want to disappear or to want the child to disappear.

It is hard to think clearly when clueless but well-meaning others offer advice. Parents may receive a lot of unsolicited advice because there is no visible reason for the child's challenging behavior. Because the signs of autism are invisible, the behaviors themselves draw attention, which can make life even harder for the family. When the signs of a child's condition are visible, such as with cerebral palsy or Down syndrome, others are more likely to show compassion.

Naturally, parents want their child's challenging behaviors to go away. However, struggling against these behaviors can be like getting stuck in quicksand—the kicking and screaming pull you in, and then you will drown. The way to get out is to breathe and remain calm. Quicksand is usually no more than 4 or 5 feet deep. If you panic you can sink further, but if you relax, your body's natural buoyancy will cause you to float. Breathing deeply helps you remain calm and makes you more buoyant. Then you can gently paddle to the side and pull yourself out. There is a parallel process for handling behavioral challenges and autism.

Since the 1980s, there has been a shift in the approach to treating autism focusing on the function of the behavior. Today, instead of just trying to stop the behavior (especially with children who have speech and language impairments), professionals trained in this approach teach parents to see and interpret every behavior as meaningful. Parents often learn to recognize what their infant needs from the type of cry. In the same way, it helps to think about what a child with autism might be asking through behavior instead of words. For example, the child may be

- Hungry

- Sleepy

- Overstimulated

- Understimulated

- Frustrated

- Avoiding something

- Feeling sick or in pain

Children who have limited verbal and nonverbal vocabularies must give their parents messages through their behavior. This is called *communicative intent*, and such behavioral messages naturally stimulate parents to wonder what is on their child's mind. When these messages are misunderstood, especially when the child is using socially unacceptable behavior to express himself or herself, both parent and child can become intensely frustrated. Parents often understandably focus on what is considered unacceptable and try to stop it.

Tension heightens for both parent and child when the parent tries to stop the behavior without understanding its intended message, and it heightens still more if the child keeps doing the same thing. The unacceptable behavior may be the only means through which the child can express his or her need or want. Trying to grasp the intent provides a starting point for parents to receive the child's message and then teach the child how to express it in a more socially appropriate way.

When you can understand why your child is behaving the way he or she is you can have empathy. Empathizing does not mean agreeing or giving in, but *understanding*. And empathizing makes it a lot easier to work on changing a behavior that is a problem. Greene (2010) explained that children with challenging behaviors, not just children with autism, are challenging because they lack skills. These skills include flexibility, frustration tolerance, and problem-solving skills. In this model, challenging episodes occur when the demands placed on the child in a specific situation exceed the child's ability to respond adaptively. So behind every challenging episode is a lagging skill and a need for that skill to solve the problem.

For example, 3-year-old Joanne, who has no speech, starts pushing her 5-year-old sister when she is tired of playing with the blocks. Realizing that her child is bored enables her mother, Christine, to empathize with her child's limited language rather than criticize her for being physically forceful. Joanne can then be asked to point to what she wants to do. As a rule of thumb, as a child develops a communication system through words, gestures, or pictures, many challenging behaviors fade away.

In addition, most children with autism have problems processing information received through their senses. They have difficulty interpreting sights, sounds, and sensations from touch and movement. They may become unusually upset, for example, by bright lights or loud noises or by being touched or moved unexpectedly or in a certain way. They might also have problems using their muscles effectively, which might cause difficulty in learning to run, jump, or hop (actions that require groups of large muscles, or gross motor skills) or button, zip, cut, or write (actions that require groups of small muscles, or fine motor skills). If a child has difficulties rooted in the sensory system, then sensory integration therapy may be able to help correct the problem. In *The Out-of-Sync Child*, Carol Stock Kranowitz helps parents to understand and address these issues.

Understanding that a child is always trying to communicate something often serves to defuse the buildup of tension between parent and child. Often I have observed parents relax visibly when they start thinking this way about their child. Doing so makes it possible to look at how to change behaviors that are problems while remaining relatively calm. The chart detailing challenging behavior shows some possibilities.

Challenging behavior	Possible function
Crying, whining	To get attention, to get out of doing something, to indicate pain in the stomach, to express frustration
Throwing things	To express anger, to hear the sound it makes, to see how others react
Hitting oneself, head banging	To get attention, to express frustration, to avoid doing something, to experience the internal sensation
Biting others	To express overstimulation, fatigue, hunger, and so forth; to get out of an activity; to engage others
Flopping on the ground	To get something (e.g., more french fries), to get out of doing something, to receive stimulation

A Brief History of Behavioral Principles and Autism

The focus on behavior seems to be the most common viewpoint whenever autism is discussed. The almost universally negative connotation is that something must be stopped or extinguished. Since the 1960s, behavior management has dominated the discussion around the treatment of autism. This is simply because aggression, self-injury, tantrums, and disruptive behaviors can make family life miserable at times and education virtually impossible.

B.F. Skinner invented his own philosophy of science called radical behaviorism. Skinner's experiments on changing behavior were done in laboratories with rats and then widely replicated in other settings and with human participants. He found that behavior often did not depend on a given stimulus, as the earlier behaviorists John Watson and Ivan Pavlov maintained. Instead, Skinner found that behaviors were dependent on what happened after the response.

Radical behaviorism seeks to understand behavior as a function of reinforcing consequences in the environment. Reinforcement is primary in the shaping of behavior. A common misconception is that negative reinforcement is synonymous with punishment. This misconception is even found among some professionals who call themselves behavior specialists. Briefly, *positive reinforcement* is the strengthening of behavior through the application of something after a certain action or behavior, such as praise after a child puts his trash in the wastebasket. According to Skinner and the principles of behavior analysis, organisms, including humans, learn through positive reinforcement. However, *negative reinforcement* is the strengthening of behavior through the removal or avoidance of something. Punishment, in contrast, weakens a behavior because a negative condition is introduced or experienced as a consequence of the behavior. For an adult, for example, getting written up for lateness from work would be a punishment. The table on behavior and consequences illustrates these key principles.

Antecedent	Behavior	Consequence	Result
While the class works Serita is still staring at her paper.	Serita throws her paper on the floor.	Teacher walks away.	Serita gets out of the activity. This behavior is negatively reinforced.
It is time to clean up before lunch.	Serita throws her book on the floor and screams, "I don't want to!"	Teacher says, "No recess until you clean up." Serita puts her book away.	The possibility of punishment modifies the behavior.
It is time for math.	Serita takes out her book and stares at the ceiling.	Teacher waits for Serita to pick up her pencil. "Way to go Serita."	There is positive reinforcement when she picks up her pencil.

Skinner's philosophy of science is humanistic at its core. In the preface of *Walden Two,* a utopian novel first published in 1948, he wrote,

> It is now widely recognized that great changes must be made in the American way of life. Not only can we not face the rest of the world while consuming and polluting as we do, we cannot for long face ourselves while acknowledging the violence and chaos in which we live. The choice is clear: either we do nothing and allow a miserable and probably catastrophic future to overtake us, or we use our knowledge about human behavior to create a social environment in which we shall live productive and creative lives and do so without jeopardizing the chances that those who follow us will be able to do the same. Something like a Walden Two would not be a bad start. (p. xvi)

Behavior analysis grew out of Skinner's theory and was applied to a broad range of behavior later called ABA. Ivar Lovaas applied behavior analysis to the treatment of autism. Lovaas developed an extremely popular program based on Skinnerian principles at the University of California, Los Angeles, in the 1970s. Originally called the Young Autism Project, this was the beginning of discrete trial training. Because children with autism are different than typically developing children neurologically speaking, it is more difficult to engage them. As Lovaas wrote in the *Autism Advocate* in 2008, "The typically developing child is engaged in and learning from his or her environment approximately 16 hours a day" (p. 13). His program brought that intensity into families' homes with 40 hours per week of discrete trial training with additional hours of engagement by parents. This allowed the child to generalize better and use his or her skills, especially verbal skills which are a strong predictor of future success in academic as well as social realms.

Dramatic results were reported in a widely cited study published in the *Journal of Consulting and Clinical Psychology* in 1987. After receiving at least 40 hours per week of ABA for at least 2 years, 47% of 19 children with autism tested with normal IQs and were in general classrooms. Only 1 child of the 19 in the control groups achieved this level of functioning. Lovaas proclaimed that these children had "recovered" from autism. Thus began the claim that ABA could cure autism despite the reservations of several scholars that the study participants had been relatively high functioning with good prognoses and had not been randomly assigned to control or treatment groups, as in a true experiment.

Although the results were dramatic, they did not point to a cure. Instead, according to Herbert and Brandsma (2002), the exaggerated claims served to undermine the approach and mislead families and professionals. Attempts to replicate Lovaas's original results have consistently failed to demonstrate the kind of dramatic results he reported. A family whose child fails to recover from his or her autism may experience intense guilt out of the belief that they did not do enough to help their child. Promoting false hope of recovery also contributes to denial about the lifelong nature of autism. However, a balanced view about the possibilities for progress helps a family to sustain their efforts and take care of the needs of everyone in the family.

Yet it is worth noting that the approach has considerable merit and has evolved over the years since the landmark study. As Lovaas himself wrote in the *Autism Advocate* in 2008, "Traditionally, behavior therapy has been known as a method of controlling 'bad' behaviors. Our experiences and research showed that it is far more than that. Behavior therapy, as we applied it in our treatment program, was used to teach skills" (p. 14). Teachers and therapists have routinely observed that as a child gains more skills, particularly language skills, the challenging behavior decreases.

As Prizant (2009) pointed out in "Treatment Options and Parent Choice: Is ABA the Only Way" there are varying definitions of ABA. The range of practices has evolved since the 1960s. Traditional ABA uses primarily one-to-one teaching in various settings and does not focus on the core social communication and relationship challenges. In contrast, contemporary ABA involves more flexible naturalistic teaching in normal routines and activities and includes a focus on social initiation. Contemporary ABA practices, such as incidental teaching and pivotal response training, appear very similar to developmentally based approaches such as Floortime (DIR), RDI, and the SCERTS® model. The emphasis of contemporary ABA has become more naturalistic overall, with a strong developmental and child-centered focus.

In 2001, the National Research Council of the National Academy of Sciences concluded that there was no evidence that any one approach to treating autism was better than any other approach for use with young children. The National Research Council recommended that children with autism be actively engaged in intervention for at least 25 hours per week. According to their report *Educating Children with Autism,* the most important areas to focus on include

- Functional spontaneous communication

- Social instruction in various settings

- The teaching of play skills and play with toys and peers in groups

- Instruction leading to the generalization and maintenance of cognitive goals

- Positive approaches to responding to challenging behaviors

- Functional academic skills, when appropriate

Travis Thompson's *Individualized Autism Intervention for Young Children* is an extremely useful book for sorting out what is known about autism in young children and what can be done to alter its course. As an expert senior psychologist and grandparent of a child with ASD, Thompson has written a groundbreaking book based on solid theory and emerging research. As Thompson points out, autism and its treatment have become battlefields among psychology's warring factions, much to the detriment of children with autism and their families. There is no need to pick a side. Treatment that is often complicated can involve a blend of logical, child-centered approaches.

I am particularly excited about the possibilities for the Autism Intervention Responsiveness Scale, Research Edition, which is included in Thompson (2011). This scale gives professionals an in-depth guide to creating an *autism intervention profile* for each child based on the type and severity of the child's autism characteristics. By completing the profile, parents and caregivers can match individual characteristics and needs with a specially tailored blend of discrete trial and developmentally oriented naturalistic teaching.

Tariq signs for more.

I am deeply troubled by budget cuts that threaten the availability of necessary services for children with autism and their families. As Thompson (2011) noted, most evidence indicates that 25–30 hours per week of one-to-one intervention are needed over the first 1–2 years of the child's life after diagnosis in order to make significant gains in treating core autism symptoms. The time is now for professionals and families to advocate through organizations for what children need and deserve.

Understanding Positive Behavior Support

An ounce of prevention is worth a pound of cure. Positive reinforcement of desirable behavior is the best prevention for challenging behavior. It is all too easy to spend a lot of time focusing on a child's challenging behaviors, especially because any behavior that makes the child appear atypical is particularly unpleasant for parents. Reducing or eliminating such behavior may make the child appear, and actually be, more typical, which is one reason parents often focus on the problems—and so may overlook many of the child's strong points.

When a child consistently gets a lot of attention because of challenging behavior, he or she learns to engage in this behavior as a way of relating or belonging. Parents, however, often grow discouraged and feel guilty when they must constantly correct their children. Although setting limits is necessary, doing so can be balanced by noticing and praising positive behavior. This kind of effort, which has been called "catching the child being good," results in a child getting more *yes* responses and fewer *no* responses, which feels good to parents and child alike.

Galinsky (1987), a developmental psychologist, reported an informal experiment in a child care center with the parents of typically developing children, who tended to overestimate the amount of time that their child was difficult to handle and underestimated the time that he or she was cooperative. Responding to the positive builds a positive self-image and confidence. It is especially beneficial to notice and comment on positive behavior as soon as possible after correcting a child for an undesirable behavior. Doing so reassures the child that he or she is still loved and valued even though he or she has just been corrected.

Positive behavior support is a practical approach to challenging behaviors that is based on ABA and incorporates developmental principles. Positive behavior support involves a functional assessment and a behavior support plan that is based on that assessment. The assessment includes the observations of parents and professionals. The support plan includes several components, such as teaching the child alternatives to the challenging behavior in terms of communication, adjusting the environment to remove triggers for the challenging behavior, and increasing positive reinforcement of desired behavior. These techniques are among the various strategies that research has demonstrated to be effective. It is important that the assessment and the strategies be suitable for a given family's skills and willingness to use them. Details about functional assessment and positive behavior support plans are available in many excellent resources on the Internet as well as in articles and books. The National Technical Assistance Center on Positive Behavioral Interventions (www.pbis .org) is a good starting point for these resources, as well as *Positive Behavioral Support: Including People with Difficult Behavior in the Community* by Lynn Kern Koegel, Robert L. Koegel, and Glen Dunlap (1996).

In my meetings with parents individually and in groups, I have found it useful to ask them to observe when the problems are not occurring. This tends to make people stop and really think about and analyze what is going on in their homes. Here are some examples of moments when parents catch their child being good:

- When the child is doing something he or she likes to do by herself

- When the parent is doing something with the child, keeping him or her occupied

Tariq folds his hands on cue which helps him to stop flapping and connect to an activity. Photograph by Tommy Leonardi.

- After a nap
- When things are going according to schedule
- During a structured activity
- When the child is outside
- When the child is eating his or her favorite foods
- When the child is going for a ride in the car

Children need loving, positive attention along with limits. A deficit in either area will inhibit growth. This is particularly true when the challenges are great; children with autism tend to make more progress when reasonable expectations are made and parents hold to them. Conversely, unrealistic expectations may be counterproductive and discouraging to both parent and child. For parents of all children, the inner struggle over setting limits and establishing who is in control continues until the child leaves home.

At the core of many parent–child conflicts is the expectation that the child should be acting differently. Successful limit setting is based on realistic evaluations of the child's skills. Understanding a child's capabilities helps to avoid setting unrealistic limits, and it is important to understand the effect of the child's unique variant of autism on whatever limit is being considered. The child may not be intellectually able or developmentally able to do what is being expected. Reasonable expectations can be formulated with the help of other parents and professionals who know your child as well as with the help of developmental checklists. It is vital to maintain a warm relationship with your child whenever you are setting limits. This will help your child realize that you are trying to teach him or her through that connection. You in turn will feel less guilty for restricting your child. Both developmental and behavioral approaches to challenging behavior recommend teaching one key issue at a time and using broad, enforceable rules that are repeated frequently, calmly, and firmly.

When parents begin to set and enforce rules, there is virtually no way to avoid revisiting their own childhood. Most parents consciously aim not to repeat what hurt them as children. In this respect, they may be trying to be the parent they themselves once wished for. People who grew up with inflexible, authoritarian parents may strive to be flexible and empathetic and may therefore find it hard to set and enforce limits. On the other end of the continuum, those who grew up with permissive parents may have longed for more structure and rules and the security that can come from firm direction. The techniques of either of these two groups will have to be reshaped for these individuals to be successful parents.

Consider the following possible causes of your child's challenging behaviors:

- Your child may not understand what is expected.
- You child may not have a skill that is needed in a certain situation.

- Something in the environment may be interfering with your child's ability to use a necessary skill.

- A feeling, such as anxiety, or an internal experience, such as pain, may be expressed through behavior.

- A task may not be rewarding.

- Something else may be more rewarding.

There may be other reasons or needs which trigger challenging behaviors as your child's way to meet those needs, such as

- Getting an item, such as food, or being able to engage in an activity, such as watching a video or going outside

- Getting attention from a parent, teacher, or other children

- Escaping an activity, such as bedtime

- Expressing a feeling, such as fear or anger, or saying no

- Engaging in self-stimulation for fun

- Engaging in self-regulatory behaviors such as rocking, spinning, or flapping as a way to manage overstimulation or anxiety.

Functional Behavioral Assessment

Functional behavioral assessment is a process of understanding the relationship between your child's challenging behaviors and the reasons for them. This process has been mandated for use in schools by several states through their departments of education as the best approach for dealing with challenging behaviors. By performing a functional behavioral assessment it is possible to understand

- Why problems happen

- How we can change our behavior to prevent them

- How we can change environments and routines to prevent them

- What skills we can teach our child to replace the challenging behaviors

- How we can use effective consequences to decrease challenging behaviors and promote functional replacement behaviors

To begin thinking about the functions of behaviors it is necessary to consider four key concepts. First, consider the *setting events.* These are the events that set the child up for challenging behavior, such as

- Medication or medication changes

- Illness or pain

- Sleep patterns
- Diet or hunger
- Changes in routine
- The physical setting
- Relationships with others
- Communication problems
- Sensory issues

Second, consider the *antecedents,* or the events that happen immediately before the challenging behavior occurs. Antecedents may include

- Requests or directions to do things that a child does not like and/or finds difficult
- Interruptions to activities the child enjoys
- New situations or people
- Exposure to things that make the child fearful or anxious
- Loud noises, painful tactile sensations, or other types of difficult sensory experiences

When considering potential antecedents, it can be helpful to step back from the intensity of the moment and ask who, what, when, and where questions, such as the following:

- Who is around when the behavior occurs or does not occur?
- What is happening when the behavior occurs or does not occur?
- Is the child being asked to do something he or she does not like or finds difficult?
- Is the child being asked to wait or take turns?
- When is the behavior likely or unlikely to happen?
- When are transitions difficult?
- Are mealtimes difficult? What about going to bed or getting up in the morning?
- Where is the behavior likely or unlikely to occur (e.g., at home, at school, in the community)?

Third, consider the *function of the behavior,* which is typically classified as follows:

- To get desired items or activities
- To get attention or help
- To avoid/escape demands, activities, or people
- To express strong feelings or pain

- To refuse something

- To play or stimulate oneself

Finally, consider the *consequences*. In order to understand the function of a challenging behavior, ask yourself what happens immediately following the behavior. Consequences can be either positive or negative in quality. For example, a child may scream and throw things to avoid picking up his toys. A parent may respond by placing the child in time-out. The parent may believe that this consequence is negative, but it may be rewarding to the child because the time-out is a way of avoiding the demand, at least for the short term. A good way to understand the influence of consequences is to observe what happens immediately following the behavior. Then, through repeated observations, you may see that a particular consequence is reinforcing or maintaining the behavior and thus making it more likely to happen again.

Developing Behavioral Interventions

Once you have developed an understanding or hypothesis for why your child's challenging behavior is occurring or for what function it serves, you can develop strategies to intervene with a good chance of improving the behavior through learning. Positive behavioral interventions are not punishments. The strategy you try should address each component of the problem analyzed (i.e., setting events, antecedents, function of the behavior, and consequences).

- Setting event strategies take into account the individual characteristics of the child and may include physiological or sensory issues, environmental variables, predictability or routine, choices, and so forth.

- Antecedent strategies address the events that precede and trigger challenging behaviors by increasing predictability, providing choices, changing the way the parent makes requests, signaling the child to let him or her know that something is happening soon, prompting a desired behavior, providing a reminder of what to do, practicing a new or difficult behavior, using the "first–then" rule (e.g., first eat a bite of this, then you may have this), providing additional help with new or difficult tasks, and so on.

- Teaching strategies help the child develop new skills with a goal of replacing the challenging behavior. These may include functional communication skills, social skills, relaxation techniques, time management strategies, and so forth. It is important to try various methods of instruction, including verbal, visual, and even physical assistance.

- Consequence strategies are designed to lead to a decrease in challenging behavior and an increase in the use of a functional replacement. For example, if you teach a communication skill, you respond to what the child communicates; if you teach the child to make choices, you honor those choices right away; and if you promise an item or activity as a reward, you provide it right away. If you provide a negative consequence in order to reduce a challenging behavior, it should not inflict pain or humiliation. Negative consequences should be readily available and natural and should be provided as soon as possible following the undesired behavior. Most important, they should achieve the desired effect.

The chart provides an example of what these ideas might look like at home and at school.

	Home	School
Setting event	Jose got off the bus and walked in the door.	This is Tyler's first day back at school after 2 days home sick.
Antecedent	Mom was on the telephone.	Teacher said, "It's time for math."
Behavior	Jose screamed for 2 minutes and banged his head on the wall.	Tyler threw his math book on the floor, which happens periodically.
Consequence	Mom got off the telephone.	Tyler got a time-out.
Hypothesis	Jose wants attention. Jose is bored. Jose wants a snack.	Math is too hard. Tyler is out of the routine. Tyler needs a break.
Antecedent strategies	Plan to provide more attention. Keep telephone calls short. Engage Jose in a favorite activity.	Review the schedule. Provide a transition to math. Provide breaks as needed.
Teaching strategies	Teach Jose how to get attention with words, signs, or symbols.	Provide extra help during math. Give Tyler fewer problems. Teach problem-solving skills.
Consequence strategies	Give extra time on a preferred activity if Jose is patient during a short telephone call.	Give extra art work as an earned reward. Take away extra credit previously earned.

When thoughtfully done with input from various sources, functional assessment is a process for determining the relationship between events in the child's environment and the occurrence of challenging behavior. When challenging behaviors reoccur, and efforts to address them are unsuccessful, parents need to take a time-out and reengage the process to better understand why this behavior is happening and what they should do to assist their child in learning new skills. While the process outlined here is logical, it is not always easy to implement. It is often useful to get the services of a professional with training and experience in functional assessment either from your school district or independently.

Emotion Regulation and Challenging Behaviors

Emotion regulation is an internal developmental process that allows people to deal with daily stresses and challenges. Challenging behavior in people with autism has been viewed primarily through the lens of behavior management; considering the influence of emotion regulation, which is developmentally based, represents a person-centered approach with great potential for problem solving. The problematic observable behaviors that children with autism struggle with are merely the tip of the iceberg. It is respectful and compassionate to consider the internal struggle to stay well regulated emotionally that people with autism face.

An emotion regulation approach views most challenging behavior as the result of a dysregulated emotional state (Prizant & Laurent, 2011a [Part 1]). It considers biological, psychological, and social factors and focuses on developing the ability to regulate emotional arousal. It supports emotional well-being and availability for learning and socializing. Everyday life is filled with unpredictability and unexpected changes, but people with autism have a difficult time coping with these changes. People with autism also often lack control over their level of arousal. In addition, emotional memory of the feelings associated with people, places, and events is an important factor in being able to regulate an emotional response to a situation. Because people with autism generally have strong rote memories, stressful events evoke strong emotional reactions. These reactions may take the form of a challenging behavior such as refusing to do something and then dropping to the floor, or bolting.

In addition, a person's health status is critical and may contribute to any challenging behavior that he or she exhibits. If an individual is not feeling well, has not slept well, or is dealing with a chronic health issue such as Crohn's disease, he or she may have significantly more difficulty dealing with the stresses of everyday life—especially when in pain. Because individuals with autism are often hypersensitive and/or hyposensitive to various forms of stimulation, these challenges may manifest themselves in states of over- or understimulation, resulting in challenging behavior.

Problems understanding social situations that result in social anxiety also have a strong impact on emotion regulation for people with autism. It is common to feel confused by social rules and demands, and it is difficult to understand the feelings and perspectives of others. Such basic social skills like taking part in a conversation or waiting one's turn may trigger challenging behavior. Limitations in one's ability to communicate socially may also lead to socially undesirable behavior.

The goals of an emotion regulation approach to treating autism are to increase the individual's ability to self-calm and to respond to and seek assistance from others. Prevention strategies include using schedules, scheduled breaks, opportunities for choices, environmental accommodations, and individualized interactive styles. Prevention strategies include teaching replacement behaviors such as using communication supports for assistance and sensory activities or fidgets for self-regulation.

Conclusion

Although guiding the behavior of a child with autism is full of difficulties, there are also windows of opportunity to explore and understand many facets of the child's development. Simultaneously parents can look to themselves and their expectations and frustrations as their children grow. In these everyday routine behavioral events, limit setting and problem solving are attempts at finding connection between parent and child. The concepts described in this chapter can help you understand your child and guide his or her development despite the differences imposed by autism.

So what approach should a parent pick: behavioral, developmental, or blended? I think it is important to pick a good therapist or program that respects each child as an individual; that respects each family's culture and values; and that understands human development, the principles of behavior, and emotion regulation. Any of these approaches may be poorly practiced. When practiced well, assessment and analysis are done carefully by a team, data are kept, progress is evaluated, and changes are made whenever necessary.

More often than not, parents do not have real options. Access to good services is severely limited in the inner cities and in rural areas, and even affluent areas have a shortage of quality services. The general advice I give to parents is to get as much help and support as possible through public schools and agencies. Families with the means to do so can supplement with private services.

Finally, parents as well as children go through stages, and we are in stages together and learning as we go. By understanding that behavior has a function and a message, we can see our children as unique human beings as opposed to challenging behaviors that need solutions. Although parents need to be in charge, and children need to learn and follow as they develop, the reality is that we reinforce and shape each other every step of the way. Regardless of our limitations, children and parents all want the same thing—a loving relationship.

6

Surfing Your Stress

One Wave at a Time

> *Could a greater miracle take place than for us to look through each other's eyes for an instant?*
>
> THOREAU, *WALDEN*

HAVE YOU THOUGHT WHAT IT WOULD BE LIKE TO BE PHIL IN THE MOVIE *GROUNDHOG DAY?* Stuck reliving the same day for who knows how long? Do you wonder what you would do if you were suffering through the same day over and over? I have a friend who has a son with autism and medical complications. Some days his son will have horrible tantrums and bang his head, leaving holes in the wall. The walls have been patched, but the worries live on. My friend says his life feels like *Groundhog Day*—a statement that resonates with many parents of children with autism. This chapter looks at this experience with compassion for parents and their children and their stress that comes in waves that often seem unrelenting and overwhelming.

In the movie Phil is an arrogant and sarcastic weather forecaster. He spends the night in Punxsutawney, Pennsylvania, in order to broadcast the annual ritual of the coming out of the groundhog the next morning. When he wakes up at 6 a.m., he is annoyed to discover that he is trapped for a second night because of a snowstorm. But it turns out to be the morning of the day before, and everything that happened the day before happens all over again. This goes on day after day, no matter what Phil does. If he does nothing different, events repeat as on the first day. But if he changes his behavior, people respond differently, and then all kinds of possibilities open up. Either way, each day he remembers what happened the previous day.

Phil continues to live the day over again, trying unsuccessfully to seduce his

The waves keep coming.

producer, Rita. Then one day, out of desperation, Phil opens up to her. Through the intimacy, something changes. Phil begins to live each day more fully in a way that he has never done before. When he comes across a street person, he takes him out to eat and tries to keep him alive. His compassion for the old man makes him want to help people. Having suffered himself, he finally becomes able to empathize with other people's suffering.

What is so powerful about *Groundhog Day* is the window it gives people into the experience of what it would be like to make a breakthrough like this in their own lives. When they move beyond the denial and resentment over their own lives and accept their situation, then life becomes authentic and full of meaning and compassion. The pain of learning of my son's diagnosis of autism nearly 30 years ago kicked open that door for me. My awareness of my own inner life of thoughts and feelings has grown ever since.

When one cannot change or fix something, it is common to believe that tomorrow will be exactly like today. *If I just try hard enough, I'll get through it.* Thinking like this binds people to the stories of their past, clouds the present, and limits their sense of the possible. People cannot control what autism or another serious issue can do to their lives. They cannot determine what emotions will arise within them. They are often rendered powerless.

What they can do is relate to their lives differently. This means accepting that change is inevitable and believing that change is possible. Feelings come and go: happiness, sorrow, laughter, worry. A person may be fearful or worried in the morning, and that feeling may pass by the afternoon. Hopelessness may be replaced by a glimmer of optimism. Even the most challenging situation is always unfolding and shifting.

Even in pain and suffering, people can find a way to go on and keep trying to look for the possible. This is not a Pollyanna sentiment that everything will be just fine. Nor is it about replacing negative thoughts with positive thoughts. But if people go on with courage, as long as they are alive, the possibility of change is alive. People cannot control the thoughts and emotions within themselves or the universal truth that everything evolves and changes. People can however make choices about how to express or respond to those thoughts and feelings. My friend's son, for example, can be having a good day, as sweet and innocent as only a child with autism can be. And then out of nowhere, this boy will erupt in pain into a horrible tantrum, banging his head. This boy's mother and father suffer deeply, but they do not give up. They love him and each other, and they keep living as best they can and trying to help their boy.

Daily Routines

The core symptoms of autism are social impairment, communication difficulties, and a restricted range of behaviors and interests. Individuals vary greatly in terms of their symptoms in each of the domains and their severity. As mentioned in Chapter 5, the impact of autism is truly pervasive and can lead to difficulties in the routine everyday activities. These challenges impinge on the parent–child relationship and add greatly to the usual stresses of parenting. They may require of parents much more time than is required of parents of typically developing children. The only things that any child can control are eating, sleeping, and toileting. These are the most intimate and social interactions that take place in an average day. When these activities become a battleground, meltdowns often result, making harmony impossible. Let's take a look at each of these flashpoints as well as strategies for making changes while riding out the waves of stress.

To do this compassionately, it is necessary to remember that your son or daughter with ASD is first and foremost a child. As mother and author Ellen Notbohm (2005) points out in *Ten Things Every Child with Autism Wishes You Knew,* your child's senses of sight, sound, smell, taste, and touch can be so sensitive as to be physically painful. Concrete thinking can make language confusing; therefore, your child is visually oriented and needs your patience and a focus on abilities rather than impairments. The overloaded senses or emotional frustrations that trigger meltdowns or blow-ups can be as horrible for your child as for you.

Eating

Feeding your child is one of the most intimate and rewarding activities a mother can experience. Difficulties in this area can have a profound effect on the mother–child relationship. It can be heartbreaking to carefully prepare a meal and then have it rejected over and over again; this may lead to maternal depression before your child is even diagnosed. Accepting this feeling does not need to lead to helplessness. Although this experience is painful, it is more easily understood if you understand the ramifications of autism at mealtimes. This understanding will make it possible to make progress and repair the mother–child bond. Fathers who are involved in preparing and cooking meals report some of these same painful experiences.

Many children go through a fussy eating stage, and even most adults have foods they do not like and will not eat. However, many contributing factors lead to extreme food selectivity in children with autism, and the result may be nutrition and health issues. Extreme food

Tariq eating Cheerios, one of the few foods he would eat for years.

selectivity goes well beyond what parents of typically developing children would call fussy eating—it implies eating very small quantities of food and/ or only eating from a very limited range of foods.

Sensory issues play a major role in eating habits. In terms of taste, the hypersensitive child may object strongly to certain textures or temperatures and may then gag in response. The hyposensitive child may prefer spicy or hot foods. The sensory-seeking child may lick or taste inedible objects or enjoy very spicy or hot foods (Kranowitz, 1998). Deficits in fine motor skills may cause difficulty using eating utensils. The texture or consistency of certain foods, such as mashed potatoes, may seem intolerable because of tactile oversensitivity, a phenomenon called *oral defensiveness*. To a picky eater, food may look, smell, or taste yucky.

Smell makes up a large part of people's sense of taste. A child with autism may have an extremely keen sense of smell, and the odor of food they do not like can make them lose their appetite. This tendency toward selectivity and routine can cross over into other senses. Some children only eat foods of a certain color or only eat from a favorite container or plate. When it has so many possible causes, a child's refusal to eat can easily be interpreted as misbehavior. Parents need to take a step back to identify the possible causes of their child's reactions to food. An occupational therapy evaluation can be very helpful in understanding a child's sensory profile and his or her reactions to various situations.

Whatever the cause, a child with autism who is a picky eater has a very limited repertoire of foods. He or she may prefer crispy foods, such as crackers or fried chicken, or soft foods, such as applesauce or pudding. Merely settling down to eat may be a challenge. Just sitting still may take all of the child's focus. Impairments in oral motor skills as well as gastrointestinal problems and reflux may also be factors. These issues are discussed in detail in *Just Take a Bite: Easy, Effective Answers to Food Aversions and Eating Challenges!* by Lori Ernsperger and Tania Stegen-Hanson.

It is important that mealtime be a pleasant family activity. Otherwise, children with autism tend to interpret their parents' requests at mealtime as additional demands and intrusions and tend to refuse these requests. Thompson (2008) suggested several rules for mealtime. He stressed the importance of modeling appropriate mealtime behavior by eating with your child. Having a regular routine in a positive atmosphere while sitting around the table together establishes mealtime as a pleasant family experience in which relationships help to solve problems. Building routines that work is central to living with autism and simultaneously taking care of everyone's needs.

Thompson (2008) also recommends varying the appearance, texture, and taste of foods that are offered. For example, offer at least three items from different food categories, such as meat, starch, vegetables, and fruits. By varying items as early on as possible, you will be able to lessen your child's tendency to insist on an extremely limited repertoire of foods. Small servings are suggested because your child may be more likely to try an item. If a child finishes one of the items and asks for more, you can then say "Finish your dinner" and wait to see whether he or she does. Then immediately give more of the preferred item. No matter what, avoid giving your child more of a preferred item when he or she whines or cries, as this consequence reinforces crying and whining.

Thompson (2008) also advised parents that coaxing your child to eat more will lead to more resistance. Children will eat when they are hungry; if your child eats very little at one meal, he or she will be hungrier at the next. If you are concerned about nutrition, consult your child's pediatrician about adding supplements to his or her diet. Finally, it is important to avoid high-calorie sweet snacks between meals; small healthy snacks are highly recommended.

The goal of the Floortime strategies described by Greenspan and Wieder (2006) is for the child to take charge of solving his or her own problems. So if the child resists eating anything except for a few items, she should choose the food she wants if it is reasonably healthy. Once the child is in charge, eating is no longer a power struggle. Then adults can empathize with the child's positive feeling of being in charge and with how hard it is to try something new; it may be scary because it does not feel good in the child's mouth or it may be yucky to touch.

Whatever the case, you can break the challenge down into little steps. For example, you might try adding something new every few days by embedding it in something the child already likes. An example would be mixing a small amount of vegetables into mashed potatoes. Some parents even grind vegetables into a paste and mix it in other foods so it is less noticeable. Another example would be using a favorite salad dressing to make the taste of chicken interesting and enjoyable. If the problem is not a new taste or texture, but rather a child's distractibility and difficulty sitting still, then a different strategy is needed. In a situation like this, feeding may have to resemble action-oriented play. For example, a parent or teacher may pretend that the fork is an airplane flying around as the child opens his or her mouth. What was a toxic struggle becomes a game in which the airplane lands in the child's mouth. Parents of older children can reinforce the importance of trying new foods by granting children more time with their favorite activities, such as an extra bedtime story or more time on a new computer game.

Taking small steps is the best approach. A first step to introducing a new food might be simply placing the food on your child's plate. If even that leads to problems, you can start by placing the food on the child's plate for only a few seconds. As soon as your child is successful with that first step, give a reward. Rewards can vary but should include praise and a motivator, such as a small amount of a preferred food or time doing a preferred activity.

When using the Floortime model as a guide, whenever you are setting new limits or challenges for your child to work harder and try something new, it is important to add more Floortime to encourage your child to be assertive and in charge, especially in making choices about food. Use a lot of preparation, including pretending and then trying the new thing with firm expectations and a positive reward. Use more Floortime to keep a cooperative attitude and build on your child's desire to please you, which helps him or her move to the next rung of the skill ladder. Take small steps and be sure not to turn eating into a power struggle. If a child is hypersensitive to tastes, smells, and textures, it may help to let him or her play with the food and get used to it on a sensory level. A reward for just tasting a new food could be extra dessert or a favorite activity. Another idea would be to dress up a new food, such as a string bean, with catsup if a child likes French fries with catsup.

The use of Social Stories (Gray, 2000) can also be helpful. In this technique, a parent or teacher writes a story about a new food and how much people like it. Social Stories use a verbal and visual approach to help a child prepare for a new activity. Using a favorite character, such as Barney or Spiderman, or a respected role model, such as a fireman or athlete, can get a child interested enough to taste

Running together, one of the activities we could do together

a food. The Social Story might involve alternating mouthfuls of a child's favorite food with mouthfuls of the new food. For example, the child could have two bites of a favorite food after each bite of the new food. Like all strategies, this should not be a power struggle but rather it should be done in a playful manner.

Evidence from a study in England should allow parents to relax a bit about the whole eating issue. This study confirmed that children with autism tend to be extremely picky when it comes to what they will or will not eat, but it does not seem to affect their growth and development (Emond, Emmett, Steer, & Golding, 2010). In general, children with autism eat fewer vegetables, fruits, sweets, and carbonated drinks than their typically developing peers. In this study, this had no bearing on energy or calorie intake and resulted in no significant nutritional shortfalls at age 7. Although there could be a chance of nutritional inadequacy, this was not the case for the majority of children in the study. Worried parents should consult their child's pediatrician.

Sleeping

You may be exceedingly tense and irritable if your child is difficult to get to bed, takes a long time to fall asleep, wakes up during the night, cannot sleep without you, wakes up very early in the morning, or sleeps at the wrong times. Sleep deprivation may cause significant problems. Decreased alertness and excessive daytime sleepiness can impair your memory and your ability to think and process information at home or work. Disruption of a bed partner's sleep may cause relationship problems, such as the need for separate bedrooms, conflicts, moodiness, and so forth. Poor quality of life may include an inability to participate in enjoyable activities, such as watching a favorite television show. Sleepiness can also contribute to injury on the job or while driving an automobile. Learning how to help your child to sleep better can improve life for you as well as for the rest of the family.

Although sleep problems are common in all children, they affect up to 80% of children and youth with ASD. It should not be surprising that there is a high correlation between sleep problems and challenging behaviors during the daytime. The core features of autism have a profound effect on a child's sleep patterns. Problems with getting to sleep can be connected to a desire for sameness. This may include being upset with the evening transition to bedtime as can any change in the typical routine, such as trying to sleep without a parent or falling asleep in the car on the way home from an activity. In addition, problems with communication can cause poor understanding of the routine. Tactile sensitivities may also be a factor; certain textures of bedding or pajamas may be arousing or relaxing, and these should be carefully considered.

Problems staying asleep can also be due to symptoms of autism. Any slight change in the environment, such as a parent leaving the room or turning off the television set in another room, may cause awakening. Hypersensitivity to sound can cause difficulty getting to sleep or awakening from sounds that others do not notice. There can be worries, difficulties calming, hunger, illness, or gastroesophageal reflux. Any of these may make it extremely difficult to return to sleep after being awakened.

The common belief is that everyone needs 8 hours of sleep (Durand, 2011), but the actual amount required to be healthy and alert differs individually and by age. Whereas infants sleep about 14–15 hours per day, older children sleep a little less each year. For example, typical preschoolers average 11–13 hours of sleep per night and do not take regular naps after age 5. Information available at the National Sleep Foundation (www.sleepfoundation.org) is extremely helpful in understanding sleep requirements for various age groups.

If a child with autism does not sleep restfully, then the whole family does not sleep restfully; therefore, it is important to attempt to develop good sleep habits (sleep hygiene) as early as possible. According to Durand (2011), good sleep habits include the following:

1. A regular bedtime and a regular time to awaken, with a 30-minute routine that includes calming activities such as reading a bedtime story or listening to music

2. Regular exercise during the day but no intense physical activity in the evening

3. Reduced noise and light in the bedroom as well as a consistent temperature

4. No caffeinated drinks or foods within 6 hours of bedtime

Behavioral interventions are the treatment of choice for sleeping problems. The first step involves observation in the form of a sleep diary for about 2 weeks; information to record includes how long and at what times the child is sleeping. Associated medical conditions such as seizures or gastrointestinal problems should be taken into account. Behavioral interventions include the following:

• A daily sleep schedule should be used.

• A security object, such as a teddy bear, should be used.

• A bedtime routine should be followed to help the child become calm and relaxed and fall asleep. Television, videos, computer games, and so forth should be avoided, as they provide excessive stimulation.

• The child should learn to fall asleep by himself. If he does not have this skill, the parent can gradually transition out of the room.

• If the child awakens at night, she should return to bed with minimal attention. It is important not to encourage the child to be dependent on the presence of an adult in order to sleep.

• If a child has a pattern of going to bed too late, waking the child up an hour earlier than usual may help to make him tired earlier, thereby gradually shifting his bedtime.

• The treatment of any medical conditions that may be interfering with the child's sleep should be a priority.

If you are unable to make progress in terms of sleep hygiene, you can consider the temporary use of medication in consultation with your pediatrician. It is important to consider the benefits and risks of medication and to see this intervention as part of the learning process for your child. Although these recommendations are simple and straightforward, implementing them may be extremely trying for you. Habits that were easily formed, such as falling asleep with a parent, may be extremely difficult to change. It is important to view this kind of situation with compassion for yourself and your child.

Toileting

A brief history of potty training is helpful in putting this issue into perspective. In the 1950s, moms were using cloth diapers, so they were highly motivated to potty train. Moms trained their children to go in the potty by learning their children's schedules and observing their signals prior to eliminating. They would place their children on the potty when signals indicated that they needed to go. In effect, toddlers were training their parents when to place them on the potty.

The children would start to make the connection between the physical sensation that precedes elimination and learning where to do their business. This method worked, and children were trained at the average age of 18 months because they were physiologically ready.

The convenient disposable diaper was invented in 1950 but was not widely affordable until the 1980s. Parents no longer had to use cloth diapers, and therefore they were no longer so highly motivated to potty train their children at an early age. Simultaneously the child-centered approach toward potty training was emerging. This approach involved respecting the child's wishes and needs, which meant waiting until your child was ready to potty train.

Disposable diapers are now the norm and are considered a necessary expense. With more women working outside the home, parents are no longer motivated to potty train their children to reduce the work load. Although most parents want their children potty trained as soon as possible, it is challenging to find time to fit it in. As a result, the average age of potty training keeps increasing. The average age for potty training is now about 30 months, within an overall range of 18–60 months.

The child-centered approach to potty training is now the norm. Parents are advised to respect their child's wishes and needs, wait for him or her to be ready, and not force the issue. Relax and use Pull-Ups, because your child will use the potty when he or she is ready. According to the American Academy of Pediatrics (2009), your child is ready for toilet training when

- Your child stays dry at least 2 hours at a time during the day or is dry after naps.

- Bowel movements become regular and predictable.

- You can tell when your child is about to urinate or have a bowel movement.

- Your child can follow simple instructions.

- Your child can walk to and from the bathroom and help undress.

- Your child seems uncomfortable with soiled diapers and wants to be changed.

- Your child asks to use the toilet or potty chair.

- Your child asks to wear "big-kid" underwear.

For a child with autism, however, there are complications. The common reason, for these complications is difficulty in processing sensory messages (Kranowitz, 1998). For example, some individuals may be overresponsive to sensations, making the noise in the bathroom overwhelming or the feeling of the toilet seat against their skin uncomfortable. They may even be afraid of falling into the toilet. Children with these challenges tend to avoid the toilet in order to avoid the problem. Other children may be underresponsive to sensation; they may lack the body awareness to know that they need to use the potty. Yet another subgroup of children seek out sensation; to these children, it may feel good to wear or sit on or even smear warm squishy fecal matter. They may like the strong smell. They are unaware that this type of stimulation is not socially acceptable.

From my years of listening and supporting parents at the Center for Autism in Philadelphia, I know that toilet training is experienced as a huge hurdle. It is physically and emotionally demanding for parents, particularly when their child's same-age relatives and neighbors have been trained. The incontinence often results in families feeling even more alienated socially. What I learned from Dr. Ruttenberg is that children with autism train later unless there are medical complications. Although readiness is important, Wheeler (2007) advised making toilet training a priority after 4 years of age.

Reassuring parents who were afraid that their children would never be toilet trained always seemed to relieve them and help them relax a bit, continue to change dirty diapers, and do the work of training their children. I also recommended using children's books about potty training as well as videos to teach and prepare children for the learning process. Parents found these steps very helpful. The children of most parents in the support group at the Center for Autism were trained by the time they finished the program and before they started kindergarten. One by one, as a child trained, this was always a cause for celebration in the group.

A big decision is when to switch from diapers or Pull-Ups to training pants. With the latter, the cleanup is messier, but the child must be able to feel the wetness of the clothing in order to learn. It is important to teach daytime urine and bowel control first. In order to teach nighttime control, do the following:

- Limit fluid intake in the evenings.

- Have a regular bedtime with a consistent bedtime routine.

- Teach the child to use the toilet immediately before going to bed.

- Teach the child to use the toilet anytime he or she is awake and during the night.

- Have the child toilet immediately on awakening in the morning.

Smearing feces is a common problem many parents dread. As with many behavioral challenges, the most effective approach is to prevent this from occurring. Prevention may include very close supervision. If a child finds playing with feces enjoyable, any unsupervised moment may be seized as an opportunity. This may even be true for a child who is using the toilet. Once a child has smeared feces, it is important to promptly clean and disinfect the area and the child. Try to minimize any social interaction or talking, as this attention may tend to reinforce the behavior. Although it may be difficult, it is important to avoid lecturing and emotional reactions. Wheeler (2007) recommended using a picture sequence for the routine or a Social Story that shows the correct behavior. Preventing future incidents can be accomplished by patient teaching, increased supervision, and rewards for using the toilet correctly.

For many children, toilet training is accomplished relatively easily when a few of these effective strategies are used. Some individuals may require a more lengthy training that utilizes several techniques. Some children may experience regression or setbacks after being toilet trained. These setbacks may occur after an illness or accident, medication changes, changes in sleep patterns, increased stress or anxiety, and so forth. When setbacks occur, it is important to identify possible causes of the regression. Any possible medical problems should be discussed with your child's pediatrician. Also, it is important to help your child adjust to any changes that have occurred through the use of pictures, Social Stories, comforting objects, relaxation exercises, and so forth. Then return patiently to using the strategies that were successful when your child was trained initially.

Meltdowns

Whereas mothers tend to feel the most responsibility and the most pain around the daily routines of eating, sleeping, and toileting, fathers tend to respond most intensely to tantrums and meltdowns. Being the disciplinarian is a conventional male role, and fathers therefore tend to feel particularly powerless in a traditional sense. As one father I know states regularly at fathers groups, "My father was the commander-in-chief. I tried that with my son. It just doesn't work." This is not just an old fashioned approach. As recently as the 1980s, ABA commonly included aversive conditioning techniques such as water sprays in the face, yelling "no," and other punitive methods.

Now, using the techniques of positive behavior support, both parents and professionals can go far beyond punishing meltdowns and make real improvements in behavior. This requires parents and professionals to agree on an action plan based on the approach discussed in Chapter 5. It can be extremely difficult to think through and plan this approach in the heat of the moment when a child may be kicking and screaming and even possibly injuring himself or herself or a parent. These behavioral and emotional outbursts are a major source of stress for families and conflict between parents.

More often than not when there are regular meltdowns, parents as well as teachers initially report that they see no pattern to the outbursts. This is actually very unusual, because in most instances specific things around or within the child trigger or set him or her off. Part of analyzing the function of a behavior is keeping a record of observations about these outbursts, which may include aggression, meltdowns, or self-injury. The record should include what happened immediately before each incident as well as immediately after.

Sometimes the trigger is something in the future, such as when a child has a meltdown when asked to put on his coat because he is anxious about going to the dentist. It is important to remember that anxiety is almost inseparable from autism and that learning self-calming techniques is effective in preventing future meltdowns. The trigger may also be something internal, such as an earache or toothache or abdominal pain; a child with limited verbal skills who is in pain will be even more irritable than a child who can say what is bothering him. It is important to remember that when these observations are carefully reviewed with a knowledgeable behavior analyst, special education teacher, speech or occupational therapist, psychologist, or so forth, a pattern is usually detected that may include more than one trigger.

Conventional wisdom would have you believe that all you need to do is just ignore your child's outburst. In order to do this effectively you need to stay calm, which can be extremely difficult when your child is screaming, yelling, hitting, and crying. Durand (2011) provided parents with detailed guidance on using the techniques of positive psychology to implement behavioral strategies to help stay focused under the extreme stress of a meltdown. Having a plan while teaching a skill or replacement behavior can go a long way toward making real progress.

For example, it can be tempting, when trying to get your children ready for the school bus, to give in (just this once you tell yourself) and turn on the television (which they are demanding) to make the moment go easier. Although sometimes it may be all you can do, remember that this reinforces the very behavior you want to change and makes it more likely that the behavior will happen again in the future. A better approach is to wait out the meltdown and calmly tell your children that once they are ready for school they can watch a cartoon until it is time to go to the bus stop. In this way you are using a preferred activity to reinforce the behavior that you are trying to teach.

Experts such as Greene (2010), Thompson (2008), Durand (2011), Glasburg (2006), and Baker (2008) all concur that the best way to handle meltdowns is to prevent them from happening in the first place. Yet this only makes sense if you understand that the behavior communicates a need for a child without the skills to communicate it in another way. Once a tantrum or meltdown begins, a parent or teacher has no choice except to attend to it, which then reinforces it and makes it more likely to occur in the future. In addition, once this level of arousal is reached, it can feed on itself and continue until it has run its course. Prevention involves determining what triggers the problems and teaching the child skills that will achieve the same needed result. Greene provides listings of lagging skills and unsolved problems available for download at www.explosivechild.com. Considering *why* a child with ASD has challenging behavior is the way to start helping. Viewing challenging behavior from this perspective is insightful and compassionate.

When to Consider Medication

If behavioral strategies do not yield positive results, then it is wise to consider adding medication to the behavioral support plan. Many parents struggle with the option of using medications to help treat their child's challenging behaviors. This is an agonizing decision, especially when one must weigh the risks and benefits for a young child whose brain is still developing. There are no easy answers. Many children with autism benefit from medications that help behavioral strategies or self-regulation work. Others have tried many medications with little to no positive results.

The Autism Speaks Autism Treatment Network created the Medication Decision Aid, which includes answers to frequently asked questions. These materials can be extremely helpful to you in sorting out issues and clarifying your values and goals. You can then talk to your child's doctor about various options as well as their benefits and dangers. If your child is already on medication, the Medication Decision Aid could help in the reevaluation process. This toolkit can be downloaded from the Autism Speaks web site (www.autismspeaks.org). Again, I would be remiss not to mention that parents in inner cities and rural areas have very limited access to doctors who are experienced in using medication to treat children on the autism spectrum.

Wandering 2011

A Fall 2011 episode of the television show *Parenthood* highlighted the issue of children with autism wandering away from home. According to an April 2011 press release from the Interactive Autism Network (2011) 50% of children with autism wander. This press release also reported that the behavior peaks at age 4. Among families who experienced wandering, nearly 50% said that their child was missing long enough to cause grave concern about safety. This survey validated the idea that wandering is a critical safety issue for the autism community. The tendency of children and adults with autism to wander or bolt puts them at risk for trauma, injury, or even death. According to the survey, more than one third of children who wander are unable to communicate verbally or by writing or typing.

Wandering was ranked among the most stressful ASD behaviors by parents in the Interactive Autism Network study. Many families of children who elope are prevented from enjoying activities outside the home because of a fear of wandering. Many parents experience sleep disruption due to a fear of wandering. There were many nights when Cindy and I would fall asleep outside Tariq's door to make sure he did not wake up and wander off without us knowing it. Families have traditionally received very little professional support or guidance about wandering, but this is finally beginning to change. At the 2011 convention of the Autism Society of America, Kyle Bennett, Jack Arnold, and Dennis Debault presented their insights and research on the issue. Dennis Debault has posted helpful material on this issue on the web site www.autismriskmanagement.com.

When the Bough Breaks: Residential Care

My son's condition continually drove me places I could never have imagined. After Tariq's ninth Christmas, I faced the reality that his condition required round-the-clock care. That year he knocked down the Christmas tree; there were broken ornaments and shards of glass everywhere. In an instant, the festive mood had been vaporized. We were trying to live like any other family, but it just was not possible.

I had thought I could handle things better than parents whose children with severe autism were placed in residential schools. Now my life was teaching me otherwise. Years of disturbed sleep and round-the-clock vigilance had brought me to the horrible realization that I had reached the end of my rope. Any unsupervised moment could lead to disaster—ranging from bolting toward a busy street to smearing feces like an infant to climbing out a window. In hindsight I marvel at how I coped for so long. I do not think I could do it again.

There is no holiday for you when you have a child with autism. Your resources for coping are never on break. Meanwhile, school is closed, your child's caregivers are with their own families, and you are with your child 24–7. If you cannot find support, you feel alone. The most painful feelings emerge when the world is celebrating and you have no respite.

In the past the parents of children with severe disabilities were counseled by physicians to institutionalize their infants. They were often even discouraged from bonding with their children. This was later shown to be detrimental to the parents and children alike. Some families were even advised by professionals not to visit their children, because that would make it harder. The children disappeared and became a shameful family secret.

Now the pendulum has swung the other way. Parents are expected to care for a child at home regardless of the severity of the situation—irrespective of how it affects each family member. Professionals constantly emphasized the need to do more for Tariq. This did not help with my guilt or with the acceptance that I was supposed to reach. I thought I had a defect that kept me from accepting my son. I cried almost whenever I was alone. The word *autism* stuck in my throat . . . the A word.

It is not always possible to care for a child with severe medical or behavioral needs at home, so some families need other options to survive and to meet their child's needs. It is my experience that it is hard to find support when this is the case. Residential care is still seen as it was in the 1970s by parents as well as professionals. Even among parents of children with severe disabilities, there is opposition to considering such an option. People who keep their children at home are often regarded as better parents. The system and the community tend to tout them as exemplary and look down on those who make other choices. The preconception is that asking for needed residential care is putting a child away. For this combination of reasons, many parents never hear about other ways that their child may be cared for safely and with dignity.

In fact there are options, and I was fortunate to discover them before I broke. My wife Cindy had worked at Bancroft's residential program in New Jersey for children and adults with developmental disabilities. She helped me see through the stereotypes I had read about in the late 1970s. At that time, the horrendous conditions at state institutions such as Pennhurst in Pennsylvania and Willowbrook in New York were exposed. The trend to deinstitutionalize children and adults with mental illnesses and ID began—as it should have. Many children and adults with disabilities could in fact do better in community settings.

Still, there need to be humane options for children whose needs cannot be met in the home of a typical family. Where we live in eastern Pennsylvania, there are several fine private schools with residential facilities, such as Bancroft, Devereux, Elwyn, and Melmark. The children at these schools come from all walks of life. We are fortunate to have these nationally known schools in our area. Children come here from many states for this specialized care.

Most children and adults with disabilities do not belong in residential facilities any more than most people who are aging belong in nursing homes. Fern Kupfer, a mother who has experienced this with her terminally ill child, wrote about this in *Before and After Zachariah: A Family Story About a Different Kind of Courage*. Perhaps we all share a fear of what may happen to us if or when we are no longer able to care for ourselves. As a society, we certainly need services for families who choose to care for dependent members in their homes. Likewise, we need accessible housing for people with disabilities who can live independently as well as good group homes. In addition, we need pediatric day care for medically fragile children. Some children require a school with residential facilities, and as Kupfer helps readers to understand, this possibility should not be shrouded by shame and blocked by preconceived notions. In early 1988, I was awake with Tariq in the middle of the night. As I rocked him back to sleep, he was innocent and peaceful as his eyes closed. In an epiphany, the thought came to me that *if he could speak and reason,* he would not want me and the rest of the family to spend the rest of our lives how we had been living. He knew I loved him, and I knew he loved me back. Everyone who ever sees us together can see that. But he could not tell me that it would be okay for him to go to a residential school. I had to wrestle with that alone, and I knew I would have to face myself in the mirror for the rest of my life.

We gradually came to understand that a residential program was actually a less restrictive environment for Tariq. There he would be freer to run and play and learn in safety. He would not have to be tethered constantly to someone's arm. He was not being put away and abandoned or forgotten. We could visit him regularly, and he could come home for overnight visits. If he made progress, as some children do, he could come back to live at home. If a child needs this level of care, then the family has a right to it, and there is state and federal funding to provide it. As I discovered after reaching this painful conclusion, many people unfortunately have to fight a legal battle to get this care for their child and a reasonable life for the rest of their family.

I cried and cried as I struggled with this decision about my son's care. Having to prove that my baby was damaged enough to deserve this care was torture. Without Cindy to support me, without the Center for Autism to support Tariq's needs, and without a lawyer, it would not have happened. There were no witnesses to support the district's contention that my child did not need this care, so the hearing was never held. When the funding for the Devereux facility was approved through due process in June 1988, I packed his clothes and a few toys. It was the hardest thing I had ever had to do. I remember sitting on his bed with my head in my hands. It was no victory—Tariq would not finish growing up under my roof.

Canoeing; if I stop paddling, Tariq will stand up.

Because of his sleep problems, Tariq was assigned to the room right next to the night duty residential counselor. A buzzer would go off if he left his room, and the old converted farmhouse at Devereux's Kanner Center, which housed about 15 other children, was encircled with a 6-foot fence. Now it was someone else's job to be vigilant at 3 a.m.—someone who was paid to be awake and who went home to sleep in the morning.

Looking back, I have no doubt that it was the best I could have done for Tariq and for our family. Tariq has gone on year by year and made slow, steady progress within the expected trajectory for a child with autism and severe cognitive disability. He has grown up in a safe environment. I see him regularly and am involved in all decisions about his care. He remains generally happy and healthy. On a daily basis, he is never far from my thoughts and feelings. He is as much a part of our family as any other member.

Surfing Your Stress

All along the spectrum, the stress can come at you in waves from little everyday challenges such as brushing teeth to meltdowns that can be physically dangerous. One mom told me how every window in her home had been broken and replaced by Plexiglas. Another mom, referring to her son with Asperger syndrome, told me, "I'm ready to pull my eyelashes out." She was that frustrated and at the end of her rope. "I'm on empty. My child's got Asperger's and severe depression. I need to talk to you." She was hearing things coming out of his mouth that made her scared for his future.

What can parents do with that stress? It can get frightening, but I try to help people look right at their feelings. Avoiding the problem might actually intensify the suffering around it. But if you look right at it instead of trying to push it away, then you can look at your possibilities and choices in the situation. If you do not want something in your mind (your thoughts, feelings, urges), then it will be there. Avoiding your reactions only works in the short term. In the long run, things intensify. Stress just keeps coming back.

Try this little experiment in thought stopping. How many times have you thought about chocolate in the past week? Now use all of your mental powers not *to think about chocolate for 60 seconds. What happens?*

As you tried to suppress your thoughts, what happened? Did they become less heavy and float away? Did they become more pressured and frequent? Many people in this situation start thinking about, visualizing, and even tasting and longing for chocolate. Some are able to substitute thoughts of something else, such as ice cream. Some can block out the thought completely, but this is relatively rare. Experiments such as this one have been done in psychology laboratories and replicated many times. If you were not able to block your thoughts about chocolate, you can see how useless or counterproductive it is to try to block thoughts you do not like. ACT has a different slant on dealing with stress. Too much struggling with stress is like kicking and screaming to get out of quicksand—the more you kick and scream, the more you get sucked in.

Chances are that if you focus on your values, you will struggle less with stress and living the life you have now in the present moment. So instead of struggling to stop your thoughts and feelings, this approach helps us harness the energy of the waves of stress to move in the direction of our values, which include parenting, marriage, health, community, and spirituality. Identify a goal you are working on that is in line with your values. For example, you may want to strengthen your marriage by finding a way to spend more time together, or perhaps you want to use the principles of positive behavior support to understand your child's meltdowns. Here's how to do this:

- Look at the big picture. Notice the stress in your mind. Notice the tension in your body. Notice the stress in the world around you.

- Notice your values and which one you want to move toward.

- Choose a goal that will take you toward one of your deepest values.

- While noticing your stress, let those thoughts, feelings, and sensations in. Breathe right into the tension in your body slowly and mindfully.

- Imagine yourself perched on top of that stress with your eyes fixed on the value. You may be dealing with a meltdown and thinking calmly about your choices. Or you may be confident in your approach and thinking about your marriage with the goal of finding a way to spend some time together when the wave passes.

In this process, you are opening up to your thoughts, feelings, sensations, and impulses as you discern what can be changed and what cannot. This is the ever-evolving process of accepting and living for what is really important. Ride that wave in the direction of your waves. People spend a lot of time in moments that have already happened and thinking about things that have not happened yet. As you are reading this, this moment is the future of the moment you just experienced, and that moment is now the past.

This is what being attuned to your child is all about—being in the present moment, so that those connections can happen. They may not happen as frequently for a child with autism whose condition affects his or her ability to relate to others. But connections do happen. It happens for me with my son when he is happy to see me. This is how his autism speaks to me. It feels the same way when I come home and my daughters say hi. Those moments of connection light up my life. When does it happen for you? Just looking for that can help you enjoy those moments as they are happening.

Trying this takes a willingness to look at your own experience in terms of how you experience the day-in and day-out process of raising a child with autism. It takes a willingness to see and hear your child's point of view, whether it is in words or actions, and respond to whatever is happening. This journey is not just about raising children; it involves learning from them. This focus on relationship helps to improve outcomes as a study by Mahoney and Perales (2005) documented. The study included 50 mother-child pairs with young children diagnosed with ASD. Weekly sessions over a year's time helped mothers implement a relationship-focused intervention, called Responsive Teaching. Out of the entire sample of children over 60 percent made cognitive improvement. In addition, 70 percent of the children made improvements in expressive language, and 80 percent made improvements in receptive language.

This is conscious parenting and a means of getting closer to your kids and letting your family thrive. As you get to know yourself in the parenting relationship, there is tremendous meaning and growth. In moments of connection we can even stumble on happiness. The inner lives of parents have been grossly neglected in the treatment of ASD. The stress and the spectrum of emotions that come with it—fear, guilt, anger, and pain—have no exit. If you are willing to feel that, and ride out the waves, they subside and come again. It will not be an easy life, but it can be a good life. You can find light in the process. These are my deeply held beliefs and what I hope to help my readers find.

Gentle surf subsiding

7

Parents and Professionals

A Partnership in Child Development

> *Educate each child according to his ways.*
> PROVERBS 22:6

IN THIS ANCIENT WISDOM FROM THE BIBLE IS THE GUIDING PRINCIPLE OF SPECIAL EDUCATION. What parents need from professionals is empathy for their situation and good services for their children. When they do not receive that, they usually get angry. From my experience as well as from the experiences of other parents, I have found that professionals who lack feeling and hope and who seem to just be doing their jobs provoke sharp resentment. It is rare to meet a parent who does not have a horror story about a doctor or the system. However, professionals who are compassionate and hopeful and who take a special interest in the child and the family are kindly remembered and effusively praised.

A meeting with the Devereux staff in 2000

The anger and anxiety parents experience when they seek help can be intense, confusing, and energizing. As many can attest, it would be next to impossible to get through the maze of obtaining services without the energy and determination that derives from these uncomfortable feelings. Anger in particular can be a double-edged sword—inevitable and necessary but at other times an obstacle to progress. This chapter looks at the challenges and opportunities associated with helping children become all they can be while navigating the educational system.

The outcomes for children and families are best when parents and professionals work with mutual respect and shared decision-making power. Parents are true authorities with unique and intimate information to contribute. Professionals, in contrast, through their training and experience can offer expertise and a broad perspective that parents do not have. Each has only partial knowledge about an individual child, and complete expertise is possible only in partnership. Their combined viewpoint is the best on which to base decisions, plans, and goals.

Parents' relationships with professionals are born of necessity during a time of crisis and are rife with opportunities for misunderstanding and conflict. No one wants to spend countless hours having his or her child diagnosed and treated in offices, clinics, hospitals, and special schools by doctors, therapists, psychologists, teachers, social workers, and so forth. You simply want someone to fix your child and your dream—to take your pain away. As many mothers have told me, "I imagined being a soccer mom, and now I am a therapy mom."

Parenting is very personal, and many questions may lead parents to doubt themselves or wonder whether they are doing enough or even blame themselves for their child's lack of progress. Mothers especially wonder whether they are doing the right thing. These are understandably difficult waters to navigate, and parents are understandably impatient with professionals who do not seem to grasp the intricacies of the situation. Their loss of the intimate private world of the parent–child relationship is an unrecognized casualty in the process.

Professionals, in contrast, have their own stresses, having to deal with administrative pressures, paperwork, large caseloads, upset parents, and their own professional goals and ideals. Professionals also have emotional reactions while diagnosing and treating children. As they bond with children and work for their progress, they experience many of the same emotions as the parents—from excitement about a child's new achievement, to discouragement at a child's lack of progress, to anger when they are powerless to provide the services they know are necessary.

Unfortunately, most professionals who work with children have had little formal training in how to understand parents' natural reactions to disability and are unsure about how to work with the parents and the child as a unit. When a parent is visibly anxious or depressed, professional observers quite naturally speculate about what effect this might have on the child's development and want the parent to calm down and cheer up. What is often missing is the realization that accepting these feelings helps to facilitate the parents' grief and helps the child, as the parents learn how to face the future with hope and enjoy being with their child.

As the parent of a child with spina bifida, professional writer Gilbert Gaul helps others to understand why these early experiences with professionals are so intense. In *Giant Steps: The Story of One Boy's Struggle to Walk,* Gaul writes about how parents do not readily give up the heroic image of the physician. They want to believe that doctors are next to God so that they can heal their children and make them whole. If their expectations were not so high, it might be easier to change them, and there might then be less anger, which routinely accompanies unmet expectations. Although it is easier said than done, parents are forced to accept the limitations of medical science in order to function as partners over the long haul for their children.

Yet as parents try implementing this principle, they discover that today's medical model of providing services in public and private agencies has resulted in barriers on both sides of the partnership. Services are provided from the top down, and expertise and decision-making power lie squarely with the professionals. Some parents have had negative experiences with professionals or authority figures. These can be carried over to new situations, making trust and collaboration difficult. Parents who are also professionals have a special view of this dilemma that can be helpful for others on either side of it. With a foot in both worlds, I have often served as an interpreter between one and the other. Not unique in this regard, I merely stand upon the shoulders of those who came before me as I try to pass that wisdom forward to those who come after me.

A Unique Perspective

No matter who you were before your child was diagnosed with autism or other special needs, you are not prepared for what is to come. It can help to hear from people you think know how to handle things—perhaps with less anger, worry, and frustration than you. In 1992, at a family conference for parents and professionals in New Jersey, Paul and Penny LeBuffe talked about their experiences in a workshop entitled—"From Mental Health Professionals to Special Needs Parents."

The LeBuffes worked at the Devereux Foundation in West Chester, Pennsylvania, a day school as well as a residential facility for children with severe disabilities, many of whom could not be cared for at home or in public schools. Tariq was a student there from 1988 to 2001. Penny LeBuffe had been a residential counselor and supervisor and then an admissions representative. Paul was a research psychologist. They found themselves not as prepared as they had imagined for parenting a child with special needs. Telling their story to hundreds of people helped them find meaning and purpose in life. Penny credited Ann Turnbull, a well-known parent-professional from the University of Kansas, for pointing out that academic degrees can sometimes be a hindrance. An academic may start out expecting to have an easier time, only to find out that he or she is just as overwhelmed as the parents he or she has encountered in a professional capacity.

Penny's first conversation with a service coordinator about her daughter Katie was seared into her memory. Like so many parents, including me, she could recall exactly what was said. "It was like being run over by a truck," Penny said. Until Katie's sixteenth month, the LeBuffes thought they had a Gerber baby, but then her vocabulary stopped developing. Katie kept cruising around, holding on to the furniture without walking independently. In their search for confirmation that something was wrong, they were told that they were overanxious. Being told that they were anxious was not unusual, but these parents knew something was wrong. Katie's pediatrician had guaranteed that she would walk and was alarmed when she did not.

After 2 years, Katie was found to have a rare neurological disorder. It was a terminal condition, and she was losing the skills that she had developed. The people in the audience at the LeBuffes' talk gasped when they heard this. "I didn't know what to say to make Penny feel better," Paul commented. The grief had to take its course, as they contemplated whether their daughter would be happy, whether she would have friends, and whether she would ever live outside their home. These concerns are common and follow parents to every interaction with professionals.

Geneticists told the LeBuffes that there was a 1 in 4 chance that they would have another child with the same disorder. In a stroke of good fortune they surely deserved, the couple had already conceived their second child, Denise, by the time they found out what was wrong with Katie. Paul told the audience that day that the new baby kept them "sane." Many couples I have met have spoken of healing their pain and anguish by conceiving a typically developing child. Unfortunately, others are terrified to try again or tempt fate and lose the genetic lottery for a second time, having another child with autism.

Some professionals seem unaware of the intensity of parents' emotions or unable to respond with compassion. Parents may be holding hands and wiping away tears as they sit through a meeting. Perhaps the couple is being asked to recount the child's early development. Although professionals may indeed be so overloaded and swamped with paperwork that they cannot read every report, this all-too-common experience is hard to accept. No matter what your education or prior experience, there is no way to bypass the pain. It can even be harder for professionals, who may expect to have an easier time because of their education and experience.

Paul and Penny concluded their talk by challenging the practice of professionalizing parents by asking them to serve as cotherapists and coteachers, leaving them little time to hold and cuddle their children and each other. This is where Floortime is valuable in guiding loving, growth-inducing relationships. The LeBuffes' story is reminiscent of *Parents Speak Out,* edited by Rud and Ann Turnbull. The editors and contributors to this book are all professionals as well as parents of someone with a disability. Their perspectives highlight the fact that even loving parents who work in the field sometimes feel overwhelmed when dealing with the system (Turnbull & Turnbull, 1985).

David, a physician and the father of a boy with leukemia, spoke to me frankly. As he put it,

> When you're dealing with your own child, things suddenly hit home . . . you don't appreciate what someone else goes through until you experience it yourself. In a way, being a physician was a disadvantage. As a layperson, you tend to attribute more abilities to doctors than they actually have. The limits of medicine are far greater than most people realize. As a doctor, I knew that everything isn't curable. Someone who is not a doctor is better off because it is easier to have faith in the medical establishment when you are not a member of that establishment.

As physician Paul Abend stated in his unpublished presentations, he did not want to be his son's doctor, but he had to because no one seemed to know how to take care of his son's complex medical needs. This devoted father founded the New Jersey Autism Think Tank to help his family and others. The Think Tank brings together world-renowned pediatric specialists via videoconference to help with the tough situations faced by families whose children with autism have medical issues that often trigger violent and self-injurious behaviors that result in their families living under siege.

From Birth to Diagnosis: The Medical Perspective

Let's take a closer look at how misunderstandings arise between parents and professionals so that we can see how to close the gap and develop a working alliance. Many children present a complex clinical picture for doctors. The obstetrician presides at the birth, and the pediatrician is on the front line thereafter as the child is seen for immunizations and checkups. But unless the child is diagnosed at birth or before (as in the case of Down syndrome, for example), parents usually suspect a problem before anyone else. Because every child is unique and development is often uneven, the doctor may have no choice but to wait and see. Likewise, both parent and doctor may unconsciously minimize the problem because neither party wants it to exist.

When there is fear and worry, parents are hungry for reassurance, and doctors may be reluctant to confront them with the possibilities. Doctors, like parents, can deny their observations or the implications of those observations in order to avoid the pain and the agonizing obligation to tell the parents. As Norman Cousins (1989) pointed out, the physician–patient relationship is a powerful medicine. Parents who are worried about autism may long for a closer link to their child's doctor in order to help themselves manage their fears while waiting for answers.

The child's developmental problem and the parents' suffering touch doctors and may make communication awkward. In *A Difference in the Family: Life with a Disabled Child,* parent and professional Helen Featherstone (1980) reports on her interviews with several physicians who clearly saw themselves as lightning rods for parents' denial, anger, and anxiety. This may explain why many parents complain about getting shuffled around until finally getting a straightforward diagnosis. Even in the most clear-cut situations, some form of denial usually arises as a spontaneous expression of grief.

As psychologist and parent Ken Moses (1985) explained, the loss is so personal and elusive that few parents are aware at the time of what they are experiencing. Physicians may take this personally when they have to convince parents what is best for their child. But along with the doctor's truth, parents need validation of their own truth—that life at that moment has been changed forever and that the loss of their perfect child is momentarily unacceptable. Imagine being asked to trust and believe someone who is telling you that one of your worst nightmares has come true!

Complex developmental problems often require assessment by various specialists, so evaluation at a children's hospital or university medical center when accessible is the best way to get the expertise needed. The primary pediatrician may be slow to make this referral, believing that the parents are not ready for it. Doctors are understandably cautious and often would rather go slowly and wait and see, not wanting to err in such a serious matter. Proper treatment depends on an accurate diagnosis, but parents are eager to find out what is wrong and move on and fix their child. It is unavoidable that these different perspectives generate uneasiness on both sides. Parents' anxieties can be further heightened when doctors use medical jargon instead of down-to-earth language, and using this language may be a way to avoid painful feelings.

Being rushed in and out of the examining room compounds the problem. Many of the horror stories that parents tell have a recurring theme—an overly negative prognosis. "The doctor in the hospital said that my child would never talk . . . would be a vegetable . . . would never live independently . . . would need to be institutionalized" are commonly heard. Even if a doctor has not given such a prognosis, a parent may assume it in the dark, devastating moments that first follow the frightening news. Pediatrician T. Berry Brazelton recommends in his talks that physicians first help the parents find the child's strengths and delay a realistic discussion of prognosis to a postdiagnostic conference, giving parents time to absorb the diagnosis.

I discovered inadvertently how radically my perceptions of professionals changed over time. As I have mentioned, I was furious when Tariq was diagnosed with autism. I thought my head was going to explode. I remember wanting to reach across the table and strangle the people who were saying that my little boy would never be normal. Yet when I returned with Tariq for a reevaluation 4 years later, they seemed like kind, caring people. I could see concern in their eyes, and I wondered why they looked so different from the first time I had seen them, when they had seemed cold, distant, and aloof. The main difference was in me: I was over the shock of the diagnosis—not to mention the fact that Tariq, and they, and I were all 4 years older and presumably wiser.

Many of those who tell the angriest stories have never confronted or revisited the people in their stories. They may unconsciously need their anger as an exterior focus, a means of protecting their spouse and their child from that anger. I only revisited that hospital because my lawyer recommended a reevaluation by the same team as evidence for a due process hearing. The reevaluation turned out to be serendipitous, because it turned off an angry tape playing in my head. My anger had not been wrong or bad, but it was not good to displace it onto others or to hold a grudge. I was relieved when I was able to let it go and breathe normally again.

Some people may find my outlook on the medical profession too forgiving. This may be true in some cases—but doctors are people too, and they can be good, bad, or mediocre; moreover, even the best make mistakes and have weaknesses. If you are dissatisfied with your child's pediatrician, I recommend that you discuss your problems with him or her and try to resolve them. You can ask for an extended consultation so that your doctor will have plenty of time for your discussion and you will not feel rushed in and out.

If discussion does not resolve your problems, then seek out another doctor you can trust and rely on. You need that kind of relationship with your child's pediatrician for yourself as well as for your child. Other parents of children with autism are a good source of referrals. *Children with Disabilities,* edited by pediatrician Mark Batshaw, Nancy Roizen, and Gaetano Lotrecchiano, may also be helpful as a source of medical information. Dr. Batshaw himself was developmentally delayed and had learning disabilities and attention deficits. He credits his mother's devotion to his development as the motivation for his eventual success, and he became a developmental pediatrician because of his desire to help other children like himself.

Early Intervention: The Educational Perspective

Day by day, after a diagnosis, parents live with their children and learn to love them as they are. Although grief can be prolonged and can reoccur throughout the life cycle, the most intense reactions are usually short-lived, lasting at most a few months. After that time, most parents are strongly motivated to find the best programs they can to maximize their child's achievements. Once goals have been readjusted, most parents find meaning and joy in their child's accomplishments, no matter how small. A brief history will place this process in context.

Just as parents have no control over autism, they struggle to get the services to address it—even though services have become more accessible since the passage of the Education for All Handicapped Children Act of 1975 (PL 94-142), which was championed by parent organizations. Prior to 1975, children with disabilities had no guaranteed or protected rights to public education; the programs that existed were rarely found in public schools. Some children with autism stayed home, and others went into state institutions. This law mandated a free appropriate public education for all children with disabilities. It ensured due process rights when agreement could not be reached between families and school districts. The law also mandated that each child have an IEP and that this plan be implemented in the least restrictive environment, which means that a child with autism should have the opportunity to be educated with typical peers to the fullest extent possible.

After years of research documenting the effectiveness of early intervention, the Education of the Handicapped Act Amendments of 1986 (PL 99-457, "The Preschool Law") expanded services for infants and young children who have disabilities and their families. Congress intended more and better services to young children with special needs and their families from birth until 5 years of age, when children enter public school. PL 99-457 recognized the unique role of families in the development of children with special needs.

Then the Individuals with Disabilities Education Act (IDEA) of 1990 (PL 101-476) was passed. This act mandated transition services from school to adulthood, defined assistive technology, and added autism and traumatic brain injury as categories of disabilities. Prior to 1990, children with autism were included in other categories, such as neurologically impaired, learning disabled, emotionally disturbed, or mentally retarded. Thus, there was no accurate count of how many children nationwide had been identified with autism.

Many parents report long searches to find information about autism, early intervention, preschool programs, speech and occupational therapies, and community resources such as respite care. The search for services can be even longer and more torturous in inner cities and rural areas, where shortages of experienced professionals are common. Because early intervention services are federally mandated, many parents can find them, but they may not be adequate; others may find them only with persistence, advocacy, and sometimes legal representation.

Despite being federally mandated, none of the laws mentioned here have been fully funded, and thus states and local school districts have been left to fill in the gaps. This often leads to conflicts with parents. In this important respect, parents and professionals are set up to be frequently at odds. In addition, because school districts in the United States are funded by local taxes, there are huge disparities in the quality of schools based on the per capita income of the residents. Injustices and inequities abound.

For example, Salena's 2-year-old son Hakim was diagnosed with ASD. Salena had read about breakthroughs that were possible using the PECS. When she requested this intervention through her son's early intervention program, she was told that no one there knew how to do it. Yet this just was not true. The State Department of Education provided training to early intervention programs and preschools. Fortunately for Hakim, his mom did not accept what she was first told and called an advocate who gave her the information she needed to assert her son's rights. Consequently, Hakim got the PECS and improved his communication, and his challenging behaviors decreased.

Injustices such as these are far too common, but they should not occur at all, and parent groups can help keep them to a minimum. Exchanging information helps parents to be more assertive in advocating for their children's rights. This struggle is worth it; those who refuse to give up are often rewarded, such as Christy Brown's mother, whose son was able to write a book by holding a pencil with his left foot despite being severely paralyzed by cerebral palsy. Study after study has shown that when children receive early intervention services, they progress more rapidly and further than children who do not receive such services. Parents can generally see this progress during the preschool years, prior to age 5, and are heartened and relieved to witness their child's growth.

Once parents find a program for their child, there is usually developmental progress and hope for the future. Strong bonds often develop between parents and their child's therapists and teachers. These bonds are often closer than those with the child's physicians. Doctors are the messengers of the bad news, and it may be hard for parents to think of them as caring professionals. In contrast, teachers and therapists are usually seen as allies as parents come to accept their child's condition, including its limitations and possibilities.

Tariq's primary therapist, who was new to working with children with autism, arrived on our doorstep one Christmas Eve with a present for him as well as one for my daughter—a sensitive gesture that I will never forget. Professionals who show their attachment by doing something beyond their job description make a huge difference. Likewise, parents who show their appreciation through cards or small gifts to teachers and caregivers are warmly appreciated.

Clearly, professionals who share the heartbreaks and triumphs with children and families can be extremely helpful. Not all professionals have this capacity but many do, and their compassion makes a big difference for families. I encourage people to look for these traits in the professionals they choose for guidance. Of course, professionals do not have the same kind of responsibility as parents or the same emotional investment, yet their acceptance of and devotion to children can be an essential inspiration. Confidence in the treatment relationship is critically important. The input of good professionals transcends philosophy and methodology. Having the right professional team working together for a given family and child can be critical in offering the guidance and encouragement needed to navigate the many and complex issues along the spectrum.

Building Partnerships

In *Parents and Professionals Partnering for Children with Disabilities: A Dance that Matters,* Janice Fialka, Arlene K. Feldman, and Karen C. Mikus liken the parent–professional partnership to a dance as a way of analyzing the complexity of these vital relationships and their development over time. The authors draw on their years of experience as parents and consultants to build partnerships. Their developmental approach to improving the working relationship between teachers and parents is both realistic and compassionate (Fialka et al., 2011).

Phase 1: Colliding and Campaigning is about the awkward beginning, when parents do not really want to be there and the connection with professionals is fragile. According to the authors, parents and professionals begin to campaign for their own perspectives on the child, the problem, or the intervention. Much like politicians during an election year, each side pushes for its own agenda, and views may be polarized.

During Phase 2: Cooperating and Compromising involves apprehension and uncertainty, but there can also be more of a balance and some hope. With some level of trust, a spirit of cooperation can emerge. There is an expectation of working together to best meet the needs of the child; therefore, there is less stepping on toes. The partners can begin to really share their worries, dreams, and suggestions. Trust grows if both partners follow through on agreements, and if they cannot, they inform the other of the obstacles and look for solutions.

Phase 3: Creative Partnering and Collaborating is based on honest questioning and listening. In this phase, partners tend to share their interests, needs, fears, worries, and hopes openly and honestly. They are secure and safe enough with each other to share what is below the surface because each feels truly valued by the other. When a parent–professional team reaches this level, the possibilities for problem solving and solutions are maximized. The sheer volume of information about autism can be best sorted through with teamwork. When you type "autism" into Google, you get 91 million results. Type "autism web sites" and you get 6,530,000. Many parents spend endless hours surfing the Internet, hoping to find the one site that will make a difference. I wonder whether the number of books is more manageable. When searching "autism" on Amazon, I got 7,111 hits. Real teamwork can really help when knowledge and resources are pooled in the best interest of your child.

School Years: Entering the Mainstream

The transition from preschool to kindergarten can be excruciating for parents. Because of the myth that the window of opportunity is closing for a child's progress, there is a sense that time is running out. As McGarry (2011b) wrote on the Alternative Choices blog,

> I knew that my original ideas about helping children with autism were totally inaccurate. I think a lot of people share the same perception that I did—that early intervention is not just the best, but the only opportunity to help children with autism learn and grow. Now I know that is far from true.

> A lot of people have this idea that there is some sort of invisible "window" of time when it is possible to help children with autism. After about age five or six the "window" closes, and any further therapy or other efforts are useless. I think we need to take this idea of a "window" and throw it out the window. Early intervention is extremely important, but there is no age when a child shuts off and can no longer improve. I am now opening myself up to more experiences working with older children and teens on the spectrum, because I've realized that it is never too late to impact the lives of people with autism.

After their child is diagnosed, most parents, myself included, hope and pray that the child will catch up by kindergarten. Some children with autism can be included in general kindergarten classes. Some need related services, such as speech and occupational therapy. Others may need smaller specialized classes or even special schools. Parents and educators often disagree on what is best for the child. When placements are made for the convenience of the school system as opposed to the needs of the child conflict results. There may also be disagreements over related services, including behavioral support, that schools should provide.

Another common concern is the inclusion (as much as possible) of children with disabilities with their same-age peers, which is mandated by federal legislation. It is common to hear educators say that parents are unrealistic, whereas parents in turn complain that educators' expectations for their child are too low. These differences in expectations are frequently a sore point in the parent–professional relationship.

One of many resources on the topic, *You're Going to Love This Kid! Teaching Students with Autism in the Inclusive Classroom,* by Paula Kluth, Ph.D., provides strategies for including students with autism in both primary and secondary school classrooms. First-person accounts by students with autism give insight and show educators how to adapt classrooms to support student participation in classwork, school routines, social activities, and more. Inclusive education involves a humanistic approach and teaching techniques. Communication, behavior, and learning problems need to be understood in context and within relationships.

Kluth (2011) observed how students with autism are often a catalyst for change and creativity. Inclusion may help teachers think more carefully about the design of the lesson, the ways in which students can participate, and engagement for everyone. The concept of meeting students where they are at every turn makes this approach to inclusion compatible with the concepts of Floortime, RDI, SCERTS®, and developmental approaches in general. The language and practices of inclusive education respond to the diversity that exists in every classroom.

If a child's needs cannot be met in a typical classroom with added support, he or she may be better served in what is called a *self-contained classroom*. This may actually be less restrictive than being in a general classroom with a one-to-one aide. Also, a nonverbal child who does not have a reliable communication system and whose behaviors are extremely challenging may be disruptive. Hence, there needs to be a range of options to meet the complex needs of children with wide-ranging manifestations of autism. Another stumbling block that needs more consideration is the resistance to accepting inclusive education in a school culture that is often competitive, individualistic, and authoritative. As can be seen all too clearly in the world, culture changes slowly and only with respect and patience for the others' point of view.

Social Skills

A common myth is that children with autism are not interested in relating to others. Nothing could be further from the truth, but the social development of children with autism is qualitatively different from that of typically developing children. Children with ASD are missing skills that are essential for developing peer relationships, such as

- Opening and closing a conversation

- Initiating interaction with other children and joining play

- Understanding facial expressions and body language

- Observing and imitating social behavior in specific situations

- Predicting and understanding the emotions and reactions of others

These are not easy skills to explain to someone who does not understand them. Most people learn them intuitively at a young age through exposure to real-life situations in their families, on playgrounds, and in classrooms. Children with ASD, in contrast, have extreme difficulty acquiring the basic social skills that come naturally to most people. In this sense, autism can be understood as a social learning disorder. In order to learn these skills, children with ASD must be taught them explicitly and practice them over and over.

It is critical that parents and educators make a concerted effort to teach social skills. Instead of enjoying unstructured play periods, children with ASD thrive on routine and structure because they know what to expect and how to deal with things. If they are not taught the necessary skills, over time they tend to become anxious and depressed and might avoid social situations. If this happens, they will carry these problems into adulthood and may spend their lives feeling lonely and rejected. To grow into a well-adjusted adult, a child with ASD must learn basic social functioning.

Social skills make possible a broad range of relationships in families, schools, communities, and the workplace; therefore, social skills acquisition should be included as part of the IEP of every child with autism. Regardless of how much or how little language a child might have, these skills can be improved. These skills can be taught and practiced during every part of the day. An approach that parents and educators can use is Social Stories, which are short stories written to help children (and adults) with autism to anticipate and prepare for specific situations (Gray, 2010). By rehearsing social interactions, individuals can reduce anxiety, improve behavior, and build relationships. So far, evidence suggests that carefully developed Social Stories make a difference in helping people with autism cope with social interactions.

Should You Tell Your Child that He or She Has Autism?

Parents often agonize over whether and when they should tell their child that he or she has autism or Asperger syndrome. *All Cats Have Asperger Syndrome* by Kathy Hoopmann is a children's book that can be extremely useful in helping a child to understand autism and that he or she is on the spectrum. Children with autism initiate contact when they want and need it and in their own way. They do not necessarily follow you around and nip at your heels like a puppy. This endearing interpretation uses photographs of cats to help readers of all ages see how children with ASD are different from other children socially. Learning to understand that difference helps to establish contact with your child in the present moment and build a rewarding relationship.

Recently I was counseling a father who was struggling to accept his 9-year-old son's ASD. I mentioned *All Cats Have Asperger Syndrome*. When I saw him a few weeks later, he related that he had left the book on the coffee table and his son had read it. His son approached him and announced, "I think I have Asperger syndrome." Needless to say, this father was relieved and shed some of his own shame about himself and his different kind of son.

If your child had a virus, or asthma, or diabetes, you would not keep it from her. If she has autism or Asperger syndrome or ADHD or OCD, telling her is still the right thing to do. Your child needs to know. You need to be comfortable discussing your child's diagnosis intelligently and unemotionally. This means working to get past being tongue-tied when people ask you to explain autism. Talking about the diagnosis does not need to be *the* talk. It is actually better to share information as things come up. For example, "We are going to occupational therapy to learn ways to calm down when your head hurts from all the noise around you."

Stephen Shore (2010) has posted an interview on YouTube about telling a child about his or her diagnosis. In his opinion, a child is ready to know when he or she begins asking questions such as why it is hard to have friends, or why writing especially cursive is difficult, or why certain noises bother him or her more than other people. Not beginning to talk about your child's differences will have a negative impact on his or her self-esteem, because by this point your child will know that something is going on. Stephen has developed a four-step approach to broaching this topic:

1. Discuss the strengths and challenges your child is experiencing.

2. Align your child's strengths and challenges. For example, your child may have poor handwriting but be very good on the computer. A good way to compensate may be to do writing assignments on the computer.

3. Make nonjudgmental comparisons by looking at friends and family members and how they compensate for their challenges by using their strengths.

4. Reveal and discuss the diagnosis by talking about how your child's set of challenges and characteristics line up with those of people with autism or Asperger syndrome.

Stephen stresses that there is no particular age at which to begin discussing your child's diagnosis. There is no need for a sit-down talk. Stephen recalls how his parents used the word *autism* matter-of-factly, just like they would talk about brown hair or blue eyes, and this is what he recommends parents do with their children. Start with the positive aspects of ASD, such as what your child is really good at or knowledgeable about. People with ASDs often have an incredible memory for detail, especially on their special interests. They are usually very honest with other people and say whatever is on their mind. It is important to tell your child all of the good things about him that you would never want to change.

You could then explain in a matter-of-fact way that having an ASD just means that a person's brain works a little differently, which makes some things harder but some things easier. Children with ASD often get stuck on a behavior or topic and have difficulty understanding how others think and feel, so they need extra help with this. Stress your love and devotion to helping your child become all that he or she can be. These issues will come up repeatedly in various contexts, so it is important to realize that just one talk will not suffice.

Lauren Yaffe (2006) wondered how to answer her 7-year-old daughter Katie's question "Do I have Asperger syndrome?" Lauren had left *Asperger's Syndrome, the Universe and Everything* by Kenneth Hall, a 10-year-old with Asperger syndrome, lying around. Lauren struggled but answered honestly, "Yes, you have Asperger syndrome." Katie was actually relieved. She already knew that she thought differently than other people, and she liked the idea of being special like Kenneth Hall. Her mother worried that she would tell everyone that she had Asperger syndrome, and Katie did just that. In the process, Katie helped her mother by continually pointing out the wonderful qualities that go along with having Asperger syndrome. Of course, the process of wrestling with one's identity and how one defines oneself goes on for mother and daughter.

Do You Need to Stay Angry?

Once your child is diagnosed and you are receiving services, you are introduced to the autism debates. Is it vaccines? Is it something in the air or water? Also, as previously discussed, experts argue with one another about the best way to treat it. ABA? Floortime? RDI? What's a parent to do? Moms are in up to their eyeballs with all of the work of this; dads feel isolated. You need good services. As one father recently asked me, "Do we need to stay angry?"

I do not think parents need to be chronically angry people, but they do need to be engaged, involved, and active. The debates and the anger can distract from what they need to do. The mom is saying she cannot rest; there is never enough help. The dad is saying he wants to live now and plan for the future. They are both right—they just have different perspectives. It is essential to understand the other person's point of view. It does not work to tell somebody not to worry so much, or not to be so pissed off, or to take one day at a time and not think about the future. People ruminate about things that have happened and worry about things that have not happened. The hardest thing is to just be in the present, be with your kid, your family, and your partner.

Parents need to figure out the best way to live each day, think about the long haul, and yet stay actively involved. The debates and the anger are because they feel so bad, and there is no exit from autism. They want to have a solution; if there is no solution, they want to have a villain. There are no easy answers to these questions. But there are ways to live and love with autism. That is the direction I think we need to keep focused on in everyday life.

Conflict between parents and educators is common, and I would like to offer some suggestions on how to handle the anger and bridge the gap. Unfortunately, criticism of parents is common within the culture of schools. Just like parents, however, teachers are rewarded and encouraged by children's successes. Problems in learning and behavior, in contrast, leave them frustrated, sad, and unsure of their competence. Because no one wants to feel inadequate, is it any wonder that parents and teachers spend so much time and energy blaming each other for a child's difficulties? This dynamic is of course intensified in special education.

How do you get rid of or channel the huge amount of anger you feel when you have to fight the system to get the services that your child needs? A mother wrote to me saying that she felt like she could explode. "I get so drained and discouraged at all the fighting you must do to give your child what he deserves. It just isn't fair!" she stated.

You do have plenty to be angry about. Human hardship is not distributed equally, as Rabbi Harold Kushner wrote in *When Bad Things Happen to Good People*. I remember how angry I was when my son was 7 years old. I had a hard time accepting that he would need services for the rest of his life. It took time and support for me to move past that reaction.

Sometimes even the children who are the closest to typically developing but still need specialized services and programs can be very challenging. It may seem that if you just keep pushing, you will get there. Certainly many parents have felt drained and discouraged about the fighting they need to do to get their child what he or she deserves. It can help to think about what other feelings you may have besides anger. Is there fear? Sorrow? Worry? Guilt? What would be there if the anger vanished?

Parents who have children with autism try to make sense out of the condition: *If we are decent people, how could this happen to us? Why do we have to push and fight for what seems only fair?* Trying to be patient by holding the anger in only prolongs the pain. You may have tried other strategies, such as

- Venting your angry thoughts

- Trying to calm your mind

- Changing your thoughts

- Distracting yourself

- Hitting pillows instead of people

Chances are that these techniques have not worked well, if at all.

Eifert, McKay, and Forsyth (2006) debunked common myths about anger. The number one myth is that anger and aggression are instinctual. Although human history has often been marked by senseless rage and aggression, successful evolution is based on cooperation not conflict. Behavioral scientists have concluded that there is nothing in the human brain that compels us to act violently. Behaving aggressively is one of many choices a person can make when angry. Another insidious myth is that venting anger is healthy. Yet years of research have shown that blowing off steam is not beneficial but in fact is counterproductive. People who vent their rage tend to get more angry, not less, when they do so. People on the receiving end of the outburst get angry in response. It can become a toxic cycle that may be replayed over and over with no beneficial result.

Anger can be beneficial when it is a warning signal that something is wrong. It can be a catalyst for positive action to solve a problem. People can patiently ride the waves of anger that come and go while choosing to live according to their values. This starts with noticing anger, which does not mean liking it or agreeing with what is triggering the thoughts, feelings, sensations, or impulses. The more a person may try to get rid of the anger, the stronger it may become. In the situations described here, such as dealing with school districts, there is value in being an assertive mother or father in order to get your child with autism the help he or she needs. You can choose what to say and do in response to the problems that come up.

If you just keep complaining, you may start believing that the universe is fundamentally unfair. Then you will remain chronically angry and embittered, walking around with a chip on your shoulder. However, many parents have been able to use their anger to activate and energize themselves in the struggle to get the best possible services for their child with autism. In this way parents can actually make the world behave more fairly toward their child.

From Anger to Assertiveness

There is a continuum of problem-solving styles from passive to assertive to aggressive. The characteristics of each of these styles were described by Alberti and Emmons (1982) in *Your Perfect Right,* a classic self-help book. *Passive* problem solvers allow other people to treat them, their ideas, their feelings, and, most important, their child, in whatever way they think best, without challenge. They do what others want and not what they themselves think is best. They may avoid the conflict necessary to solve the problem, but in doing so they give up their child's rights. Resentment and anger can accumulate. People who use this style talk to others with a great deal of respect but little confidence and merely wait and hope for the best services.

Aggressive problem solvers stand up for what they want without regard to the rights, thoughts, or feelings of others. Through aggression, they claim their rights by attacking, viewing their rights as superior, and establishing a pattern of fear and avoidance in their opponents. Aggressive problem solvers talk to others without respect and often come across as cocky and hostile when demanding what they want. The goal is to be neither passive nor aggressive but rather to strongly, clearly, and considerately express your point of view.

The *assertive* parent of a child with autism thinks and acts in ways that back up the child's legitimate rights. An assertive parent can express strong thoughts and feelings without putting down the thoughts and feelings of another. He or she can attack a problem with respect for the professional's knowledge and establish a pattern of respect, thus avoiding the buildup of anger often caused by miscommunication. The assertive parent is both respectful and self-confident and persistently pursues a child's needs.

One mother told me how angry she gets when professionals do not understand her. The problem reminds her of difficulties she had with her mother while growing up. Once she could refocus on her daughter in the present, she was able to calmly and clearly express her thoughts, which usually helped to resolve the problem, at least to some degree. Anger is often a reflection of the hurt. With time and support, parents can gain perspective and learn assertiveness. Children with autism teach you patience—with them, with yourself, and with the world around you.

When I conduct workshops for parents and professionals on building partnerships, I ask participants to share the feelings they experience during a typical day with their child or one of their students. Their responses are very similar. In the ensuing discussion, the walls come down as each party gains an appreciation for the other's role and perspective. It is not uncommon to hear professionals say that it is a relief to go home to typically developing children. One teacher remarked that every afternoon when she picks her children up, she hugs them and gives thanks that they are healthy and growing typically. Parents who hear comments such as these feel a lessening of the emotional distance between themselves and professionals. Although educators are trained to be affectively neutral, this can undermine the partnership. It is not possible to work diligently with a child and not develop an emotional bond; parents can and do appreciate this attachment.

Hearing how much educators care, parents are often impressed with how many children and unique needs they take care of in an average workday. In addition, they wonder how professionals have enough left for their own families. Likewise, when educators hear about parents' frustrations directly, they are more understanding. When they contemplate what it would be like to go home to a child who does not sleep through the night, is not completely toilet trained, or is medically fragile, then a different attitude and tone pervades. Parents are impressed with how difficult it would be to deal with so many angry, frustrated, desperate people who want answers that are beyond the professionals' control. One lesson from this training activity is that professionals as well as parents need to share memories, dilemmas, and insights as they learn.

Outside of a structured situation with a facilitator, this kind of dialogue may be difficult to begin in everyday life. The schools in which parents and professionals meet, as Seligman and Darling explained in *Ordinary Families, Special*

Children (2007), are the turf of the professionals, and parents often find them intimidating. Not to mention the fact that in team meetings to plan a child's program the parent or parents are outnumbered by teachers, psychologists, social workers, learning consultants, and various therapists. Such a setup does not promote the equality of parents' input. The professional views tend to dominate— not necessarily in the best interests of the child. This is why every parent is called on to develop skills in advocacy and reach out for help when necessary.

A parent is the most effective service coordinator for a child, because he or she knows the child the best. Although it might not seem fair that the parent is thrust into this position, accepting this responsibility is key to getting the best program and services. Children whose parents are involved every step of the way generally get more than children whose parents get discouraged by the difficulty of navigating the system. Involved, informed parents who communicate assertively can build and maintain good working relationships with professionals. As your child grows and his or her needs evolve over time, these relationships become invaluable.

Unfortunately, there are many occasions when merely being assertive is not enough and it becomes necessary to acquire an advocate for your child. Of course, parents must learn as much as possible about their child's disability and how to work through the maze of available services. Here are some tips if you are having trouble resolving a problem:

- Gather information. It is vital to know all you can about your child's autism. Become familiar with the treatments and educational programs available to children with autism. It is also wise to learn about your rights and those of your child under federal laws and the laws that govern special education in your state. The more you know, the less likely it is that you or your child will get lost in the shuffle.

- Make a plan. Keep in mind what you really want to get for your family. It is a good idea to prepare notes before a meeting or telephone call. Think through several options so that you are ready to discuss whatever is offered to you. Contact parent advocacy groups for support, and consider the possibility of taking an advocate with you to help you stay objective as well as to let the person you are dealing with know you are serious.

- Take action. Have your notes in front of you when you call schools or agencies, and take notes on every contact with the date. If you cannot reach the right person, leave a brief message. Do not assume that you will get a call back. Be prepared to call persistently every few days until you get results. When you do get through, state your ideas simply and assertively. If the person needs to get back to you, ask when you will hear back. If you have not heard by then, call back. The person you talked to may be overworked or may be avoiding you, so be persistent for as long as it takes. It is often true that the squeaky wheel gets the grease, so do not go away until your problem is resolved.

- Take it further. If you do not get satisfaction, ask to talk to a supervisor. If that does not work, then take your problem to the director of the agency or the school district's director of special education. If that fails, then call a legal rights or advocacy group to represent you. Your notes about the problem, including the dates of all contacts, the names of the people with whom you spoke, and what you were told will be extremely helpful if you have to go this far. However, many problems can be resolved before legal proceedings are necessary if you follow these steps.

Cutler and Pratt (2010) provide detailed guidance to parents dealing with the special education system. Becoming a confident, knowledgeable advocate is a developmental process. These authors cut through the numerous myths and obstacles that block the way to better education. Barbara Cutler is a veteran advocacy expert who draws on 30 years of professional expertise and powerful insight as the mother of a son with autism.

Although these are general suggestions, I highly recommend that parents channel energy into parent organizations, such as the Autism Society of America, the Arc of the United States, Autism Speaks, or local support groups. Connecting with other parents who are either just starting out on this journey or further along can be priceless. You may also want to channel energy into advocacy that helps other families. Sometimes the best way to help yourself is to help others.

The link between parents and the professionals who serve them as physicians or representatives of agencies and school systems is vital and yet challenging. The anger that can energize you is often as hard to let go of as the dream for the perfect child, yet carrying it for too long can make you weary. In your encounters with professionals, you may be challenged to relive and rework your own childhood experiences with authority figures. By doing so, you can work in partnership with professionals and set the stage for your child to grow into all he or she can be.

8

Big Boys Don't Cry

The Secret Life of Men

> *A boy may cry; a man conceals his pain.*
>
> NELSON MANDELA, *LONG WALK TO FREEDOM*

HE HAD BEEN TALKING FREELY ABOUT HIMSELF AND HIS CHILD AND THE DEMANDS OF EVERYDAY LIFE, AND THEN HE STOPPED AND LOOKED UP AT THE CEILING. The other men in the room, seated in a circle along with me, waited patiently and curiously for Ted to continue. We had gathered in Columbus, Ohio to discuss the challenges for fathers of children with disabilities. Before long the waiting became uneasy, so I asked Ted if there was anything else he wanted to share.

Still looking at the ceiling, he answered hesitantly, "There's so much I want to say, but if I say any more, I'll cry . . . and I don't think I'll be able to stop."

It became obvious that he was looking up to keep the tears in his eyes from overflowing. As he slowly lowered his head and faced the other men, a tear rolled down his left cheek. What occurred was an awkward but tender expression of male emotion. The man who was sitting on his right reached over and put his arm around Ted. This incident was the catalyst for the other men to open up, with tears in their eyes and deep feeling in their voices.

Ted's openness released the other men from the taboo against expressing their feelings. Is it because they have held it in so long that men believe that if they cry the tears won't stop? Are they afraid to violate the male code and be considered weak or feminine if they don't just suck it up and deny that anything is really bothering them and that they are hurting? Why is it relatively easy for men to talk about their kids or school systems and so hard to talk about themselves? Clearly it is hard to sit still and listen. Men jump into problem-solving mode, especially when they lack the words to express what they are experiencing. Yet they yearn for connection, and given time, they can open up.

Reflections on Male Emotions

Why are men such a mystery to themselves and one another as well as to the women and children in their lives? As I learned from my own father, who had grown up in an orphanage, "Boys cry on the inside." Leading a men's group is a special challenge because men's emotions are so routinely cloaked. It begins early in childhood. Boys want desperately to fit in and are terrified of being called a sissy. It helps to remind men that women appreciate the strength it takes to open up.

I remember clearly the first time I ran home crying at 6 years of age after a fight with another boy in our neighborhood. Instead of being comforted, I was ordered to go back out there and handle it myself because "big boys don't cry." Being more afraid of my father than the neighborhood boys, I went back out, got in a few licks, and never ran home crying again. I learned that day not to talk about what upset or frightened me.

In *Finding Our Fathers,* Sam Osherson helps readers to explore the enduring impact of fathers on the lives of their children and their key role in their children's identity. How men deal with women, other men, and children can often be linked to unresolved matters with their own fathers. In the world of work, men are also influenced strongly by their fathers. Many men, as well as women, struggle alone with their relationship to their fathers in order to arrive at a sense of completion in this central relationship. Most men I have met want to be better fathers than they had and want their sons to feel closer to them than they felt to their fathers.

I was 29 years old the first time I saw my father cry. It was also the first time since my childhood that I could not hold my tears in. My brother Don, 6 years my junior, died in a car accident in 1977. Understanding this loss and what I learned about my father, my grandfather, and myself puts my own male development into perspective. I had recently married for the first time. I am the oldest of my parents' eight children, and Don was fourth and still living with my parents at the time. It was a cold, windy December night. I was careful to avoid the patches of ice on the road as I drove home from a party.

I went to sleep expecting to hear from Don early in the morning, as he and I had spoken that previous afternoon and had planned to meet and go jogging. When I woke up to the telephone ringing early that Sunday morning, I expected it to be him. Instead it was my mother telling me the news—my brother had been in a head-on crash in his pickup truck. Someone had skidded on the ice. The other driver was in critical condition. Don was gone.

"He was going to call me this morning," I kept repeating to her. She asked me to come right away. My head was spinning, but I sprang into action. As I dressed hurriedly, I kept thinking it couldn't be. That telephone call was supposed to be him. The frigid December air filled my lungs as I started my 1971 Volkswagen Beetle. The ride, which routinely took 20 minutes, went quickly. I needed more time, but there was none. My family's home loomed before me.

When I pulled into the driveway, my father came out to meet me. He had been waiting for me by the window. He ran across the frost-covered grass to me and hugged me, weeping profusely. I could feel his chest heaving next to mine and his whole body shaking.

This was the first time he had hugged me since I was a little boy when he got home from work and sat me on his lap. It was the first time I had ever seen him cry. I had seen him mad and sad, and more often grumpy, but never in tears. It was my first confirmation that Don's death was real—I would never see my brother alive again. In that outpouring of male emotion I was released—if my Daddy could cry, then so could I. But not yet. I had to help my parents.

My memories of my mother that morning are not as clear, probably because I had seen her cry before and knew what her sobs sounded like. It did not take a death to release her tears, and her normal mood usually returned in a relatively short time. This time, though, she was devastated. She would become physically sick with her grief for many months. For more than 20 years she got sick every year on the anniversary of my brother's death.

A little later my grandfather called: "Hello, Robert . . ." His voice broke, and he just sobbed uncontrollably. The other man in my life who never cried, my other male role model, was in tears. I wanted to console him, but I did not know how. Later that day he managed to hold it in, yet I saw the pain in his eyes. I kept busy that morning calling relatives and friends and asking them to pass the word along. I was upset; my voice shook, but I did not cry. I felt that I had to be strong and help my parents. As the oldest, this was my job, and I wanted to do it well.

In the afternoon I went home, got in the shower, and turned on the warm water . . . and then the tears came. My whole body shook as my tears mingled with the warm water and washed over me. I had not willed them to start, and I could not will them to stop. After what seemed like a long time, my body slowly stopped shaking. My mind, my heart, my whole being was inundated with grief. All of my muscles had been heavy, but now they were relaxed.

The days that followed blur in my memory, but my images of Don's funeral are crystal clear. I can still see the sadness and the tears and hear the sobs and consolations of my grandparents, my aunts and uncles, my cousins and friends, and Don's many friends. The church was filled with people in shock—there is something unusually compelling about the sudden death of a healthy young person with his life in front of him. Add to that Don's naturally pleasant disposition and engaging smile and the dimensions of the loss become more defined.

People kept asking me how my parents were doing. Nobody asked how my brothers and sisters or I were doing. Actually, I did not have words for how I was doing. My brothers and I were the pallbearers, and my sisters were with my parents and grandparents. They were crying, and we were sucking it up and acting, or rather pretending, to be brave.

The casket was heavy with our family's grief. When we put it down at the gravesite, I burst out sobbing, even though I was trying to hold it in. I recall my brother Rich putting his arm around me in a firm yet gentle way, and gradually I regained my composure.

As I understand now, that outpouring of feelings by my father, my grandfather, and my brothers was the beginning of the growth of my emotional life as a man—as a more authentic person. I wish there had been an easier way, but this was the path my life took. Then Tariq by his very existence challenged me to grow further.

Tariq's autism led me to explore my relationship with my father. Fathers are the most influential men in the lives of both men and women. Boys and men often connect through competition, sometimes inflicting wounds or reopening old ones in the process. Osherson (1986) presented this as a normal but unpleasant tension between men and boys as well as between fathers and sons. Men have a desire to connect despite having been taught to shun vulnerability to avoid being hurt. This explains why men seem more comfortable expressing their feelings indirectly through stories about their struggles rather than by directly stating their feelings.

I remember how excited I was as a young boy when my father came home from work. How little and insignificant I felt when he was mad at me, and how terrified I was when he would take off his belt, and yet how warm and wonderful it was when he would put me on his knee and say, "How's Daddy's little boy?" I remember the many conflicts with my father over politics and lifestyle when I was in college and in my younger adult years. Over time we eventually reconciled many of our differences and learned to respect those that remained. Many men find it difficult to open up with their fathers or even to talk about this with other men.

When my father died peacefully at home after a long illness in 2000, I read a short excerpt from e.e. cummings about his relationship with his father. It captured my feelings towards my dad so well. Cummings wrote that his father was a true father because his dad loved him. So, cummings loved him back. As a child he worshipped his father. In his youth he battled his father, and as men they understood each other. Through it all they loved each other.

For me, it was true. I adored him as Tariq still adores me. As a teenager and a young man, I battled him over everything from the Vietnam War to the civil rights movement to religion. I have mourned that it was not the kind of battle I can

My dad felt the same way about me that I felt about Tariq.

ever have with my son. At the end of his life, however, I was fortunate to understand him and myself a little better. His mother had a stroke in childbirth and never recovered. She never cared for him, as she needed to be cared for herself. Orphaned by the age of 8, he was never mothered and grew up in an orphanage. He was nurtured by his sister Selma, who was only 13 at the time. Yet he was determined to give his children a better start. He proudly raised eight of us and told me how proud his father would have been to have seen that.

Working with Men

Men are supposed to be the strong, silent gender, and most if not all of their experiences with intense passions are alone, unspoken, and unshared. What a relief it is, I have found from my own experiences, to tell your story and to feel empathy from other men. So often men just want to be heard and appreciated as friends. I have been able to develop this skill at opening up through my own therapy as well as by participating in and leading groups.

I have learned how to relate more quickly and deeply, particularly with men, in both my personal and professional lives. Perhaps it is listening a little differently or asking one more question and waiting a little longer for the answer that makes my interactions richer and fuller. Instead of avoiding what makes me uncomfortable in my everyday personal relationships, I have become more able to wrestle with my difficulties as a husband, son, brother, father, or friend.

Several years ago I was counseling the parents of an adult child with autism and ID. When I met the young man's father, I asked him what it meant to have a child who was named after him and who had autism. "You know; you've been through it," he responded. How often men make comments such as this as a way of joining with another man but still avoiding really sharing what is going on. Opening up is not usually considered manly.

I responded, "I know what it's been like for me. Can you tell me a little about what it's been like for you?" That is all it took— that one more question—for him

Tariq and my grand pop

to open up about his disappointments and his worries about the future. What bothered him most was that his son could never be fully independent and that his other son and his daughters would feel burdened by looking after their sibling after their parents were gone. These worries about the future are common for fathers as well as mothers. Once he told me these things, I could help him.

The New Man

Men frequently react in extreme ways, and fathers of children with disabilities such as autism fit this pattern. They are either very involved or withdrawn and virtually absent from interactions with professionals—with the majority seemingly uninvolved. Based on this observation, many professionals assume that fathers do not wish to be involved. Is this really the case, or do men grieve and cope differently and hence react and involve themselves in different ways?

Men are often poorly represented at IEP meetings, conferences, and support groups for parents of children with autism. Where are they? Usually they are at home watching the children so that the women can attend, but as the primary caregivers the women still feel overburdened and stressed out. The men, at home, think they are helping out. They generally prefer to help out by doing things as opposed to connecting by talking about the stresses and strains of everyday life. What a bind for both men and women to be in.

Until the 1970s, the role of fathers in child development was largely ignored in the professional literature. Although they were regarded as providers and protectors, fathers were not expected to be involved in daily parenting, with the notable exception of discipline. Who of a certain age, for example, doesn't remember hearing "Wait until your father gets home!"? In emphasizing the undeniable importance of mothers, social scientists lost sight of the father and the larger family context. The word *parent* became synonymous with *mother*. This same trend applied to fathers of children with disabilities. Consequently, the literature about these fathers is limited.

By the time fathers were rediscovered, many men were frustrated with their traditional roles. They found that the duty to be a successful breadwinner sometimes choked the natural instinct to nurture. They realized that they could be tender and nurturing with their children and provide discipline, too. As more and more women began to work outside the home, fathers out of necessity became more involved in the daily care of their children.

Cross-cultural studies reported by anthropologist Wade Mackey (1985) showed that when men spent time with children alone, they behaved much like women in their physical interactions, particularly in terms of nurturing. This was true on every continent and in every social class regardless of the gender of the child. The model of the indifferent, unavailable father figure was not sustained. Check this out for yourself the next time you go to the playground and see a father alone with his child.

Developmental psychologist Michael Lamb (1997), a leading scholar on fathers, reviewed studies that revealed some significant differences between mothers' and fathers' behaviors with their newborn infants. Mothers spend more time attending to the infants' basic needs, whereas fathers tend to play more. Fathers are also more vigorous and rougher in their play than mothers. Both fathers and mothers adapt their play to the child's developmental level, which implies that fathers as well as mothers are sensitive to child development.

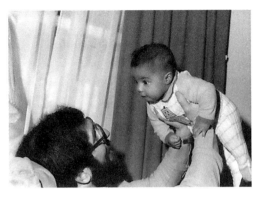

Tariq and I engage in typical father–son play.

Lamb (1997) also found a consensus in the professional literature that mothers and fathers initially respond differently to a child with a disability. Fathers seem less emotional and traditionally focus more on long-term problems such as the financial burden. Mothers respond more openly with their emotions and are more concerned with the challenges of the daily care of the child. Fathers who are less involved in daily interactions with their children tend to have a prolonged period of denial about the disability and its implications. The growing literature about men reveals that men express their feelings differently.

It has been presumed in the professional literature that fathers have higher expectations for their sons and therefore are more disappointed when these sons cannot live up to their dreams. It is a strong blow to the male ego when the father has no heir apparent to his throne. The mother, likewise, has been unable to produce an heir, and both have been deprived of a chip off the old block.

Strong scientific data shed some light on these generalizations. Sociologists Morgan, Lye, and Condran (1998) conducted a study of 15,000 families and concluded that a family constellation with a boy is most likely to keep the parents together. Having a son tends to draw the father into a more active parenting role, and having more than one tends to cement the involvement. Morgan also reported a startling statistic: He estimated that each son in a family reduces the parents' risk of divorce by 9%.

In terms of social support outside the marriage or primary relationship, the trend is to socialize with other couples, as described by Stuart Miller in *Men and Friendship*. Women, in contrast, show a strong tendency to maintain their circles of friends. Having a child with autism, which tends to isolate parents even more, makes it even more difficult for men to maintain and build connections with other men. What do you do when you cannot brag about your child's accomplishments in the way other men do? What do you even say when you are asked how your child is doing? How do you handle that choked-up feeling you get when you are searching for the right words? This is part of the secret life of men who are raising a child with autism.

I wanted to be a better parent than my father when I held my son Tariq for the first time in 1979. I also expected Tariq to become a better son, a better man than me. I looked at my son and saw myself, only better. His diagnosis of classic autism with mental retardation shattered that reflected vision like a broken mirror.

This broken mirror leaves many fathers, especially those of boys with autism, feeling powerless and shamed. They love their children and do not want to fail them. This sequence occurs for men generally, as described by psychologist David Wexler in *Men in Therapy*. Hearing from fathers helps open up powerful and liberating conversations.

When it comes to emotions, there is a male imperative to suck it up. Expressing tender feelings is traditionally seen as weak. So men tend to cry on the inside. On the outside they may be grumpy and irritable, but on the inside they are hurting. Life does not stand still and wait for them. Their families need them to express themselves and to show up and be present day after day.

Because expressing vulnerable feelings violates unwritten and unspoken codes of the male gender, asking a man how he feels evokes an automatic "I don't know" response, resulting in frustration and distance for his partner. What helps men to express themselves, especially when they are living with a child with autism?

What I have found in my work is that men can begin to learn to express themselves in groups of men or even in one-to-one conversations. Many men prefer to open up to a female therapist because they find this less threatening. Without the fear of performing poorly or being wrong there is a sense of safety from shame. When this opening up happens, men can later begin to express themselves with women. Then, because it is okay to open up in treatment, they can open up in general, particularly to their female partner. Opening up to other men may be harder and may be more easily facilitated in a group led by either a man or a woman.

Asking a man how he feels is not necessarily an effective way to get him to talk. Try to say things in guy talk to help, such as

- Tell me your story.

- What's it like for you? (Curiosity works better than empathy.)

- Tell me more.

- I need to know to be closer to you as your friend/wife/brother/etc.

- Your child needs you.

- It takes courage to open up, and I admire you for that.

- Let's figure out a plan to go forward.

Most men in a supportive environment with other fathers readily discuss their frustrations as men and as fathers and the strain that their child's autism has placed on their marriages. Many openly confess that their wives are dissatisfied with how they are handling things. They also divulge that they have worried privately whether their marriage will survive. The romance seems long gone for many, along with most or all of their sexual relationship, and they have little hope of bringing it back. Most of them have never really talked like this before to one another even if their children go to the same school or they live in the same neighborhood. They always comment on how much more open they are in the presence of other men. Listening and disclosing needs to happen slowly for men, as they are more easily overwhelmed by tender emotions. Living day by day is how I grow and help others.

Getting into the Real Stuff: Connecting Through Anger

There is a typical male code for handling overwhelming emotions. What are men expected to do in the face of an overwhelming experience such as autism? Keep the lid on emotions, take charge of practical details, support others, and take on the challenge as a chance to problem-solve or even a test of traditional masculinity are all part of the script. However, men are not supposed to lose control, to openly cry, to worry, or to express overwhelming sadness.

In *Uncommon Fathers,* Robertson (1995) worried that his anger would overpower his love for his daughter Katie, who was born with severe brain damage. He found himself more cheerful when he was actively involved with his wife in helping to meet Katie's needs and wants. Standing by and watching his child's struggle and his wife's pain was more heartbreaking than pitching in and helping. Robertson found a parallel in *Beauty and the Beast,* in which a spell is broken when the hero comes to love another human being as much as he loves himself. In caring for a child with special needs, a father can learn about love and break the grip of the grief.

"When I hug my son, he doesn't hug me back," said a father at a conference in Cincinnati. Ten fathers of children with developmental disabilities and two male behavior specialists who worked with their children sat around a table one Friday evening waiting to hear what I had to say about being the father of an adult child with autism. They were wondering what it would be like. Only a few had ever been to such a gathering. All 10 fathers had children on the autism spectrum ranging in age from 6 to 24. Before the discussion began I told them that nothing they said would be wrong. They seemed relieved; then I invited them to share their experiences.

It was no accident that "When I hug my son, he doesn't hug me back" resonated in their hearts. Autism at its core is a social disorder of relating and communicating. Mothers have the same heartbreaking moments. It is just that fathers are far less likely to verbalize their experience.

It is a myth that children and adults with autism do not connect to other people. But they are not easy to bond with. Another father shared that his 7-year-old son connects in some ways and not others. This was a rare opportunity for fathers to bond with one another and experience fellowship.

It felt good to create that space for men by sharing bits of my own journey. Some of their children were nonverbal, some spoke slowly, and others could not stop talking. One father mentioned that his son, who was slow to speak, forced others to slow down. Because their children connect and speak differently, parents have to pay attention closely. They engage their parents in a different way.

The men talked about their struggles and what they were learning. For example, the type of discipline many of their fathers had used with them just did not work with their own children. Some spoke of the "belt lessons" they had received, and others described the shame they had felt when they had not met their fathers' expectations. One man shared how he was still learning to be a father after 5 years. Others were finding that they could not shape their children into who they had expected them to be. They were making new dreams, yet they worried about the future. Sharing that he was never known for patience, another man spoke of how much more patient he was becoming with his son, who "spoke in slow motion." One 18-year-old still loved to wear Barney T-shirts. His dad found sweetness and innocence in that but worried about him being targeted by bullies.

Finally we discussed things they enjoyed doing with their sons and daughters. Some were not sure, so I just encouraged them to search and explore for those moments that might not be planned. Another man shared how he had decided to take his son, who was nonverbal, with him on a Saturday morning while running errands. He enjoyed having his boy along, but he was not sure whether his son actually liked it. Warm memories of riding with his dad opened up because he had really enjoyed that one-to-one time with his father. When he got home, he wrote on Facebook about having a good time running errands with his son. Several friends wrote back saying that they too had loved running errands with their dads. He had stumbled on happiness with his son.

My approach was not focused on replacing negative thoughts. It was not sugarcoating their often exasperating lives. It was not ranting about the injustice of it all, although that was allowed to happen freely. I tried to help these men find balance so that they could be honest about the frustrations and sorrows that come and go while also seeing and feeling the moments of meaning and happiness that also come and go. When people are open to living in this way, they find real happiness. This is what it is like to be a father or a mother of a child with autism. But even more, this is what it is like to live.

In April 2011, I was the guest speaker for the opening of the Autism Resource Center by the Ontario Arc. When I met with the fathers and male therapists, one man burst out, "I am just so angry!" His voice shaking, he expressed what other men in the circle were thinking and feeling:

> When I get home and approach my son, he pushes me away. I can't stand it anymore. He just wants his mother, and he pushes me away from her too. The other day I told my wife I am ready to sign my parental rights away.

Alex loved his son but hated how hard it could be to connect. Once the anger was out on the table, the whole group of men seemed to open up. Inside the shell of anger, the men found fear, sadness, guilt, and shame. Their honesty with one another opened the door to possibilities for connecting with their children. The man who started the discussion did not come to disown his son—he came to find out what he could do to improve his relationship.

Another man talked about how getting on the floor with his son and just tickling opened the door to the possibilities of playing together. Others shared what they could do with their children and how to follow the child's lead, and those still at a loss got ideas and inspiration. They planned to meet again. The next day at a parents' workshop, I met Alex's wife. Jen approached me to say that Alex had come home determined to find ways of connecting with their son. Maybe now she could get some breaks. She was so grateful that there was now a fathers group in their town, and the men have met monthly ever since, sharing their struggles and their successes.

Understanding Male Depression

Terrence Real's landmark book *I Don't Want to Talk About It: Overcoming the Secret Legacy of Male Depression* helps explain why men hide their emotions from everyone, including themselves. Real (1998) understood typical male symptoms—difficulty with expressiveness, workaholism, alcoholism, abusive behavior, and rage—as attempts to escape depression. But manifesting pain differently than girls or women and directing it outward hurts the people they love.

Girls and women tend to internalize pain and blame themselves. Boys and men, in contrast, tend to externalize pain, feel victimized, become angry, and act out. Among girls or women, depression is usually overt and includes symptoms of hopelessness, helplessness, and despair. Both men and boys, in contrast, experience a covert form of depression that is manifested by an emotional numbness—not just feeling bad but really not feeling at all. This numbness has been termed *alexithymia,* and it represents a difficulty identifying and expressing feelings. Levant (Levant & Pollack, 1998) estimated that close to 80% of men in the United States have a mild to severe form of it.

"Men may excel at building empires, but we're not much for taking care of ourselves," according to Geoffrey Cowley (2003). Generally speaking, men are not very good at taking care of themselves. As a striking illustration, consider that women live 5 years longer on average than men, who are less likely to receive needed medical care as well as social and emotional support. Much of the gap in life expectancy has to do with how hard it can be for men to admit or even recognize their vulnerabilities. According to the National Institute of Mental Health (2009), more than 6 million men experience clinical levels of depression each year. These statistics are the modern confirmation of what Thoreau wrote in *Walden* during the 18th century: "The mass of men lead lives of quiet desperation" (2012, p. 4).

What comes up first in conversation for fathers who have a child with autism is the stress that men live with. It is easy for a man to say that he is stressed. A man does not want to say that he is depressed, but he will admit to being stressed and worrying about the future. I keep asking, "What's it like for you now?" They talk about the shock, the disbelief, the refusal to believe that there is anything wrong with their sons or daughters. Some even say that refusing to believe the diagnosis has hurt their wife and family. There can be guilt and determination to make up for it. Of course men worry about the future. Where will their kids live? Who will take care of them?

The cure for this covert depression, according to Real (1998), is overt depression. He saw grief as the cure. While depression freezes men's emotions, sadness flows. Sadness and anger are feelings that will run their course. Tears come and taper off if one does not hold them back. The gender code deprives men of their hearts and therefore must be challenged. According to psychologist Pollack (1998), this is a "gender straightjacket" (p. xxiv). The fear of vulnerability blocks the connection and intimacy that most men actually long for. In my work, I help men to find their softer side through exploring their relationship with their fathers and their children. More often than not, sharing pain is the way to lessen it. If a disconnection from feeling is at the root of male depression, then connection relieves it. As I continue to see in myself and others, taking care of a child with autism can drive and inspire a man to grow to his fullest potential.

Finding Our Fathers

It is important for men to reflect on their own fathers—especially on some of the warm moments that often bring up some of the painful ones. The point is for men to go into their minds and hearts and then share it. Sharing the experience of being a son, because of the shame so often experienced in that relationship, can be the most difficult challenge in opening up. Some men have fathers who are no longer alive; others may not be on speaking terms with their fathers; and addictions or other problems have ruined still others' father–son relationships. The shame, anger, sadness, and loss that men often express when they are able to relate their experiences as sons are similar to the emotions that they are experiencing in their relationships with their own children. It is usually a relief to talk about these vital experiences that have been bottled up.

On a snowy January night in Richmond, Virginia, 75 fathers of children with autism turned out for a presentation titled "The Father Factor." They came ostensibly to hear me talk to them about the issues they face day and night with their families. They did more than listen. First they showed up, and that turnout alone said something. It said that their local chapter of the Autism Society of America (www.asacv.org) recognized the need for programming that spoke directly to fathers. It said that men responded when they were spoken to directly. It happened because some mothers had discovered the presenter at a national conference, planned and organized the event, and encouraged the men to attend.

After a brief talk about my background as a son and a father, I asked the men to share their stories with one another in small groups around the tables at which they were seated. The energy level in the room rose as they connected with one another. In every small group, men commented on how alone they had felt and how much they enjoyed meeting one another. Many had never attended an Autism Society event before. Those who had mentioned that there had been few if any men present, so they had just listened.

Tariq and my dad at Tariq's 20th birthday party

A short, compelling video, *Fathers' Voices,* about men raising children with disabilities, was shown. The film, which is from the Washington State Fathers Network, focuses on four dads, including the father of a child with autism, and how their lives have been dramatically changed because of their children. Filled with the powerful message of the movie, the men opened up in their small groups about their own thoughts and feelings. I asked them to recall their sweetest memories of their own fathers and the male role models they carried with them. These insights were then offered within the larger group of all who were present.

Here are some of the highlights:

- "When I was really unhappy, he advised me to quit my job and be my own person."

- "We can always come together around baseball even though we are not close."

- "When I played Little League, my dad was always hiding behind a telephone pole telling me where to be on the baseball diamond."

- "My dad took me on trips and let me use a map to help him navigate."

- "Dad taught me how to shave, and now I shave him in old age."

- "When he was deployed overseas in the Army, my dad would bring back toys from overseas and make us find them."

- "Watching him care for my mom, who has Parkinson's now, makes me proud of my dad."

- "My dad gave me what he thought was my first drink and told me how proud he was of me now that I had turned 21."

Finding Our Sons and Daughters

In Richmond, as I do with all of the fathers I meet, I discussed how men can apply what they knew about fatherhood from their own lives to their overwhelming mission of raising a child on the autism spectrum. What stands out is men remembering the time they spent one to one with their fathers doing simple things: doing chores, running errands, going to baseball games, fishing, and so forth. Many had lost sight of what they could do with their children while overwhelmed in the world of therapies, special education, and doctor visits. Recalling special memories with fathers and male role models helps people think about how they can relate to their own children according to their individuals wants, needs, and abilities.

Even though they cannot fix the autism, there is a sense of hope that fathers can do something about their relationship with their child. After 2 hours of open and honest discussion, men lingered, talking and holding on to the moment. There are plenty of good men in the autism community, and not just in Richmond. I have taken notes from the men in the support groups I facilitate for fathers of children with autism and other special needs as well as from dads in my psychology practice. In groups they have the opportunity to help one another and to experience the fact that their difficulties are normal in their situation. They experience acceptance from other men when they open up and share their pain. I will share here some of their stories.

"If my dad gave up on me, I'd be the school janitor. I was mad at the world. My dad helped me to find my passion, and helped me to overcome my obstacles." This comes from Frank, who has a learning disability and whose son has Asperger syndrome. Today Frank is the successful executive of a Fortune 500 company:

> When my son was first diagnosed, I thought he might never make janitor. Now 10 years later, he is doing well, and it looks like he can go to college [with a support program]. I took a lesson from my own father about how to believe in him.

But just like the automobile commercials that state "actual mileage may vary," the symptoms and outcomes vary. "They tell me it's hard to be the father of a typical kid. I wouldn't know." This comes from Larry, who has a son with Asperger syndrome and another boy with PDD. He feels depressed when school is out and his children cannot go out and play with the other children, for they do not know how to interact.

My dad tells Tariq to look at the camera on family day at Devereux.

Maurice, who has a child with Down syndrome, shares his dilemma:

I come here and talk with you guys, and I get my feelings out. I feel cleansed. Then I go home and act like a husband—it's like I think I get points for being remote. So that's how I have been acting. I hear what you guys are saying about opening up at home, but I still act like my wife and kids need me to hold it in and appear strong. I'm not sure I can get over that. I'm not sure I want to.

Jeff also has two children with autism:

You can't fix it, so you learn to live with it. My wife feels like she is to blame, and I haven't been able to help her get over that. We try to give each other hope, but it's hard. She says I don't smile enough. I'm not sure I can remember the last time I smiled. I love my boys so much, but between me and my wife it's like one beggar who found a piece of bread sharing it. I just want to smile more.

It's a delicate balance of hope and reality—accepting the news about a child's condition and working for the best. Men struggle with their anger through this process. "My fuse is much shorter now," according to Sal whose son is on the severe end of the autism spectrum. "I've started to exercise, and now my fuse is getting longer. I've just got to be nicer to my wife and children. Julie accepts me, but I don't always deserve her. I can't melt down. I'm there taking care of my family the best I can. Someone has to be the rock. I cry when I'm alone in the car, but I stay rational at home." What helps? The men I talk with tell me they want to be appreciated for their loyalty to their families. They want to be recognized for trying their best.

They are learning as they go. Here are a few of the lessons fathers have shared with me:

- "I have a different relationship with work. It's not my whole life anymore."

- "My daughter has taught me to appreciate life in a profound way."

- "I have learned to see past what my son isn't and focus on who he is."

- "My children's smiles are my smiles—they light up my life."

- "My father had a horrible temper. I was determined to do better. My daughter's disability taught me to accept what I could not change without bitterness."

- "I am a fixer, and I can't fix this. There is no wrench to pull out of my toolbox. I have learned to just be there for my family."

- "When I get home at night and my kids run to greet me and laugh—that is the best part of my day."

James May, the retired founder of the Fathers Network, put it this way: "The old myths are far flung—and deeply held—that men are hard driven, inexpressive, pragmatic creatures, devoid of strong emotions or the capacity to nurture, always more at home with work than with their families." Numerous articles and photographs on the web site shatter these stereotypes. There people can read accounts by many fathers about their journeys through grief and depression as they love and care for their children.

Professionals who are not sure what fathers in this situation need should get them together as a group and ask them. The ideas collected in *Fathers of Children with Special Needs: New Horizons* by James May can be a helpful guide. The fathers can tell you everything you want and need to know, but you have to question and listen skillfully because the male imperative to be strong in the face of tragedy can be tricky to overcome. In a males-only meeting, it is more likely that fathers can take off their armor and get to the real stuff inside.

Make a Plan

It is obvious that men have a different tone of voice than women and a different way of connecting. Male intimacy is different from female intimacy but not defective. Connecting with other fathers can have a dramatic and powerful impact on a man's ability to interact with his partner and his children. Although men certainly need to learn how to listen and open up, they relate best through action.

It is hard for men in general and fathers of kids with autism in particular to admit that they need help. They want to be able to handle things, but the truth is that they lead a really difficult life. Men respond better to having some kind of action plan. So the action plan I give people is this: Find something you enjoy doing with your child. You may have to start with something your child enjoys that you yourself are not really into. But start with that. Make contact. And from that contact, find the things you both enjoy doing together. That is your action plan.

When you first try to do it, it may not be easy or natural. Observe whatever happens in your mind—your thoughts, your feelings, your impulses, and the sensations in your body. Are you getting stiff and sore? Are you having trouble breathing? Observe while you are engaging with your child, and then talk to somebody about it. That way, the next time you come back to a meeting with moms and dads or a meeting with just dads, you have something to contribute. That can be another part of your action plan. I encourage men to have conversations with other men about how to connect with their son or daughter. Watch how other people join in; watch how you connect.

I recently got an e-mail from a father in upstate Pennsylvania who told me, "You've changed my life." I was incredulous. He said, "You gave me the assignment to find something I enjoy doing with my son 5 years ago and I did it, it changed my life. I have a relationship with my son now and it feels so good to me." Parents do not control autism; there is no cure, and it waxes and wanes often unpredictably. Some kids make dramatic progress, and some make only a little bit. What parents do have a lot of control over and a lot of impact on is their relationships. Focusing on your relationships is an action plan—try it, and see where it can take you.

9

Ordinary Couples, Challenged Relationships

Another Developmental Process

BECOMING A PARENT FOR THE FIRST TIME CHANGES OUR IDENTITY FOR-EVER. Moreover, everything changes once a couple has a baby and is faced

> *Although marriage is for grown-ups, very few of us are grown up when we marry.*
> JUDITH VIORST, GROWN-UP MARRIAGE

with adjusting to the 24/7 care of an infant. Gottman and Gottman (2008), in a 13-year study of 130 families, reported that within three years after the baby's birth two-thirds of couples experienced a significant drop in marital satisfaction which affects the care of the baby. "Being with Baby tasted so sweet, but being together as partners turned bitter; increases in conflict and hostility soured family life" (Gottman & Gottman, 2008, p. 16).

Although most of my professional experience is with heterosexual married couples, I have also counseled unmarried, remarried, adoptive, and same-sex couples. What follows are general observations and descriptions of research that are applicable to various parental relationships but that also consider the uniqueness of each family.

After children arrive, there is a balancing act between caring for their needs and putting time and effort into the maintenance and growth of the marriage. Family life can be a test of love and resilience, so understanding each other's needs and wants is vital to the success and survival of any marriage. Children can add to a family but subtract from a marriage relationship if partners do not attend to each other along with the child. This transition in the life of the family is challenged even further by autism. Dealing with autism can keep parents tired and edgy. As Josh Greenfeld, the father of a child with autism, wrote so poignantly in *A Child Called Noah*, "There is a strain on any marriage whenever a baby is sick. And we always have a sick baby" (1970, p. 79).

Noah was the most famous child with autism of the 1970s and 1980s. Greenfeld wrote very candidly in detail about his marital problems with Fumiko Kometani, also a writer and winner of the Akutagawa Prize, Japan's most prestigious literary award. He detailed their efforts to get Noah the best treatment possible as well as the pressures this placed on their older son, Karl Taro Greenfeld, who in 2009 wrote his own open and honest story of what growing up with Noah was like in *Boy Alone: A Brother's Memoir*.

A successful marriage or partnership is based largely on a basic faith in the relationship by both parties. This kind of devotion is often what makes it possible to work out problems or get through the tough spots. When a child is born imperfect or when a disability or chronic illness is discovered, the resulting emotions put the relationship on trial. Greenfeld experienced his son's autism as a demoralizing symbol of a biological failure to produce a healthy child. Even when two people share the same sorrow, their individual pain and unhappiness may drive them apart.

The chronic stress that raising a child with autism entails can affect relationships at their weakest points. This is just as true for families who have volunteered to adopt children with special needs or provide a foster home. While divorce rates are complicated, it is generally reported at approximately 50% for first marriages and close to 75% for second marriages (Marshak & Prezant, 2007). Although the findings are inconsistent, there is general consensus among experts that although divorce rates are comparable, there appears to be more reported marital distress among families of children with special needs (Seligman & Darling, 2007).

Together you and your partner dreamed of a healthy child, but after the diagnosis you face a life dramatically different from what you imagined. Your overwhelming feelings, both individually and combined, are normal and natural in the situation but very difficult nonetheless. The needs of the child are often complex and illusive. Searching to find the services and the best available treatment can be a long, hard journey. When people get wrapped up in the stresses and strains of everyday life, relationships inevitably suffer from a lack of attention. Communication problems; a lack of time and energy for personal, marital, and family activities; and social isolation affect many families. When autism is discovered, powerful emotions surface and often test the foundations of relationships.

How can partners understand each other in the wake of such devastating pain? For a relationship that is fragile or unstable, autism or other special health care needs or disability can be the last straw. However, couples with strong cohesive marriages may become closer and more loving, and those in relationships that have not yet been tried by adversity may develop increased closeness and strength. Some families disintegrate, whereas others thrive despite their hardships. People can emerge from crisis revitalized and enriched. Hope for relationships really can spring from the crises people experience when their child has a disability.

A Diagnosis of Autism Is Not a Prognosis of Divorce

For a number of years it was widely reported in the popular media and therefore generally accepted that there was an 80% divorce rate among parents of children with autism. Oprah, Dr. Phil, Jenny McCarthy, as well as major autism organizations and others who should have known better regularly reported this. Even the popular television show *Parenthood,* which generally depicts Asperger syndrome accurately, had an episode called "Date Night" that reported this statistic as fact in 2010.

For years, I have gotten telephone calls from journalists asking me for the source of this 80% statistic because they cannot find it. I know of no source for this statistic which has become an urban legend. Some dropped it and some just used it anyway, but Dave Girardi (2007), editor of *Autism Spectrum* magazine, wrote a story about the myth after speaking to me and confirming that there was no source. People considered this to be another strike against autism: It was the reason marriages failed! This seemed to be believable because the incredible stresses in these relationships often lead to tensions between parents, and the relationship can feel fragile as a result. The myth certainly called attention to autism, but it did not reflect the reality that most families cope courageously with their challenges while passionately loving their child.

Exaggerated statistics generate pity for parents, but distorting the facts does not help families who are struggling to cope. Furthermore, it does not help families to actually get the support they need. Quite the opposite—this myth can engender more distress and hopelessness and even possibly become a self-fulfilling prophecy. It also creates the image that the autism community is filled with deadbeat dads who are abandoning their families in droves. I feel personally insulted by the myth. What is the actual evidence for the impact of autism on relationships?

To the best of my knowledge, there were no autism studies specifically related to marriage or relationship status prior to 2007, although there were studies about other conditions and special needs in general (see Seligman & Darling [2007] for a review). Data began coming in 2008 from the Easter Seals' Living with Autism Study. This survey was conducted by Harris Interactive, a market research firm, in cooperation with the Autism Society of America. Easter Seals surveyed 1,652 parents of children ages 30 and younger who had autism and 917 parents of typically developing children ages 30 and under. They asked about daily life, relationships, independence, education, housing, employment, finances, and health care. It should be noted that this was not a peer-reviewed study, so its findings were not published in a scholarly journal. However, its findings are similar to those of other studies that have been peer reviewed.

The Harris Interactive research showed that families living with autism are significantly less likely to be divorced than families with children who are typically developing: 39% of parents of typically developing children were divorced compared with only 30% of parents with a child with autism. Of the parents of children with ASD who were divorced, only one third reported that their marriage ended because of having a child with autism and managing those special needs. It is interesting to note that the divorce rate was 36% among parents of children with Asperger syndrome compared with 32% among parents of children with PDD-NOS and 27% among parents of children with autism.

With regard to the broader context of living with autism, the study documented that mothers and fathers wrestle with worries about many facets of life. They are painfully aware that the lifelong supports their child may need do not exist as of this writing for adults who do not have intellectual disabilities. They are dramatically more concerned about the need for supports than parents of typically developing children—nearly 80% say they are extremely or very concerned about their child's independence as an adult compared with only 32% of other parents. This is especially true when it comes to children's financial independence, quality of life, social and interpersonal connections, and employment and housing opportunities—and with good reason.

Hartley, Barker, Seltzer, Floyd, Greenberg, Orsmond, and colleagues (2010) analyzed data on marriage and divorce from 391 families of adolescents and adults with ASD from Wisconsin and Massachusetts. These families were part of a longitudinal study and were interviewed at four different times between 1998 and 2004. The data were matched with data from a comparison group of families with same-age typically developing children. The researchers found that parents raising a child with autism had a divorce rate of 23.5% compared with 13.81% for parents of typically developing children. Hartley and colleagues concluded that the parents of a child with ASD are at an increased risk for divorce when the child was between 8 and 30 years old.

Freedman, Kalb, Zablotsky, and Stuart (2011) published the first population-based study on relationship status among parents of children with ASD. The objectives of this study were to examine the association between having a child with an ASD diagnosis and the relationship status of the parents and to identify factors that contribute to the greater likelihood of a child with ASD living with two biological or adoptive parents. Data for the study came from the 2007 National Survey of Children's Health. This was a nationally representative sample of 77,991 children ages 3 to 17, of which 913 had an ASD diagnosis.

Freedman and colleagues (2011) found that 64% of children with an ASD were living with married biological or adoptive parents—far different than the 80% divorce rate often reported by the media. None of the statistical models suggested a lower incidence of intact families among children with ASD. In addition, and in contrast to the Easter Seals study, the severity of the child's symptoms neither increased nor decreased the likelihood of the child living with two biological or adoptive parents.

In June 2011, Elizabeth McGarry, an intern at Alternative Choices where I practice psychology, wrote a blog about this research that was posted as a guest blog by the Autism Society of America:

> As a college student, I have learned a lot of what I know about the world from surfing the Internet. Whether I'm checking out tomorrow's forecast or the latest YouTube sensation, I rely heavily on my laptop to tell me what I need to know. Although I never want to believe that it could let me down, the truth is that the Internet can sometimes be more of a conniving trickster than a trusty friend. It's

so easy to believe everything that is out there, especially when an article is well written and seems reliable. I like to think that I am an expert at spotting false information, but my first day at Alternative Choices I learned that I, too, have fallen victim to a myth that has gained a lot of popularity over the last few years. (McGarry, 2011a)

Elizabeth went on to summarize the research. Several hundred people, mostly women, commented on the Autism Society of America's Facebook page. Here is a small sample:

My parents are still married and we all love my brother to death.

I think having an autistic son has made our marriage stronger because we both love him and know we need to work together to make the best life for him.

Contrary to popular opinion, it has actually made our marriage even stronger and we are dedicated partners in our commitment to our children's welfare.

After our daughter's diagnosis, the first question everyone asked was if the father was still in the picture? If I were the father of an autistic child, I would be very offended.

My wife and I will be married 25 years in September and my son turns 21 in August so almost all of our married life has had autism in it . . . is it always hearts and rainbows . . . NO . . . but none of us are guaranteed a perfect life and [we] also recognized that after the diagnosis it wasn't about us anymore. Life was bigger than that.

I'd be lying if I said the thought never crossed my mind. It's a tough boat to sail if both parents aren't working together and supporting one another.

How Parenting Changes Couples

Children with autism are after all just children, and couples raising children with autism are after all just couples. Let's take a step back and look at how any child changes a couple. By and large, people marry or commit to a partner largely unprepared for the potential disappointments, heartbreaks, and possibly shocks of their lives together. They may not know their deepest fears and expectations about being in a relationship. As Viorst (2003) pointed out, either consciously or unconsciously people ask or expect more than the relationship can give them. The daily fireworks and passion of the early days changes as people face their real lives and grow to accept their flawed and imperfect partner.

Although the birth of a couple's first child brings astounding joy, the partnership or marriage takes a big loss in terms of sleep, sex, and privacy. A man may feel shut out by what Winnicott (1993) called "primary maternal preoccupation"—a consuming attachment to one's infant, which he saw as a normal sickness from which most mothers recover. (He was talking about the mothers of typically developing children!) A woman may also feel this, and both man and woman

Tariq dances with me and Cindy at his 20th birthday party.

may wonder, *Who comes first?* A mother may be exhausted from lack of sleep and anxious about her infant's health and development. Fathers tend to see themselves as assistants or helpers.

A father may be sad and feel deprived of the exclusive connection the couple once had. He may feel jealous of his infant and embarrassed and ashamed of that feeling. He may just be grumpy and irritable and unable to express his more tender and vulnerable emotions. Viorst (2003) described children as an anti-aphrodisiac, as both partners may be so stressed and exhausted that sex loses its appeal. Even the parents of typically developing children describe marriage as being on the back burner. For parents of a child with autism, these experiences can be more intense and can last indefinitely.

The Impact of Autism

"It seems like every time the phone rings I jump." Not a week goes by without the parent of a child with autism echoing these words in my office. Is it a telephone call from the child's school asking that the child be picked up early because of a meltdown? Could it be another injury on the playground or in the classroom? Has the child had another seizure? Is the teacher calling to report that many assignments have not been completed? When you are living on the edge so much of the time, all of these are possibilities, or maybe it is not bad news after all.

Let's consider the traumatic emotional impact of a child's disability on the family. According to the *DSM-IV-TR,* trauma is a personal experience that involves a threat to one's physical integrity. Trauma can also result from witnessing such an event or from learning about an event that has happened to a family member. Autism itself is not life threatening, but having a child with autism often produces the symptoms of trauma in families. Although reports of traumatic stress related to developmental disabilities have only recently appeared in the professional literature after 2000, this concept can provide a lens for understanding what families go through.

As the child grows, a bad day is often lurking in the shadows. For example, if the child has a tantrum in the supermarket that attracts attention, or bolts across the street without looking, a parent or sibling may react intensely—triggering palpitations, shortness of breath, dizziness, and even flashbacks to other even more stressful incidents with the child.

Parents may experience nightmares and disturbed sleep as well as a sense of despair. They may spend long periods of time on edge and behave irritably with each other as a result. Obviously this affects their relationship. But families are resilient, and with support and effective intervention, some sense of order and predictability can be restored to their lives, and thus the overpowering sense of helplessness and powerlessness can be alleviated.

Although you cannot control what happens, you do have a lot to say about how you handle things. If you jump the next time the telephone rings, remember that this is a normal reaction for people who have a child with autism. This is everyday life in their homes. Just take a breath and recognize that your fear is about *what may have happened*. Take another breath and meet the moment that is happening: If there is a problem you will find a way to deal with it, but maybe it's just a friend calling to say hi.

Autism and Parenting Stress

For decades research has documented conclusively that parents of children with special heath care needs experience more parenting stress than parents of typically developing children. Prior to 2000 there was little research comparing parenting stress across parents of children with various health conditions. However, in one of the few studies on this topic that does exist, Gupta (2007) found significantly higher levels of stress among parents of children with ADHD and developmental disorders such as autism than among parents of children with HIV, parents of children with asthma, and parents in a healthy comparison group.

Besides the type of disability, the family's resources for coping and support systems were factors in the level of stress. Whether parents were biological or foster parents did not make a significant difference in their stress level. Likewise, ethnicity did not contribute to a higher stress level, but lack of literacy in English and low parental education did. According to this study, stress results when a child's physical, cognitive, and emotional characteristics do not match parental expectations (Gupta, 2007).

In addition, Schieve, Blumberg, Rice, Visser, and Boyle (2007) found that parents of children with autism scored higher on the Aggravation in Parenting Scale than parents of children with other developmental problems, parents of children with special needs without developmental problems, and parents of typically developing children. The additional stressors identified for parents of children with autism included communication challenges, difficult behaviors, social isolation, problems with self-care, and lack of community understanding. Parents of children with autism reported three main areas of difficulty: finding their child harder to care for than same-age typically developing children, being bothered by things their child does, and giving up more of their life than expected to care for their child. The researchers concluded that these families would likely benefit from family-centered treatment.

Unfortunately, most treatments focus almost exclusively on the child, primarily in terms of the behavioral realm, and do not address the other needs of the family. Blackledge and Hayes (2006) concluded from their review of the research that parents have high rates of depressive and anxiety disorders and that these needs are largely ignored. The focus in parent training is managing the child with autism. The parents' painful thoughts and feelings are congruent with the extreme and unrelenting difficulties of their lives. The researchers emphasized accepting difficult thoughts and feelings while clarifying values and goals. Moving toward those goals significantly reduced anxiety and depression in this study.

Fathers of children with special needs, including autism, have long been ignored by researchers. As far back as 1984, mothers who reported receiving more adequate support from their spouses reported fewer symptoms of depression, reported happier marriages, and had higher scores on quality of parenting (Bristol & Schopler, 1984). These researchers cautioned that ignoring the needs of the entire family may also be detrimental to the child with autism. Family-focused intervention, as opposed to child-centered intervention, was reported to be related to long-term successful family adaptation.

Flippin and Crais (2011) discussed the pressing need for more effective father involvement in early autism intervention programming. Their review of the research on fathers indicated that since the 1960s fathers spend more time than fathers of previous generations with their children and are more directly involved with their care in a coparenting role. In stark contrast, they are not more involved in early intervention programming for their children with autism. Mothers almost exclusively participate in autism research and early intervention services. The high stress levels reported by mothers may be the result of taking on the dual role of caregiver and intervention provider. Important to note, however, is that fathers' stress levels are not being routinely studied, so there is no valid point of comparison.

Flippin and Crais highlighted the unique contributions and challenges of fathers of children with ASD. For example, fathers' use of higher level vocabulary and their different communication style with children may complement those of children's mothers. Fathers are often frustrated because they think they do not know how to play with their children with ASD, but the active rough-and-tumble nature of father–child play can be instrumental in the development of a child with ASD. Fathers reported that their child's acting out behaviors, such as tantrums, were the greatest source of stress. Mothers in contrast reported their greatest stressors to be regulatory problems with sleeping and eating.

Turnbull and Turnbull (1985) suggested that high parental stress levels have cascading effects on all family members, including typically developing siblings. In focusing almost primarily on mothers, researchers and professionals may be inadvertently increasing the burden on moms. Although working hard may provide a respite for fathers, who seem on the surface to have less stress, increased involvement by fathers may have positive outcomes for all family members.

In Their Own Words: Why Would It Be Hard to Be the Mom of a Child with Autism?

Groups have the power to teach in a special way. When I meet with groups of fathers, I regularly ask them why it would be hard to be the mom of a child with autism. They readily speak up about what they have observed in their families. In most cases they have not previously verbalized these thoughts and feelings. My goal is to evoke empathy in men for their partners and thus improve their ability to relate and communicate in daily life. At conferences, these workshops often run overtime, and women are usually waiting outside the door for their partners, wondering what they are talking about.

Why don't men talk about this stuff at home? Can women understand what men don't say? As many men tell me in response to these questions, "You've got a point there doc, but there's nothing I can do about the situation, so I gave up talking about it a long time ago."

According to a Native American proverb, you can only begin to understand a person after you walk a mile in his or her moccasins. For this reason, I have developed role reversal exercises in order to help men and women understand each other. Role reversal diffuses the tension between the genders by allowing each person to experience the problems of the opposite sex within a group of their own gender.

Here is a sampling of what fathers tell me:

- A mom since she carried the child in pregnancy may blame herself for why the child has autism and for how the child may or may not be progressing.

- A mother's bond to her child is more emotional, and mothers really miss this part.

- The tasks of everyday child care fall more on the woman even if she is working full time outside the home.

- Mothers are more sensitive to the child's needs and more protective.

- Men don't know how to show support and express feelings, which makes women feel more alone.

- Mothers have more time together with their child, and this can be very demanding.

- Women have more personal care needs and less time to take care of them.

- Women often sacrifice their careers and don't feel appreciated for doing this.

- Caring for a child with autism takes time away from a family's other children, and mothers feel guilty about this.

- Women shoulder the burden of most interactions with the system to get services and feel responsible for the outcome.

- Moms suffer burnout from the goal of raising their child to adulthood.

- Women want to talk about other things too—not just the child with the disability.

- A mother needs more physical help when the man is home; they're worn out from the everyday grind.

- Women want men to play more with the child and get to know more about him or her.

- Women want men to take the children out and give the woman some free time for herself.

In Their Own Words: Why Would It Be
Hard to Be the Dad of a Child with Autism?

When I talk to mothers about this same topic, what emerges as the main need is the women's desire to be understood more by the men with whom they share their lives. Many women are extremely frustrated because they feel alone with the emotional burden of their child with autism. They think that their husbands are tired of hearing from them. They usually joke about feeling like they are nagging when they keep trying to get their point across.

Asking them to look at things from a male perspective actually provides a break from their frustrations over making their voices heard. Women often have a shorter list of observations because they do not expect the men to come up with much. Nonetheless, the women hit the mark:

- Men have an extremely hard time with all of the intense emotions involved with the child with special needs. They have a difficult time expressing themselves and want women to be more rational and more supportive of their style of caring.

- Men feel unappreciated for their efforts especially for how hard they work to pay the increased medical bills and so forth.

- Denial lasts longer for men because they cannot fix the problem.

- Women are so intense that men feel like they're getting nagged all the time.

- Men don't have a maternal instinct and are more at a loss as to what to do.

- The role they expected as father and husband has changed, and they are at a loss.

- Men need nurturing too and feel left out because there is little time left for them.

- Men have a harder time bonding, especially if it's a son with autism and they can't do the things they dreamed of.

- Because a man has a hard time focusing on the child, he focuses on being the provider and puts a lot of stress on himself from this perspective.

- A man has a harder time asking for help and feels more isolated from other men.

Why Is It So Hard for Mothers to Take a Break?

Winnicott (1993) said that struggling with taking a break from maternal responsibilities is normal. Yet he was talking about mothers of typically developing children, who presumably have a little less to be preoccupied with on average than mothers of children who have autism and other special needs. So it is normal, but when it goes on indefinitely, it is not healthy.

Winnicott appeared regularly on public radio in the United Kingdom between 1939 and 1962. When asked how he knew so much about mothers, he responded that most of what he had learned had come from listening to mothers. Winnicott (1993) also wrote, "I think mothers are helped by being able to voice their agonies at the time they are experiencing them. Bottled up resentment spoils the loving which is at the back of it all" (p. 75). This tends not to work for the average man and creates a tension in the relationship.

Opening up and connecting about upsetting situations can help. However, suggesting that a mother do more to take care of herself often makes her feel worse. Listening to mothers in my practice at Alternative Choices, I hear that this can sound like just one more thing to do and another thing they just are not getting right—even more guilt!

In contrast, the average overwhelmed father seems to have less difficulty taking a break. He may also have trouble talking about what he cannot fix or act on, which offers no outlet for his partner's feelings. He may shut down out of helplessness and an overloading of emotion that he has no words for. The very same man may love his partner and children passionately, yet he may feel left out and ignored. Still, most fathers admire when the mother of their children reacts like a mother lion with her cub, doing everything possible to raise their child.

So here's a plan for men: Tell your partner how much you appreciate her and everything she does for your children. Be specific about all of the wonderful things she does and how hard she works. Ask what you can do to make her job easier. Gently keep asking and showing up to do things. This is how to be a good man in your situation. Help her to take a breath, literally and figuratively. Most likely this may help her feel better—it may even lead to her taking a break.

Bringing Men and Women Together

After the men and women at my talks have looked at life through the lens of their partners, I bring them together. When I spoke to the Southwest Texas Autism Society's 12th Annual International Autism Conference, the fathers met with me on Friday evening and on Saturday. I spoke all day about how to take care of the needs of everyone in the family when a child has autism. After discussing the journey and all of the difficulties, I had a group of five men come to the front and sit in a circle with me while everybody else just listened. I asked these men why it would be difficult to be a mom of a child with autism.

Their answers had everybody speechless. These were just regular guys from all walks of life. All of them talked about what was going on in their families, about how dedicated their wives were to their children, about what they went through every day, about how they needed a break once in a while, about the support they wished they gave. And the women were just speechless. Why? They never hear this. Guys just suck it up. Expressing their fears and worries is hard to do. They want to do the right thing. They try to do the right thing. They are afraid to talk about problems because they are afraid the discussion will not end. I assured people that indeed tears end, and discussions end, and people can continue living.

You could have heard a pin drop in that room when men were talking about why it was hard to be a mom of a child with autism. This was part of the secret life of men finally out in the open. Their partners had no clue. Then we switched roles and I got five women in the front, and we did the same thing. They talked to me, and to the hundred other people there who just listened, about why it would be hard to be a dad of a child with autism. They just nailed it. They talked about how a man's ego suffers when he cannot play sports with his son. They talked about how hard it is to come home and not be able to solve the problems that your family has. They talked about fathers who know they cannot protect their sons and daughters from bullying. They even mentioned how men tended to be very disappointed about how autism had affected their sexual relationship.

Comment after comment, when the men and women were asked to respect the role of the other, they were just hitting it out of the park. And people were just coming together warm and close. Then I brought them all together to talk about what it was like in the room now. And people felt the barriers coming down, at least for the moment. I assured them that they would come back up and they would have to knock them down again. But in that moment the barriers were coming down, and people understood one another. There was light shining into lives that can be really difficult. But difficult lives can still be good lives.

There was laughter and smiles. I pointed out that the differences in the male and female styles of relating that were expressed in the group were similar to the differences seen in most other couples, not just those who have a child with autism. Although these generalities do not apply universally, a lot of forgiveness comes from simply naming these differences between men and women, and doing this does not mean that either one is wrong.

Linguist Deborah Tannen (1990) explained in detail the different conversational styles of men and women in easy-to-understand language. As Tannen pointed out, men and women have quite different definitions of the comfort of home. The man generally has been using language all day in his struggle to succeed at work. At day's end, at home with the woman he loves, he at last has nothing to prove and wants to be free not to talk. In contrast, the woman, if she works outside the home, generally has been careful not to be too expressive all day in order to avoid being called aggressive or neurotic. If she works at home caring for children full time, she may not have had an adult to talk to. At her day's end, when she is finally with the man she feels close to, she wants to be free to talk. I have routinely seen these roles reversed in families in which the man is the stay-at-home parent.

These stereotypes suggest a splitting of love and work. According to psychologist Carol Gilligan (1982), expressive capacities are delegated to women through communication in relationships, whereas instrumental or problem-solving tasks are regarded as logical and masculine. This neat but outmoded model collapses under the weight of autism that neither love nor logic alone can heal. The stage is then set for a far deeper connection, perhaps even more intimate than would have been possible with an easier life.

People always ask: Does it get better? Does it get easier? Those are not the best questions. Do you change? That's the better question. I think that you do change; you change profoundly. If you can learn to navigate your most difficult thoughts and feelings, you get better at handling things. You can have a deeper relationship in your marriage. You can have a deeper relationship with your kids. You are then also more able to understand your typically developing kids and their individual and special needs, which I look at in Chapter 10. Raising a child with autism really takes you on a journey in which you can become wiser, more compassionate, and more loving.

What Men and Women Want

It is also important for partners to talk about what they want from each other. How can women be expected to understand what men don't say? It is easy to talk about work and sports, but other stuff is hard. Here is a sampling of what men say in groups and in conversation:

- We want the women to understand that we are trying to help in the ways we know how, and that we're frustrated when we can't make things better.

- We need more time as a couple again, to be together without the children, and have sex a little more often.

- We want women to listen to us too and be less emotional, so we can discuss problems and find solutions when possible.

- Let us take more responsibility with the child with autism. Sometimes it seems that the women can't let go of doing all the work and being overwhelmed all the time.

- It would help if you told us what we are doing right so that we could feel more secure in the relationship.

I always ask the women to speak next. Usually the women are amazed at how specific the men's group has been as well as relieved and understanding of the male perspective, which has usually gone unspoken at home. Here are some of the things that women want:

- To be appreciated for all they do.

- For men to be involved in the child's education. Women are tired of going to meetings alone. They want men, whenever possible, to take a few hours off from work to be there.

- Some time alone without the children to relax.

- Time together as a couple not just limited to sex.

- For men to develop a better understanding of their child's autism and not leave it all to them.

- To be able to talk about their feelings without the men getting defensive.

At the end of these discussions, I share how I am still learning how to listen to Cindy, Kara (now 21), and Zoë (now 19). How many things have I expected them to understand without talking about the issue at hand? How many times did I expect Cindy not to be upset because it was too frustrating for me to listen to things that I couldn't fix? They are teaching me. Often they will say, "I don't need you to do anything; I just need you to listen." This often relieves me of my knee-jerk response of trying to come up with a way to fix the problem. Sometimes they will say, "First just listen, and then there is something I want you to do."

I still marvel at how feeling heard is often all they want. I do not come across many men who experience life that way. Wanting to solve problems and wanting to be useful to the family they love is part of the best part of men. Yet men's difficulty in listening first often sabotages their best part. When they learn to listen first, they can be more helpful than they ever dreamed of. What I tell men is that learning to listen to your partner's upsets is not learning how to be more like a girl. It is about learning how to be a better man and a better father.

Often I ask everyone at one of my talks to find their partner and whisper something special in each other's ear. Many file out arm in arm, hand in hand. Some feel lonely because they are missing that connection. Each time I facilitate these discussions for couples I learn and understand more about what it takes to be in a relationship and to understand each other better. Then I bring that to each group, and each group finds its own unique way of teaching itself.

Like the participants at these workshops and conferences, you can have these discussions with partners, with friends, and in ongoing support groups. Some more involved problems are beyond the reach of these self-help strategies and can best be untangled by consulting a professional skilled in counseling couples and sensitive to the issues around having a child with autism. Although this chapter covers many of the difficulties encountered by parents of children with autism, it is crucial to remember that every relationship is unique and special and needs to be understood that way. The vitality of healthy children reinforces parents' efforts and keeps them going. Raising a child with autism may require more and not less relationship maintenance for couples living with those stresses and strains.

Polarized Couples

Often couples seem to get polarized in their individual perspectives and reactions to daily events. Recently a couple raising a 3-year-old daughter with ASD came to me for counseling because they were having problems getting along. Both expressed deep love and devotion to their daughter. She was receiving therapies and making progress. Kathy, the mom, was extremely anxious about her daughter's upcoming third birthday party. She was upset with John because he was leaving everything until the day before the party. She wanted him to buy the balloons that day, but he wanted to wait until the morning of the party so that none of the air would leak out. He seemed very irritated with her anxiety about preparations for the party.

Both of them complained that they were always fighting about trivial things. I asked them what else might be at the root of their disagreement. Kathy burst into tears. "My baby is turning 3 and there are so many things she isn't doing yet. I love her so much, but lately I just keep thinking of everything she's not doing and how she doesn't like to play with other children."

I asked John about his perspective. "I understand her condition. She is making progress every day, and I don't worry about the future yet." His rational response and moderate emotional temperature was in stark contrast to that of his partner. I asked him whether there was anything he was worried about. He paused thoughtfully. "There really isn't much time or space for me to talk about these things at our house. Kathy is always worried and I try to be positive."

I asked Kathy whether she ever felt more hopeful about their daughter's progress. She thought for a moment. She responded that she just wanted John to understand her feelings and validate them. As she explained more, John gradually seemed to understand. At this point John and Kathy were looking at each other warmly. The session was over, and they asked me for homework. John's assignment was to talk to Kathy about his worries for their daughter. Kathy's assignment was to listen and validate his concerns.

When I saw them the following week, they told me that the homework had been helpful and that their daughter's birthday party had been a big success. They were truly on the same page in celebrating their daughter's life. They did tell me, however, that the pattern of their interactions after the party had not changed. They have continued to address this issue in their counseling and in their work with each other at home. In my experience, many couples have similar difficulties and benefit from reversing roles. It takes some time, however, before they can change their pattern and live more harmoniously in their everyday lives.

Decades of research has shown conclusively that marital conflict is bad for infants and increases their chances of developing depression, poor social skills, and challenging behaviors. Dingfelder (2011) reported on interventions developed by John and Julie Gottman to prevent the spiraling negativity commonly experienced by couples such as John and Kathy. The Gottmans work to strengthen three key elements of marital satisfaction: friendship and intimacy, constructive conflict, and shared meaning. This approach can be applied to couples raising a child with autism and is also described in detail in John Gottman's book *The Seven Principles for Making Marriage Work*.

Romance and Intimacy

Whenever I speak to couples, I ask when they had their last date. It is rare that couples go out together with any regularity because of the often overwhelming demands they face. Yet those demands make it all the more necessary to find time together for the sake of the marriage, which obviously will benefit the children. "Why not have a date night?" is not a good question, as it can be hard to find a baby sitter who can handle their children. A better question is this: How do you steal some time for yourselves as a couple?

Here are some of the things that people have told me:

- Just socializing with friends, even with the kids around.

- Staying up after the kids are sleeping and watching a sitcom together.

- Taking a break from talking about autism.

- Taking turns listening to each other even if we don't really understand or fully agree on a particular issue.

- Taking a walk together, even if it's just for 10 minutes.

- Just enjoying some quiet time together.

- Doing the grocery shopping together if the children are at school or another activity.

- Being able to spend time together anywhere, even if that's at home.

Many couples are able to plan at-home dates. On a Friday or Saturday evening, after the children are sleeping, they have a candlelit dinner and watch a movie. (If your child has sleep issues, it might be possible to have a support person upstairs with the child.) These dates usually involve an agreement to talk about anything but autism.

Although marriage is often on the back burner for parents of most young children, when a child has autism the marriage is often not even in sight. It is important for couples to see that problems with their sex life are really troubles for both partners. In general, men like to have sex in order to feel close and tender. In contrast, a woman generally wants to feel closeness in order to feel sexual. It is important to see these general differences as problems to be resolved and not faults in each person. When I talk to groups of parents they always seem relieved to hear this problem talked about out loud. The sexual connection between partners is about more than just sex. It is symbolic of their closeness and intimacy.

Although there are many self-help books about relationships, I am aware of only one that addresses the complexities of relationships for couples raising children with special needs. In *Married with Special-Needs Children,* Marshak and Prezant (2007) observe that many people insist that they will work on their marriage when things get easier. However, the stress is endless. According to the authors, being consumed with the child is really not good for anyone, including the child.

Laura Marshak is herself the parent of a child with a disability. She advises readers that intimacy, romance, and sex cannot be adequately replaced by other strengths in the relationship. Unfortunately, some people become worn out and feel unworthy of attention other than as a mother, father, or caregiver. She cautions that sacrificing sexual intimacy is not entirely reasonable and that maintaining a sexual relationship may foster goodwill between partners who might not be feeling particularly desiring or desirable.

Lack of interest in sex is often experienced as rejection. According to Marshak and Prezant, stress decreases sexual desire in women but has the opposite effect in men. Women may look at sex as something else they have to do, whereas men look at sex as a stress reliever. Some women and men may even feel guilty when they enjoy themselves. Marshak and Prezant note that as women get more upset by their lack of emotional support, they tend to become physically distant from their partners. This may lead to their partners becoming more irritable and distant. As with many issues faced by couples, there is truth in both viewpoints regarding intimacy and sex. Partners who are struggling with these issues in their relationship may need to consult a marriage and family therapist who is familiar with the challenges of raising a child with autism and its impact on couples.

Grown-Up Couples

Just as parenting even a typically developing child requires giving up the dream of the perfect child, a rewarding and enduring relationship calls on parents to abandon their longing for the perfect union in which all of their needs are met and their partner is also totally satisfied. Relationships can be incredibly complex and seldom quite what people expect. It is, however, important to maintain the love between a couple when the very fabric and meaning of life is challenged by autism. For some people, the child's condition may reveal relationship problems that no amount of understanding and insight can repair or pave over, and divorce may ensue. For others, a child's special needs can be a red herring that distracts from fundamental issues in the couple's relationship. Problematic relationships can become considerably worse.

Hope for relationships can, however, spring from the crisis that couples experience when their child is imperfect. Normal crises, such as childbirth, a move, the loss of a job, financial problems, and trials in parenting, can all strain a relationship in parallel ways. Ordinary trouble differs only in degree from the strain caused by autism. Although having a child with autism is a quantum leap away from everyday problems, it is nevertheless an experience that prepares parents to learn and grow in ways they might not have imagined. Being grown up in a relationship means that partners are working hard to maintain what they have found with each other. The many voices in this chapter illuminate these essential themes.

10

A Different Perspective

Understanding Siblings

I don't believe an accident of birth makes people sisters or brothers. It makes them siblings, gives them mutuality of parentage. Sisterhood and brotherhood is a condition people have to work at.

MAYA ANGELOU

BROTHERS AND SISTERS HAVE LIFE'S LONGEST RELATIONSHIP. Most people have at least one sibling, and these bonds start early and outlast most other relationships. They go on after the death of parents and keep going after arguments that would end most friendships. Siblings share the special kind of laughter that you can only enjoy with a brother or sister. There is a love and loyalty that is easy to talk about. However, the darker side of emotional life is also there. Overemphasizing sibling rivalry tends to accentuate the negative, whereas ignoring it denies an integral part of the reality that bonds siblings.

It is a story as old as humankind. Cain killed his brother Abel. It is a story about the wish to get rid of a sibling. There is a certain amount of shame in admitting competitive and angry feelings. After all, doesn't everyone love and respect their brothers and sisters unconditionally? Everyone who grew up with siblings can access these deep mixed feelings. Most, if not all, parents aspire to have a perfect family with warm, unconditional love between brothers and sisters. Children who have a sibling on the autism spectrum cannot avoid wondering about and missing the brother or sister they might have had. Life is not fair when your parents are overwhelmed and bereaved by the unrelenting demands of caring for a sibling's special needs but usually considering your own needs to be minimal. In so many ways the feelings and attitudes of siblings mirror those of parents.

It can be hard for parents to face the experiences of their typically developing children. Karl Taro Greenfeld wrote about his little brother's inability to communicate verbally and his tendency toward violent outbursts despite his angelic demeanor. *Boy Alone* is Karl Taro Greenfeld's gripping memoir about growing up with a mixture of rage, confusion, and love. It is a raw and honest exploration of what it means to have a brother with autism. This chapter is dedicated to those brothers and sisters.

The Imprints of Birth Order and Gender

Parents are not only parents; they are siblings with one foot back in the world of their own childhood and one foot in the world of adulthood and parenting. Having a disability in the family heightens a parent's challenge to be fair to all. In this quest, grasping the lessons of their family of origin can help parents to understand the dilemmas of the family that they create.

Primogeniture historically meant that the firstborn son received the inheritance as well as a key position in the family. Yet at times, the natural order was reversed in religion and mythology when a later born son overtook the elder. When such a reversal occurs, it threatens the self-concept of the older child and can leave the younger one feeling chronically guilty. Even today, parents still long for a son to carry on the family name. Despite social advances in the realm of gender equality, the birth of a son after a daughter represents a reversal of the traditional social order, and daughters are often not valued equally. On the positive side, when both are valued equally, having a sibling of the opposite sex can be a great advantage throughout life in terms of learning how to get along with the opposite gender.

Same-sex siblings have a special kind of identification with each other. Because they are so alike, they have the special challenge to establish their individuality. Two women who grew up together tend to be more intimate and sometimes more jealous. Two male siblings tend to be more competitive. The greatest power struggles are between siblings of the same sex, and they sometimes continue into adulthood. This is especially true when there are only two children in the family and thus there is no one else to dilute or buffer the struggle.

Remembering One's Roots

When talking to parents about the issues faced by their typically developing children, I always ask them to reflect on their own lives as brothers and sisters. Of course I do the same. For example, if a baseball game is on, I remember all those summer nights on my grandparents' back porch listening to the Phillies, whether they were winning or losing. Pop was a real fan. I share those memories with my brothers and sisters and cousins. Likewise, walking past Independence Hall to my office, I remember my father taking us as children to see the Liberty Bell. Back then, you could still walk up and touch it, and we took turns putting our fingers in the crack. Recalling those memories brings back a whole world of warm, compassionate, loving feelings mixed with the inevitable rivalry and jealousy that exist among siblings.

Every time I have an involved conversation with one of my siblings, it seems that our similarities and differences come up. Fortunately, our differences naturally have a wide span through age, gender, temperament, and abilities.

Affirming our differences helps to control rivalry and serves as a way of expressing it constructively. Most people long for a balanced view of these emotions which can emerge in adulthood. In *The Sibling Bond,* Stephen Bank and Michael Kahn discussed the positive aspects of aggression and rivalry. Two brothers wrestling, for example, can represent contact, warmth, and presence.

This point reminds me of the endless wrestling matches between my brother Al and me. Al is 2 years my junior and was my constant companion until I left home for college. In a fight, a child is alive and real and noticed. In these power struggles and interactions, siblings can learn how to resolve conflicts. Yet I felt some guilt for winning, even though I was supposed to by virtue of being older and putting myself under tremendous pressure to do so. Certainly this was the downside of feeling responsible to lead and achieve. When Al and I discussed this as adults, it was a relief to know that he had not held it against me, but still I could never feel good about winning so consistently. As he has pointed out to me, our roads diverged so long ago that it is very different now, and each of us has hair that has begun to gray. Our bonds have endured.

As the oldest in a family of eight kids, I had grown up always helping my parents take care of the younger ones. The feeling of being so responsible at a young age is very common among eldest children. The pressure to set a good example is a burden at times but naturally helps one develop leadership ability. Like with most eldest children, my role was always clear, and that has been a blessing. Since my teenage years, I have found myself in leadership positions in sports, in union activities, in professional groups, and now speaking to and for parents of children with autism and other disabilities. This is no accident.

I remember teaching my younger brothers how to play baseball and being proud of their accomplishments in Little League. I remember how, at one point, they thought I could do anything. There was a certain competition among the older group of us for the attention and admiration of the younger ones. This is another common form of rivalry. Nonetheless, it is hard to admit and carries a twinge of embarrassment along with it. The oldest is by nature biggest, strongest, and knows the most, so he or she is expected to win out. The oldest may also feel guilty for winning at the expense of a younger sibling who is also loved. No wonder so many siblings report strained relationships in adulthood.

In *Mixed Feelings: Love, Hate, Rivalry, and Reconciliation Among Brothers and Sisters,* Francine Klagsbrun explores the unique perspective of each position in the birth order. Such a wide range of factors contribute to people's personalities; therefore, generalizations about birth order do not always hold up. Nonetheless, they can be used along with other differences to better understand oneself and others. In every case, sibling bonds leave special imprints that affect the way people parent their children, whether their experience fits the norm or not.

Gender, spacing, and family size are also important factors in sibling relationships. Middle children in most families tend to have a hazy role and be pressured from all sides. They have no clearly defined place, but their experience tends to produce people who are friendly, diplomatic, and good at negotiating. They usually are blessed with a sense of responsibility, connect strongly with older siblings, and are very protective of younger siblings.

The youngest, like the oldest, has a unique position and is never displaced. The child in this position feels chosen for special protection by older siblings as well as parents. The youngest is often regarded as spoiled or as the favorite, whether this is true or not. Whereas the oldest is usually expected to help with parenting, the oldest daughter is often expected to take care of the parents as they age. Several years ago I met a man who was the second child in his family but the first son. He was treated as if he was the oldest child, and that had always felt weird to him. Of course, it also strained his relationship with his older sister, who was never treated in accord with her natural position. His dilemma is meaningful in reference to how gender affects sibling relationships.

Family Pictures

Family Pictures is a novel by Sue Miller about a family with five children, including a son with autism. It is a story about relationships and forgiving told through the eyes of Nina, the oldest child—a different and much needed perspective. Randall, the child with autism, strained everyone's patience. Lainie, the mother, tried to treat him as normally as possible, devoted most of her time to his care, and seemed inseparable from Randall. David, the father, and the other children all felt neglected at times—a major dilemma faced by many families touched by autism.

One day the family received the devastating news that Randall had wandered away while on a field trip for school and had been killed by a car. I shudder, for this is still my worst fear for Tariq, and I can imagine a funeral like the one in the book. What makes this novel and the television film based on it significant is the confrontation and the subsequent reconciliation that occurs between Nina and her mother. There is much friction between mother and daughter, who have argued bitterly for years.

Married and pregnant with her first child, Nina asks why her mother had divorced her father after Randall's death. Lainie explains in a firm tone that they had both worked hard to stay together. Nina counters that from her perspective it seemed like her parents had tried to stay together only for Randall's sake, as after he died they broke up. She feels that her mother's love was conditional and summarizes it this way: "It's be quiet, be good, be happy, be well. Most of all, be well. Be all of those things, and I'll love you. I'll love you, my perfect baby" (Miller, 1990, p. 406).

Her mother responds by explaining that she wished she could have loved Randall the way she loved her other children. She explains that it would have been a gift if she could have asked the same from him as from her other children.

She acknowledges that she was not a good mother to Nina because she yelled and hit. She makes no excuses and concludes that her love for her other typical children "held me to the earth" (p. 407).

The reconciliation that results is possible between a parent and an adult child when both can speak honestly and openly from the heart. It takes courage to have this kind of dialogue, but it can liberate its participants from so many dark feelings. In speaking her mind and in hearing her mother's response, Nina begins to make sense out of her life. As the narrator, Nina reflects on her family and sees it as a portrait of courage. From this perspective, every child who is born represents an immense risk on the part of the parents. There is so much potential for pain and tragedy that any child's existence is a miracle.

I reflect on the risks my parents took to have and raise eight children—only to lose one of us in a car accident. I thought of my grandparents and their courage. My grandfather came over on a boat alone from Italy when he was 12 years old to meet his father, who was already here in America. He never knew his mother, who had died when he was only 2. During the Great Depression, my grandparents raised five children to adulthood. They lost a 2-year-old daughter to illness, which was not uncommon in those days. In fact, the infant mortality rate was 165 per 1,000 during the first year of life in 1900 in comparison to 7 per 1,000 in 1997 (PBS, n.d.).

I am not the only one who rolled the dice and lost. I think of my wife Cindy and her parents because she too lost a brother—he was only 17—in a bus accident in Israel. He was buried on the kibbutz while her family sat shivah half a world away in Philadelphia. Every family has its share of tragedy. Love is such a risk, but who would want to live without love, without a connection to others?

I often wondered what sense my oldest daughter would make of Tariq when she was grown. All parents want to be fair, and they want their healthy children to grow up loving them as parents and loving their siblings who are less fortunate in some ways. Her early years with her brother were extremely difficult. She tried so hard to play with him, and he just was not interested in her. She experienced rejection repeatedly. He would rip up her artwork at times. Her things were never safe. Smeared feces could wind up on her stuff too. I could not protect her from these experiences.

When my oldest daughter was 5, Tariq's school, the Center for Autism, invited brothers and sisters to spend a day at the school. The bus picked up Tariq. My daughter got in the car with me. Her question gave me a chuckle: "Do Tariq's teachers talk?" How could she possibly know? Her whole lifetime of experience to that point was having a nonverbal brother. She had fun with the other brothers and sisters. Although some of their siblings spoke, they were more like her brother than not. From that point on, she told everyone that Tariq acted the way he did because of autism.

One night when my oldest daughter was a young teenager, everyone else was out and she and I were having dinner together. She asked me whether I would rather have one healthy son than three daughters. What a heavy question for her! But I was glad for her sake that she was able to ask it. I told her that I would have been overjoyed for Tariq to be normal, but not in place of any of my daughters. She seemed relieved by my answer.

On another occasion when she was a senior in high school, she expressed her longing for a typical brother: "If Tariq was regular, he could tell me which guys to watch out for." Although Kara and Zoë have also wished for a typical brother, they did not live with Tariq and did not experience the same kind of impact on their lives. In this photograph, they are enjoying taking Tariq for a walk.

Kara and Zoë take Tariq for a walk.

Veteran Parents Speak Out

Several years ago I addressed a unique group of parents—Vietnam veterans who had been exposed to Agent Orange. One of the tragic consequences of their exposure to that chemical compound was that their children had a much higher incidence of all sorts of disabilities, especially those of a neurological nature, including autism. A class action court case that had awarded damages to these veterans and their families also established funds for parent training for those whose children had special needs. I was asked to focus my presentation on the issues facing parents who are raising siblings of children with disabilities. About 50 people were present—two thirds were women. After a brief introduction, I talked about Nina's comments in *Family Pictures,* especially Nina's confrontation with her mother. I asked people to share what opened inside of them as they heard that story. Here is what they told me:

- "I'm sad. I'm always yelling at my child who doesn't have the problem. I expect so much from her, and she's not even 4. I know I have to change."

- "I'm always running around trying to keep up with my son . . . . I'm never sure what I'll find around the next corner. My nerves are shot . . . my other children are really on their own. I don't know what to do."

- "My child was just diagnosed with autism. My daughter will never have a normal playmate. I'm not sure how to help her."

- "I think I talk to my healthy daughter too much. My husband doesn't want to talk about our child's problems. For years I've confided in my daughter, who is now a teenager. I know this isn't right, and I feel horrible about it, but I haven't known where to turn."

- "My 2.5-year-old has a hearing impairment. My 4-year-old looked at her the other day and said 'Why won't you talk to me?' I told her that her sister's ears were broken, and she will learn to talk with her hands. Did I do the right thing?"

Of course it was right—information liberates us all, parents and children, from some of our darkest worries. The pain is still there, however, and that is one thing that makes it so difficult to know if we are doing the right thing as parents. In 1972, Grossman reported on the first large-scale study involving college-age siblings in *Brothers and Sisters of Retarded Children*. These brothers and sisters reported that talking to their parents about the disabilities of their brothers and sisters was as difficult as talking to them about sex. Parents need to share with other adults. It does not make things all better, but it helps with the isolation. Sharing these difficult thoughts and feelings and connecting helps parents to get refreshed and go back to the important people in their lives.

So far none of the men in this group of veterans had spoken, which was not unusual in these meetings. A simple intervention often can change that. I opened the door by asking whether any of the men wanted to share. After an awkward pause, some men spoke up:

- "Our 3-year-old has just been diagnosed with ASD. We don't know what to think. My wife is really worried about the effect on our two older children, and I am too."

- "My wife tells me I don't talk about this enough, but I don't know what to do, and that's why I have nothing to say. It really makes me feel like a nothing as a father. I want to go home with something to say."

Stressing that we might be able to find many answers to these questions already within the group, I asked everyone to imagine that they had a sibling with a disability or chronic illness. What would they want from their parents?

What Siblings Want

There is the clear simple voice of the child in everyone. Everyone who grew up with siblings can access those deep mixed feelings. It can be hard to admit to these feelings especially to their parents as Mary McHugh described from her compelling personal experience and from her extensive research in *Special Siblings: Growing Up with Someone with a Disability*.

As I mentioned in Chapter 9 with regard to couples, role reversal exercises can help people think for themselves as opposed to just hearing what I as a counselor have to say. When the veteran parents imagined taking on the role of a sibling of someone with autism, here is what they had to say:

- "I would want a fair amount of attention from my parents. This could be in the form of taking my own problems just as seriously as those of my sister with special needs."

- "I want recognition of the positive without having the pressure of being the star of the family."

- "So much gets taken for granted when you're normal. As parents we make such a big deal out of the accomplishments of our special child. If I was a sibling, I would really resent it if my parents didn't notice my struggles and accomplishments." (This comment, like Nina's in *Family Pictures,* reflects the reality that the child with the disability does not have to compete for the parents' attention. From the siblings' perspective, that child always wins.)

- "I'd want my own life!"

- "I would want time alone without any responsibilities and time with my friends."

- "I would want to be treated as an individual, and I would absolutely hate it if my parents always reminded me how lucky I was. That would drive me up the wall."

- "I would want information about the disability, I'm sure I would have a lot of questions, and I would want answers."

- "That makes me think that I would want my parents to be concerned about my feelings. I would want them to ask me how I felt."

Because they are always expected to help out their exhausted, bereaved parents, siblings often feel like junior parents. Yet they find it hard to express their negative feelings about this role. They may feel that doing so would be inconsiderate or disloyal to their struggling parents. When we looked for solutions within the group, the ideas flowed freely. Just as parents need information, so do siblings. Information helps siblings to answer the questions that come from their peers or even from adults who are too uncomfortable to ask the parents directly.

Like their parents, brothers and sisters have a host of feelings that run the gamut from confusion to fear to anger to sadness to embarrassment. Sometimes their shame is so acute that siblings wish they did not even know their brother or sister who acts or looks unusual. This can be especially true if there is a strong physical resemblance between the two. Although it may be hard to express these thoughts, most siblings long to have their feelings described or confirmed in some way. It helps to relieve their guilt about having negative feelings toward a sibling.

For example, let's take the anger that a sibling might feel toward a sister who keeps messing up his video games, perhaps by pulling out the plug when he is playing with it and forcing him to start over again. The anger makes him want to get rid of or even beat up his sister, who is being a pest. Then there is the guilt that he may feel when he thinks it over and remembers that she just wants to play, does not understand how to play the game, and wants him to do something different. Surely this is an understandable cycle of emotions, but ones that are very difficult to deal with internally.

Parents who have come to terms with the darker side of their feelings about their child's disability and their own feelings as siblings themselves are in the best position to help all of their children feel whole and lovable. Research on the adjustment of siblings of children with disabilities consistently shows this. As the father of a child with autism told me, "I would want a normal family life, and that would mean doing things together as a family as well as time alone with my parents to do things or just talk." Parents frequently tell me that privacy would really matter because it is annoying to have a kid who does not understand any better constantly getting into my things. It would also be good to get a break from all the worries and responsibilities. A sense of humor in the family could really help with this.

There was a resurgence of hope among the veterans at my talk following their open expression of feelings. They had captured the essence of what siblings themselves say in interviews and what is recommended by professionals. As parents did this brainstorming with me, the mood of the group shifted. Feeling empowered, people were eagerly copying down the ideas they had shared. Whenever I discuss sibling issues with parents, this role reversal technique seems to be helpful.

Given that everyone wants to be a good parent to their children, and people get a sense of their needs when they meet together and talk, then why is it so hard to do this? Stressed out and out of breath much of the time, it can be hard for parents to hear the voices of their typical children. It can be really, really hard, and sometimes they run out of gas. People always tell me, and I am sure other parents get this a lot too, that they do not know how I have survived having a child with autism. Sometimes that makes parents angry, but I think people are saying that they admire the strength and courage and love exhibited in such quantity by the parents of children with autism and other special needs.

As Shakespeare wrote in *Hamlet,* "Nothing is either good or bad, it's thinking that makes it so" (Act 2, Scene 2). Talking about these things is one way in which parents can find the good side, take care of themselves, and replenish their energy. And they can take better care of their children by learning to take care of themselves. That sounds simple, but there is something more to take into account. Autism can disrupt the usual occurrences in the family life of brothers and sisters.

Some time back, I met a man who was very concerned about the unsettling outlook for his 3-year-old daughter. She kept calling her older sister, who was

6, "the baby." The 6-year-old was visually impaired and had a developmental disability. Although it seemed weird to this father, in this case the younger daughter functioned at a much higher level than her older sister. Her way of looking at things was in accordance with the reality she experienced.

Disability had reversed the natural order. Her father had explained the disability to his younger daughter, but she still called her older sister the baby. That will stop when the younger girl develops the capacity to understand the abstract concepts involved. She will nevertheless be uncomfortable at times. In the same way, all of my own daughters feel like Tariq is the baby. In a functional way, what is historically false is actually true in terms of the role that the children play in the family. The younger, typically developing child loses both a playmate and a role model as well as the attention she would have naturally gotten as the baby of the family. When parents are sensitive to this, they can help their children understand.

Kara and Zoë eat pizza with Tariq.

When the healthy child is born second, parents are quite naturally thrilled with his or her development. However, this is a double-edged sword. Every achievement can remind parents of the limitations of their first child. Without warning, the inner confusion and turmoil may be reignited. In this way, the feelings can reverberate through a family. Physical resemblance is another tricky area. As my oldest daughter moved toward adolescence, I noticed that she got uncomfortable when people commented on her resemblance to Tariq. Her reaction bothered me at first. I wanted her to have the warm feeling I had when people told me that I looked like my siblings. Indeed I still want that for her. I realize that she was responding partly from her own fear that something might be wrong with her—a fear revealed by every sibling of a child with a disability whom I have interviewed. When the disability is invisible, such as with a learning disability, autism, mental disorders, or intellectual deficiencies, this worry seems even more prominent.

Children with autism are also siblings. They too may experience anger and resentment, especially if they are aware of their condition and frustrated with their differences. I have counseled young people with autism who are jealous of their typical siblings' friendships and social lives. Every child comes into the world with parents who are fantasizing a perfect child. Each one is the recipient of that fantasy, but no one's life can be magical. The child with autism, like a typically developing child, bears the weight of his or her parents' expectations and may experience them as unfair.

The Meaning of "Rain Man"

A certain level of mystery shrouds sibling bonds. The 1988 movie *Rain Man* provides a compelling illustration of this theme. Dustin Hoffman's masterful portrayal of Raymond focused attention on individuals with autism. When *Rain Man* was released around Christmas of 1988, I was interviewed for a parent's perspective on the movie for a local television station. Tariq had just turned 9 and was home for the holidays, as he had recently begun residential school.

We appeared on the evening news together. My oldest daughter was only 7 at the time, and she was too shy to be interviewed, but she showed up in the background. At the end of the interview Tariq hugged me and then gave the reporter a high five. It was a warm and memorable moment that I have preserved on tape as one of our own family pictures.

Unlike Raymond, Tariq and many children with autism cannot read and write or memorize the phonebook. Nonetheless, this movie depicts a character transformation in Raymond's brother that has meaning and relevance for siblings. Raymond's brother Charlie is an angry hustler who is calloused and self-centered. His mother died when he was 2, he is estranged from his father, and when the movie begins he does not know that he even has a brother.

He feels that nothing he does is good enough. When his father dies, Charlie discovers that he has been excluded from a $3 million inheritance. In his quest to find out why, Charlie discovers that he has a brother, Raymond, in an institution. He kidnaps Raymond in order to bargain for his fair share of the inheritance. Because of his autism, Raymond lives in a world without a typical perception of human relationships. He unwittingly provides his brother with someone he cannot con and forces Charlie to confront his own stunted emotional development.

What is ironic is that Charlie begins to find himself and his feelings as he struggles to relate to Raymond. Raymond does not seem to crave or accept attention or affection, but Charlie begins to appreciate his brother on their long car trip together from the Midwest to his home in Los Angeles. At one point in the film Charlie remembers that when he was little and got scared, he thought someone called the *rain man* could save him. During the trip, Charlie discovers that the rain man in his fantasy was his brother *Raymond,* who remembers singing to Charlie as a young boy.

Eventually Charlie comes to love Raymond for the unique person he is and comes to want the best for him. He tells Raymond's guardian that he is no longer furious at his father or about the money. Instead he now wishes that his father had told him about his brother so that he could have known him growing up.

By making a genuine connection with his brother, Charlie is transformed. Raymond cannot be like the typical brother, but Charlie proves to himself that through his brotherhood with Raymond he can have genuine relationships.

Siblings Speak Out: Another View of the Mountain

A mountain looks different from every direction. It could be a slow-rising chain of hills from the north and a granite wall from the south. There might be a creek on the east. The rocks, the trees, and the soil may be different depending on the approach. None of the views may match, yet they are all views of the same mountain. The same is true of families; what any member sees is determined by his or her vantage point. The challenge of autism fits this metaphor. Age, place in the birth order, gender, native abilities, emotional temperament, parents' attitudes, and individual history all make each person's position unique. There is much one can learn from the questions brothers and sisters ask and what they say about their experiences from a young age.

In *Voices from the Spectrum* Cindy and I asked siblings to write about their experiences. Their contribution to this book of essays was deeply felt. Our daughter Zoë, 11 years old at the time, surprised Cindy and me by writing an essay, even though she did not enjoy writing at the time. Even though Tariq was living in a residential setting when Zoë was born, she remembers being afraid of him when she was little because he was very big compared to her and would steal her pizza or ice cream. She put it this way: "My brother always hogs my dad . . . Whenever we go canoeing: dad hogger. When we go hiking: dad hogger. Every time he is around and I try to go near my dad: dad hogger" (Naseef, 2006, p. 160).

Lydia Liang was also 11 years old at the time. Her younger brother had cerebral palsy as well as autism. She wrote about her resentment:

> Since I didn't understand what his problem was when I was little, I thought he was just being rude and misbehaving. These feelings have stayed with me and I still think this way a lot . . . I try to find positive things about my brother and really there are some . . . it's great when he can make me laugh . . . I tell myself these things and I try to be grateful and not resentful that I have this unique brother . . . he is my brother and I love him. (2006, pp. 156–157)

Katherine Flaschen, 16 at the time, wrote about her perspective:

> You know how they say life's not fair? Well mine definitely isn't. It's always the same: DJ first me second. As long as he's happy, my mom's happy, as long as my mom's happy, my dad's happy, but what about me? Where do I fit in? . . . I've succumbed to his charm, too. In fact, I think I take more pleasure and pride in his accomplishments than anyone else. I watch in complete adoration every little thing he does. (2006, pp. 149–151)

Tariq with his younger sisters

Kimberly Bittner was a special education professional who shared her experiences:

> My little sister is my hero—she has always been . . . Growing up with a sibling who has special needs is not an easy road . . . Being the oldest, I became like a second mommy to Kristy . . . I gave up a lot to play such a large part in Kristy's upbringing. (2006, pp. 141–144)

The Sibling Slam Book, edited by Don Meyer, gives voice to the perspectives of brothers and sisters who have grown up with a sibling with special needs. These teenagers talk about real life in funny, smart, and poignant ways. They talk about what is weird, what is fun, what is annoying, and what is cool about having a brother or sister with special needs such as autism. It is clear from this book that siblings cannot be easily categorized. Their diverse opinions are full of wit and wisdom as they describe their trials, tribulations, and joys from an insider's point of view.

In *Thicker than Water,* Don Meyer provides an outstanding collection of essays by adult siblings of people with disabilities. As Meyer comments in the introduction, it is clearly not *Chicken Soup for the Siblings Soul.* For some of the authors being the brother or sister of a person with special needs is a good thing. For some it is not a good thing. For many others the experience is something in between. According to Meyer, "It's a mixed bag: they have a deep, abiding love for their sibs who have disabilities, but it is a devotion which is never easy" (2009, p. xi).

Emily Marino shared an experience that I have frequently heard from siblings. She related how her brother Peter, who had fragile X syndrome, scared off some of her ex-boyfriends. In her words, "Peter was my litmus test of whether or not the guy was true boyfriend material. Let's see nice to Peter? Nervous? Too nice, insincere?" (Meyer, 2009, p. 32).

Another sibling wrote about having a violent and chaotic childhood because of her older brother's severe challenging problems. Her parents refused residential placements, and for 18 years this woman lived in fear—the kind of fear that can rip any family apart. As an adult this woman was not emotionally able to be directly involved with her brother's care seemingly because of challenges to her mental health that had resulted from her childhood experiences. This essay is a difficult read but an important contribution towards understanding a sibling perspective.

Gallagher, Powell, and Rhodes (2006) noted the wide spectrum of feelings that brothers and sisters experience:

- Siblings may fear that they might catch the disability. Siblings may also be concerned and worried about the future for their brother or sister or their family as a whole. Siblings may also be afraid to have their own children for fear that these children may also be born with autism or other disabilities.

- Loneliness and isolation from peers is common. Siblings may feel alienated from other family members and different from other children.

- Anger is also a common reaction. Siblings may feel anger toward the child with autism, their parents, society, or even God. They may be angry because they feel ignored. They may also be angry at peers who say negative things about their brother or sister. Others may feel resentment because their parents spend so much time with the child with autism or because their own social activities are limited because of their brother or sister. Overall the situation may seem unfair, and siblings may grow weary of having to be a constant helper.

- Embarrassment may be hard for parents to understand if they deny their own shame about their situation. Many siblings report feeling embarrassed by their brother or sister with autism, especially in public. Inappropriate behavior attracts unwanted attention and triggers embarrassment. Siblings may resent the fact that the rules at home are different for them and their brother or sister who has autism.

- Jealousy may be evoked because their sibling with autism receives an inordinate amount of attention from their parents. Healthy siblings often feel ignored and feel that they have to be perfect in order for their parents to notice. This is experienced as pressure to excel.

- Guilt may arise because of very strong emotions that are considered negative, such as anger, jealousy, and resentment. There may also be survivor's guilt about being healthy and having more opportunities.

- Siblings may experience rejection when repeated attempts to relate to their sibling with autism fail and when their brother or sister is not interested in being with them or does not participate in everyday activities.

Recently I have begun to observe in my work with siblings that there are often marked variations in reaction within the same family. For example, one older sister I know enjoys being like a second mother to her little brother, Tim, who has autism. Meanwhile, Tim's older brother wants nothing to do with him. In fact, he has told no one that his younger brother has autism. In another family I know, one younger brother is always worried about his older brother with autism and the stress on his parents. The other younger brother primarily expresses anger and resentment about the inequality of the situation.

What Research Reveals

Like parents, siblings share in the broad spectrum of feelings evoked by having a child with autism in the family. Seligman and Darling (2007) concluded that the literature on families, while focusing primarily on parents and particularly mothers, suggests that siblings may be at risk psychologically even though many cope well. A major problem for siblings is being pressed into caregiving roles that they are not prepared for. They may experience survivor's guilt because their lives are in sharp contrast with those of their brother or sister with autism. The gender of the healthy siblings may also play a part in how much caregiving responsibility they are expected to take on, with a female sibling expected to be more involved.

When a sibling with a disability such as autism needs lifelong care or guidance, typical siblings can become anxious about the future. They wonder how much responsibility will be theirs. Some siblings develop somatic fears or phobias—for example, the tendency to translate small physical symptoms into a fear of cancer seems to run high among siblings, according to some studies. Children may also develop somatic complaints in order to gain attention from their parents. This may become a way of expressing a need for attention. Overall, Seligman and Darling (2007) cautioned that from an empirical point of view, the impact on siblings in terms of mental and behavioral health remains open to speculation. Whether siblings are helped or harmed by their experience and in what way is certainly a complex question.

Seligman and Darling (2007) also looked at the career choices of siblings of individuals with disabilities. Clearly siblings are influenced by their experiences growing up, and they often choose careers in which contributing to the welfare of others is key. Siblings of individuals with autism or other special needs are often overrepresented among therapists, doctors, nurses, and educators of children with disabilities. There is, however, only a modest evidence base for these conclusions. There is a danger that such a career choice may not be gratifying, as it may just be an extension of that individual's role in his or her family and he or she may never have considered other choices. If this is the case, the individual may select another career at a later point.

There has been very little research specific to siblings of children with ASDs. Yet there is evidence that the broad ASD phenotype is present in the relatives of many individuals who have been diagnosed with ASD. This broad phenotype involves more subtle impairments such as language delays, difficulties with sensory integration, and problems with emotion regulation and communication. Goldberg and colleagues (2005) compared 3 groups of children: 1) young children with ASD, 2) younger siblings in families with a somewhat older child with ASD, and 3) young children with typical development. They found genetic vulnerability for ASD in the siblings. Overall the social and communication behavior of the young siblings more closely resembled that of the ASD children than the typically developing children who did not have a sibling with autism. This was especially true in terms of joint attention. The researchers concluded that family interaction may explain some of the behavior of the young siblings of children with autism. More research is needed on how having a sibling with autism influences siblings in the early phases of their development.

In another study, Cassel, Messinger, Ibanez, Haltigan, Acosta, and colleague (2006) studied the early social and emotional communication of infants who were siblings of children with autism. They found that these infants were at increased risk for developing an ASD or more subtle other impairments, such as language delays, sensory integration difficulties, or emotion regulation difficulties. There were challenges noted with joint attention through gestures and gaze to communicate about objects or events or to ask for help. Intervention begun as early as possible has been shown to alter the course of their development in a positive way and is highly recommended. Other studies, such as the Early Autism Risk Longitudinal Investigation (EARLI) Study, are in the process of looking at the development of young siblings by studying families that already have a child with an ASD who are pregnant or who might become pregnant in the future. EARLI will closely follow families from the start of the pregnancy to the time the baby reaches age three. Comprehensive data will be analyzed to help better understand the complex causes of autism to hopefully move science towards prevention.

According to Hastings (2003), siblings of children with autism engaged in ABA had fewer adjustment problems when their sibling with autism was less severely affected. Several factors were suggested to mediate the impact on siblings, including the sex of the sibling, birth order, the age of the sibling, and whether the child with autism resided in the home or outside the home. Hastings found evidence that social support moderated the impact of autism on the development of typical siblings. There was less risk for behavior problems. Hastings concluded that siblings of all children with autism may have an increased risk for adjustment problems, whereas siblings of more severely affected individuals may be at extreme risk.

Orsmond and Seltzer (2009) expanded the lens to later stages of development by studying adolescent siblings. These researchers noted that some studies have reported siblings of children with ASD to be well adjusted, whereas others have indicated an increased risk of behavior problems. They noted that in general siblings without a disability reported greater conflict in their relationship with their sibling with autism in adolescence than in childhood or young adulthood. They found that sisters reported higher levels of depression and anxiety than brothers. A high level of maternal depression and symptoms of anxiety was also present.

Changes in the sibling relationship over time were examined by Seltzer, Orsmond, and Esbensen (2009). Other than personal accounts, relatively little is known about developmental differences in the sibling relationship in adolescence and adulthood. Researchers thought examining this time period was important because siblings are often responsible for their brother or sister with autism when their parents are no longer able to provide for or oversee their care. Previous research reviewed by Seltzer and colleagues had mixed findings: some siblings were satisfied with their relationships while other brothers and sisters experienced less closeness and decreased interactions and often viewed their brother or sister with autism as a burden. They have also reported feeling more lonely and isolated than the siblings of children with other disabilities such as Down syndrome. The symptoms of autism in terms of social interaction, communication, and behavior tend to become less severe but still problematic across the life span. Seltzer and colleagues' study appears to be the first of its kind concerning the sibling relationship in adulthood when one sibling has autism.

Because sibling relationships are characterized by supportiveness and concern, siblings of adolescents and adults with autism are in a natural position to become more involved when their parents die or become disabled. The behavioral challenges of autism have a unique impact on the sibling relationship through major life transitions such as getting married, having children, and providing care to aging parents.

Seltzer and colleagues found that adult siblings reported the same degree of positive affect as did adolescent siblings despite decreased contact with their adult brother or sister with ASD. This contrasted with sibling relationships in general, because closeness in the sibling bond tends to decrease in adolescence and young adulthood and increase in middle and later adulthood. There was no group difference in depressive symptoms. Adolescent siblings reported greater support from parents and friends than did adult siblings, and adolescents from larger families reported greater positive affect in their relationship. It was noted that brothers who had a sister with a developmental disability were the least engaged in the sibling relationship. This means that women with developmental disabilities, including autism, are at greater risk for social isolation if their only sibling is a brother.

The sibling relationship was also associated with age and behavior problems according to Seltzer and colleagues. Adult siblings were more engaged when the brother or sister with autism was younger. A brother or sister's behavior problems clearly impact the sibling relationship negatively. Behavior problems make siblings less willing to engage in activities with their brother or sister with autism, especially in public. Overall, typically developing siblings viewed their relationships with their brother or sister more positively when they were not worried about their sibling's future, an issue that is discussed in Chapter 13.

Seltzer and colleagues concluded that siblings may be less involved in their brother or sister's lives if they lack parental support, if their sibling has difficult behavior problems, or if their sibling is of the opposite gender (this is especially the case for brothers who have a sister with autism). This study established the fact that parents play an important role in siblings' relationships not only in adolescence but also in adulthood.

Supporting Siblings

In October 2008, The Sibling Leadership Network released a white paper on recommendations for research, advocacy, and supports for siblings of people with developmental disabilities (Heller et al., 2008). The following is a partial list of their recommendations:

Siblings need information about

- Their sibling's disability and its implications
- Treatments and services for their brothers and sisters
- Plans their parents have for their sibling's future

- The genetic implications of their sibling's disability
- How to effectively advocate for their brother or sister
- Services for adults with disabilities

Siblings need opportunities to

- Meet their peers
- Discuss common joys and concerns with other siblings
- Learn how other siblings address problematic situations frequently faced by brothers and sisters
- Discuss their current and future roles in the life of their sibling who has a disability

Siblings need parents who

- Understand siblings' lifelong and ever-changing concerns
- Learn proven strategies to minimize siblings' concerns and maximize their opportunities
- Provide their typically developing children with information and opportunities to meet their peers
- Plan for the future of their child with ID and involve their typically developing children in this planning
- Value the right to self-determination for each of their children

Siblings need service providers who

- Understand siblings' lifelong and ever-changing concerns
- Proactively provide brothers and sisters with information
- Create programs specifically for siblings
- Make systemic changes to include brothers and sisters in their working definition of "family"

Gallagher and colleagues (2006) presented what they called "Capstone Strategies for Parents and Siblings." Based on research and many years of experience, these strategies reflect what I often hear from parents and siblings. For example, it is recommended that parents

- Be open and honest in being available and answering questions
- Value each child individually and pay attention to the needs of each child
- Limit caregiving responsibilities
- Treat children as fairly as possible and explain any differences in discipline

- Schedule special time with each sibling
- Let brothers and sisters settle their own differences whenever possible
- Notice each child's struggles and achievements and praise him or her accordingly
- Listen to feedback from siblings, validate siblings' feelings and concerns, and involve siblings according to their wishes
- Require the child with autism to do as much as possible for himself or herself
- Teach the siblings to interact with their brother or sister in ways that are comfortable
- Make family life and activities as normal as possible
- Talk about the future with typically developing siblings

Strategies for siblings include

- Talking to others about their feelings and concerns
- Learning about autism on the Internet or in books
- Connecting with other siblings who have a brother or sister with autism or another developmental disability
- Attending sibling groups and special events
- Being open and honest with their parents about what it is like to have a brother or sister with autism
- Being open about their mixed feelings toward their brother or sister and learning that these feelings make them human
- Developing pride in their family and experiences and opportunities for growth
- Asking for help when they need it
- Talking to friends and acquaintances and answering their questions about autism when they feel comfortable doing so
- Speaking up when others tease or bully someone with autism or another disability

Siblings need ongoing support as well, and when it comes to workshops for siblings of children with autism and other developmental issues, Sibshops is the best fit. This popular model has been used in more than 200 communities in eight countries. It is an essential guide to creating and running effective sibling support programs. This model provides brothers and sisters of children with disabilities with peer support and education within a recreational context. The workshops take a wellness approach that is fun and engaging. In this supportive context, siblings can get to know one another; receive information; ask questions; and share their experiences, whether they are good, bad, or indifferent.

For parents, the fantasy of a close, cozy set of siblings is part of the image of a perfect family. Squabbles among brothers and sisters sometimes crush that dream. There can be a dilemma over whether to let children work out their differences and when to intervene. Too much intervention keeps children from learning for themselves how to resolve conflict. The key is to be able to express negative feelings without doing damage. The goal is for children to work out their own solutions whenever possible. In *Siblings Without Rivalry: How to Help Your Children Live Together,* which is illustrated with cartoons, Adele Faber and Elaine Mazlish include a chapter dedicated to understanding this. It takes patience and wisdom to let go in order to facilitate this process. Sometimes it just means waiting a moment or two. As they have grown up, I have seen my three daughters find meaning for themselves in their relationship with Tariq. They are all better women for it as they experience love and hate, rivalry and reconciliation, grief and joy, embarrassment and pride. Parents and siblings of children with autism really are all in this together, and they all have to keep working at it.

11

Family and Friends

Finding and Building Circles of Support

WHEN SORROW SENDS PEOPLE INWARD TO BE ALONE AND LICK THEIR WOUNDS, THEY CAN HEAL THOSE HURTS BY OPENING UP AND CONFIDING IN OTHERS. True friendship, as this proverb states, divides the grief and makes it more bearable. Likewise, friendship can multiply joy. It is a special friend to whom people can turn in their darkest moments for solace. Some people already have this kind of support, whereas others have to find it—from family, or friends, or people they are yet to meet.

> *A friend is one to whom one may pour out all the contents of one's heart, chaff and grain together, knowing that the gentlest of hands will take and sift it, keep what is worth keeping and with the breath of kindness blow the rest away.*
>
> DINAH MARIA MULOCK CRAIK,
> *A LIFE FOR A LIFE*

When someone close dies, family, friends, and even acquaintances rally around to offer comfort. But after a short time, perhaps because they do not know what to say or how to respond to the bereaved person, people seem to avoid broaching the subject. This is also true when something is wrong with a child's development or after a child has been diagnosed with autism or another disability. The topic may be emotionally threatening to talk about.

One of the things that parents are the least prepared for is the social isolation and alienation that comes with the diagnosis. Many report, and I myself have experienced, that it is as if there were a giant elephant in the living room. It fills the room, and it is hard to get around. It is difficult to communicate honestly when you are bereaved. People say, "How are you?" and you respond, "I'm fine." You talk about work, the weather, the news, the economy, and everything else but the obvious—the elephant in the room that is unavoidably on your mind. Given the genetic component of autism, there may be a fear that others in the family will be affected and diagnosed in the future.

Maybe the trivial chatter is just a way of saying that no one wants to be alone with the elephant and an attempt, however awkward, to acknowledge connection and express concern about a shared sorrow. As John Donne wrote

No man is an island entire of itself; every man
is a piece of the continent, a part of the main . . .
. . . any man's death
diminishes me, because I am involved in mankind; and
therefore never send to know for whom the bell tolls;
It tolls for thee.
COFFIN, 1994

When I look back over my own experiences searching for help and support in the early days of worrying about Tariq, I see that much of what I went through was fairly typical. At first I believed that if he could just start talking again, then everything would work out from there. When something is wrong with your child, you often feel like a little child yourself and you want your mom and dad to help you, to rescue you, to protect you from the hurt you are feeling.

My mother and father would counsel me to be patient, that things would work out. My mother would tell me that she was praying. They would ask me how Tariq was doing, as if he had the flu and was expected to get better each day. I would describe any little changes I had noticed. Our conversations lessened the tension I felt, helped me to get through another day, and kept me working with Tariq to help him develop. My parents could not, however, make him normal, and that was hard for them as well as me.

My grandparents were still alive when Tariq was younger, and they would reassure me too. I have a cousin my own age who was diagnosed with mild cognitive disability and whose speech came late, and my grandparents had helped my aunt and uncle a lot when Greg was a little boy. They reassured me based on how my cousin had developed. Even though he still stutters, he learned to read and write a little bit. He has a driver's license, and he held a civil service job as a maintenance worker. All in all, he has done very well for himself. My grandparents seemed confident that Tariq would be like Greg. Because of their direct experience and their love for me, I trusted their wisdom and hoped desperately that they were right.

My mother with Tariq

My grandmom with Tariq

My cousin Greg was the first person I knew with a developmental disability. We are only a few months apart in age and started first grade the same September. I can still remember the uneasy silence when I asked my parents and his why he was not promoted and I was. They had no clue as to how to explain his difference to me. There was no one to help them with that. He was just my cousin, and he still is more than 5 decades later. When I go to south Florida to speak to parents and professionals, I visit Greg. We hang out and take pictures together of the flora and fauna in the area—something we like doing together. If Greg were growing up today, there is little doubt he would have a diagnosis of ASD.

Greg's nephew, Donato Jr. (also my cousin), wrote a blog about Greg that can inform and inspire others about the possibilities in adulthood for people with autism and other developmental disabilities. Don, the founder and chief executive officer of TradeKing, an online broker, wrote

My dad's younger brother Greg brings fun just about anywhere he goes. Uncle Greg has been developmentally challenged since he was a kid. My grandparents, and then my father helped Greg look after himself for years. One has to wonder what Greg could have accomplished if he were born today. This is a fellow who taught himself to read after he got his first computer, at age 52!

After taking early retirement from his lifelong job working for Camden County,

Cousin Greg raves about how technology has improved his quality of life.

New Jersey, in August of 2005 Greg moved down to join me in south Florida while we were still building TradeKing. Greg lives in his own condo in Delray Beach, near my house and office. Greg enjoys many of his own hobbies, such as motorcycles, swimming at his beach, and photography. He helps with jobs big and small around our office. Our crew really accepts him as a team member and relies on his help to get all sorts of support tasks taken care of. With my vision problems of late, most days Uncle Greg is my ride to work and back, too.

Greg's lack of sophistication can actually prove to be an advantage. For example, it's easy for me to tell who's a good apple and who's not simply by how people behave upon meeting him. His honesty often helps him cut to the chase and see the really important things in life. (Montanaro, 2007)

Nonetheless, at the time of Tariq's birth *autism* was not part of our family vocabulary. I remember how my grandfather would put Tariq on his lap and recite Italian nursery rhymes, the same ones he had recited to me when I was a small boy. He would take Tariq's hands within his strong palms, as he had taken mine, and rub them on his coarse beard until it tickled. Tariq would smile and then squirm to get away because he did not like to be held for long. My grandmother, too, would try to hold him, and she would sing the lullabies that she had sung to me and my siblings and cousins when we were little.

So many people never tried to hold my son, perhaps shying away from what they could not understand and what was uncomfortable. They would just make small talk, and I would withdraw in the embarrassment of the moment, always remaining outwardly calm. That is why I get such a warm feeling recalling those moments when my grandparents tried to hold Tariq, despite his squirming and wriggling away. Of course I wished that he would sit still and cuddle with them, but I felt myself held by them because they never stopped trying with him.

No parent wants their child to be noticed as different from the norm. They want a healthy, happy child who fits in and makes them proud. But what do you do when your child is different? Speaking for myself, I had a hard time for years. I walked around looking out of the corner of my eye, ready to pounce on people for their reactions. Actually it was more my perceptions of their reactions. Not to mention the perpetual knot in the pit of my stomach. Like many parents of children with autism, I felt like I was battling the whole world. Life is definitely easier when you understand your own reactions as well as those of others while realizing that you are not alone.

It is human nature to notice differences. All too often people are limited by their assumptions about how people look, move, communicate, behave, and learn. When people are different, others tend to stare and compare, so realizing that the human brain is wired to notice differences that seem unfamiliar or unsettling is very useful. It is important to realize that most of us did this too before we had children with autism. For example, we stared at children having meltdowns in the checkout lines.

When Tariq starts self-stimulating (i.e., engaging in the repetitive behavior patterns that are a prominent characteristic of children and adults with ASD) by playing with his tongue or flapping, especially now that he is full grown, I automatically want him to stop and act "normal." Internally my reaction can be rather desperate, for I do not want him *and* me to be noticed as different. I also still find myself trying to avoid taking photographs when he is not behaving "normally." There is a certain image I prefer of him in my head, as much as I hate to admit that. But his behaviors are, after all, a part of him.

Even though I consider myself a veteran in terms of dealing with autism, I struggled to understand and own up to these reactions. It took some time, but eventually I learned to love my son Tariq not in spite of his differences but rather because of them. The knot in my gut is long gone. Now for the most part I can look comfortably around me. I can notice what must have been there before—the friendly faces and kind eyes of compassionate folks.

I know I am not alone. Many parents of children with special needs have told me how isolated and abandoned they felt in their own hour of greatest need. There is a longing for someone to reach out and take a special interest in your child and therefore in you. When you finally do find that real support—a gentle hand to touch you and your child and a kind heart to ask how things are—that is when you know for sure that you are not alone.

Intergenerational Grief

A young father came to me for help with his grief and told the familiar story of looking to his parents for help. His father had died when he was 7. When his son was diagnosed, he went to the cemetery, stood by the grave, and told his dad what was going on with his grandson. He cried and asked for help and for strength to carry on. He told me that he had found an emotional relief and that he has thought about his father and missed him more ever since that day in the cemetery. This made me think of how my own father, an orphan, must have missed his parents as he went through the normal trials and tribulations of child rearing. Who else would you naturally turn to for guidance—whether your child was just like other kids or not?

As time passed, and Tariq still did not speak, my parents and grandparents, my siblings, and my other relatives all kept saying basically the same thing—that Tariq would outgrow this. Instead of feeling comforted, I felt frustrated and terrified to think about how I would handle it if he never spoke again. Tariq was different from what they expected, so when he was eventually diagnosed with autism, they did not know what to say. This was understandable enough but horribly isolating for me.

I believed that I was the only person who had ever felt this way. No one could help me, I thought, because no one else had ever experienced what I was going through. I believed that it was all my responsibility and that I should be able to handle it. I did not want to burden others, but sometimes I felt like I was in a land beyond tears and beyond comfort. Everything—toys, playgrounds, clothes, and healthy children—reminded me of the little boy I had dreamed of and the sorrow that Tariq's silence presented to me. I thought I would never experience happiness or smile ever again.

Many parents start to think that others do not want to hear their problems because they have enough of their own. It is easy to get tangled up in a web of distorted beliefs as you grieve the loss of your typically developing child. You might even believe that it is too hard to find support and that it takes too much energy to explain your situation, so therefore it will be easier to just hold it in and do everything yourself. Fortunately, in most cases, the passage of time brings a gift of perspective. It becomes clear that grandparents can have as hard a time—or even harder of a time—accepting a disability as parents do, and their acceptance can take longer. They face the double grief of their grandchild's disability and their own child's pain.

This second level of grief often renders grandparents powerless to offer the support that their adult child longs for. They may despair that they could not protect or rescue their child from this fate; they may worry that they have passed on a defective gene and that it could appear again in another grandchild. They may also feel overwhelmed and guilty that they cannot help more.

Some parents report that their relatives keep bringing up the same thing. For example, Jennifer's parents could not grasp why their grandson had so many peculiar repetitive behaviors and why his speech was so limited. They were unsophisticated folks who were unaware that neurological issues such as autism could cause such problems. They kept asking Jennifer whether she had had Tommy tested for lead poisoning. No matter how much Jennifer, who was a registered nurse, disclaimed the possibility of lead poisoning, her parents would not give up. She was close to her parents, who watched Tommy when she was at work, so she really wanted them to understand and agree with her. This situation was causing her a lot of pain.

I suggested that more direct information about and involvement in Tommy's professional care might be helpful for his grandparents, and I asked Jennifer to bring them to her next therapy session. After introducing myself and explaining my role with the family, I asked Jennifer's parents whether they had any questions about Tommy. Of course they brought up lead poisoning right away, and Jennifer sighed. Jennifer's mom commented that it was getting hard for the three of them to talk about this issue. It was clear, nonetheless, that these grandparents wanted to help and that their help was needed and wanted.

In an authoritative manner, I explained that the cause of Tommy's limitations was unknown. From reviewing his records, I knew that he had received excellent care and that testing had revealed no indications of lead poisoning. I patiently explained that Jennifer was frustrated that the grandparents repeatedly brought this up and recommended that they avoid doing this. Knowing that they were trying in their own way to understand, I suggested that they visit their grandson's classroom and meet and talk with his teachers. I also recommended that they take a look at the books and articles that their daughter had collected related to Tommy's speech and language development.

Hearing this from a doctor made a difference. I was not a part of their family system and was considered an objective source of information. They could tell that I cared about their grandson. Jennifer told me at her next session that her parents had stopped talking about lead poisoning. She felt relieved and was much more comfortable when she was around them. They were reading about autism and getting a better understanding of Tommy's condition.

Looking forward to a warm, indulging role with their grandchildren, grandparents may naturally expect to have pleasure without the responsibilities of being an authority figure that they had with their own children. Being involved with the new generation can be a source of special pride and satisfaction, but when grandparents are confronted with autism, their role is not what they expected. And if they are in some form of denial, they can add to the parents' burden.

Grandparents of children with autism lose their dreamed-for grandchild who was to be their legacy to the future, just as the parents have lost their dream child. Getting to know their actual grandchild can be more difficult because they are often removed from the child's everyday life and because they may face the additional challenge of supporting their adult child in a time of tremendous need. In these ways, grandparents are affected by what happens in the nuclear family, and they also affect those family members. Because they see and hold the child less often than parents do, it takes proportionately longer for them to bond with that child. They actually need help from their adult child to understand their grandchild's condition, but it takes time for parents to be ready to lead the way.

Once grandparents understand the problem, they can be a great asset. With experience and wisdom gained from raising their own children, they may have much to offer in sharing coping strategies and in discerning which issues are linked to the disability and which ones are the normal challenges of child rearing. They may also have time to help with many of the practical demands of caring for a grandchild with special needs.

Grandparents' Stories

Recently I got this e-mail from a grandmother. The subject line was "Make a Wish, Blow Out the Candles":

> Three birthday candles are lit, a hush of quiet descends. The birthday boy stares; his father makes his wish, and blows out the candles for his son. I'm making a secret wish, too. One day, dear grandson, may you be able to blow out your own candles, so your father, my son, may find his smile!

> Fast forward three years, on my son's birthday, that wish came true. Many candles are lit, he's making his secret wish, and my grandson blows out all the candles for his father. My son, Matthew, and I look at each other and smile.

This grandmother described what she called the rollercoaster ride of autism behavior, one minute gloriously enjoying the spontaneous highs and then, without warning, plunging downward—meltdowns, aggressive behavior, inappropriate language, broken dreams.

She described another situation on the same day in which her grandson Josh and his younger sister started fighting over her bicycle, which had training wheels.

> His bike without training wheels had been banished to the shed. Although he's exceptionally strong and athletic, all attempts at riding his own bike were unsuccessful and were met with physically harmful episodes. As I witnessed the siblings fight, Josh threw down his sister's bike, started toward her to grab her, but for the

very first time, redirected the focus of his anger. Running wildly to the shed, he dragged out his old bike and screamed, "Help me, I promise I won't cry."

Josh got on; his father quietly gave him a few brief instructions, holding onto the seat. Josh pushed off from the cement patio, let go, and pedaled all the way down the back yard, applying the brakes to stop. He had mastered balance. He didn't fall! They high-fived and there it was. They looked at each other and smiled! No screaming and cheering, just quiet smiles.

A grandson on his first bike ride

Another grandparent I know is Dan Gottlieb, one of my best friends. Sam and his grandpop Dan are quite a pair, each remarkable—Sam with autism and Dan with quadriplegia. In *The Wisdom of Sam: Observations on Life from an Uncommon Child,* Dan writes with simplicity, gentleness, and keen insight about their relationship and the human condition.

So much is "normal" about them. Until you see or imagine Dan in his motorized wheelchair or read about how Sam does not know how to join in a conversation with other kids his age, or is asked to leave his mother, or is confronted by a change in the day's routine. Such is life with autism, but as this grandfather points out, the limitations do not matter, for "We are who we are." Because of his autism, Sam often notices things about the world around him more clearly than his parents or his grandfather do. It could be a texture or a color or the words used in a particular situation—something others have missed in hurrying around. As readers read about Sam's observations, they become enlightened to some advantages of autism. Dan

Dan Gottlieb and his grandson Sam

reminds readers through Sam's observations of the simple truths and passions they once knew as children. Sam's perspective, through his different kind of mind, makes him a remarkable teacher.

I met Dan Gottlieb in 1997 when he interviewed me about my first book on his public radio show "Voices in the Family." He was genuinely interested in asking me what it was like to have a child with autism who had lost his speech. He looked in my eyes, and I knew then that he was not afraid to hear the real answer. Words stuck in my throat, my eyes filled up. He went to a station break, asked if I was okay, and told me he wanted listeners to hear my story. We have been dear friends and colleagues ever since.

From more than 25 years of listening to other families of children with autism, I know that many have experiences of profound insight and learning from their children. These are precious moments that reward families' love and devotion. *The Wisdom of Sam* and Dan's earlier book, *Letters to Sam,* elevate these moments with dignity, grace, and profound meaning.

The Mind–Body Connection

Although many people conclude that it is easier to hold in their feelings and do everything themselves, this is far from the truth. In ancient Greece, Hippocrates, the father of medicine, stressed that emotional factors could be a contributing cause to disease as well as a factor in recovery. In more recent times, psychologist Pennebaker (1990) and his students have found a mountain of evidence that disclosing pain when one is suffering through a major upheaval can greatly improve one's physical and mental health. Conversely, holding it in can lead to recurrent health problems, such as colds, flu, high blood pressure, or ulcers.

Having a child with autism certainly qualifies as a major upheaval. Inhibiting upsetting thoughts and feelings is physical work, the burden of which can lead to long-term health problems. People who can open up in a group generally report that they enjoy it and learn from it. In addition, their health notably improves—which incidentally provides the scientific basis for the rapid increase in self-help groups for all sorts of problems. According to Pennebaker (1990), writing about one's inner turmoil can also be therapeutic. Writing helps people to organize and understand their thoughts and feelings. Writing in a journal with some regularity can thus be extremely helpful for people's physical and emotional well-being. By translating their feelings about events into words, people can gain perspective and understanding about themselves and about what has happened.

When people confront upsetting circumstances by talking or writing about them, they are often relieved to find out they are not alone; this in turn helps them gain insight into how they feel. According to a January 2009 press release from the U.S. Census Bureau, 54.4 million Americans, or 19% of the population, reported some level of disability in a 2005 survey which includes all ages. About two thirds of these individuals have a severe disability. These millions of Americans with a disability and their families and friends need a place to connect and talk freely. Then, with this kind of support, we can see ourselves as just ordinary people who happen to be living with some difficulties, and this may be a great comfort.

The journey to acceptance includes finding people, whether related by blood or not, who really want to listen. When someone listens to your story, it is the first step in lessening your alienation. Through telling their stories, people make meaning out of what may seem chaotic. The power in storytelling is that life is an ongoing narrative and can be best understood in this way. Telling and listening to stories is crucial to human caring and interconnection.

Telling and listening is not always easy. Some people want to avoid adversity, and they avoid others who are going through it. They may not want to be reminded of how fragile life and health can be, or they may not have enough physical or emotional resources to share. There is a true burden and even a possible health risk in listening to other people's pain, as Pennebaker (1990) documented, for the listener may not know how to handle internally what he or she is hearing. One place to find people who can listen is in support groups.

These groups are often organized in local school districts or larger geographic areas and include interested parents of children with various disabilities. Mandell and Salzer (2007) found that parents of children with self-injurious behavior, sleep problems, and severe language problems were more likely than children with less severe behavioral challenges to belong to support groups. Because the system of care is so fragmented, these groups help parents to obtain both vital information as well as emotional support. Mandell and Salzer's Pennsylvania study found that two thirds of families of children with autism have participated in autism-specific support groups. These researchers found that participants were more likely to be middle income and well educated and less likely to be African American, possibly because of cultural factors.

Finding Support in Groups

A special kind of camaraderie exists among parents of children with autism and other special needs. Although they are not related by blood, they are deeply related by their circumstances and can offer one another much comfort and understanding. I facilitated several meetings of one group near the New Jersey shore, in which children were graduating from a half-day preschool program and moving into full-day kindergarten. The subject of one particular meeting was the parents' concerns about their children moving on.

Although the meeting was held in the morning, a fair number of fathers came and participated actively. The group had agreed to videotape the session for some people who could not attend. The description that follows is based on the complete video record of what happened and illustrates the power of parent groups to provide support. I asked people to speak out about their worries. Which worries did they think would be the same for any young child, with or without a disability? Which worries had to do with their child having special needs? I knew that thinking about these questions and sorting them out has a calming effect. Isolation can be very painful, and connecting with others in a similar situation provides a soothing antidote.

A young mother spoke first. "My child started a full-time program this past fall. I was so worried. I didn't think anyone else could care for her properly. I remember standing with my husband and looking in the one-way window of her classroom and crying. She's my first child, so I didn't know what to expect. What really helped was that she came home happy every day."

The next mother recounted, "This little one in special education was the hardest for me to let go of, I think because he is my youngest. I'm not sure what life holds for me now without a child home. I'm not sure I can be as free as I could if he was normal."

A mother who worked outside the home spoke next, adding a somewhat different perspective: "What's really hard for me is how my children have their alert, fun time with another person. My time is caregiving, like fixing breakfast and dinner, giving baths, and getting them dressed. There's not much play. I mostly get to discipline them. That hurts."

A man spoke next. "We're glad to be here. When our baby turned one, he showed us how really far behind our three-year-old was. I'm really broken up inside . . ." As his words trailed off, his wife continued, taking up where he had left off: "He was really slow speaking, and we were devastated, but it's picking up now that he's in a special class."

Somehow this man's expression of emotion seemed like the go-ahead signal for the group to start talking about the harder, darker side of their experiences. The open and direct expression of male emotion often has that effect in a group. Perhaps the women hold back, fearing that the men may shut down and withdraw, leaving them alone.

Next the mother of a child born prematurely told her story. "My child was a preemie—only three pounds. I knew right away there were problems. It was difficult for her to see. She got all the early intervention therapies. Still she didn't walk until two months after her second birthday. It's been so hard; I never thought I would make it this far. Now she's five, and she's okay cognitively. It's a great relief; sometimes I cry over it. I'm glad she survived those first months. I'm ready for her to go to school full time. I need a break . . ."

Her voice trailed off; there were tears in her eyes. At this point, I asked to hear from some more of the men, who had been quiet up until now. A man who was a carpenter, who had been home for the winter because work was slow, took the ball: "I didn't know how hard it was day in and day out until now. My son is a real handful. Every time it seems that we have things figured out, he goes to the next stage. He doesn't wait for us to catch our breath or anything. It hasn't been easy being out of work, but I am glad that I've gotten to learn all about him at this early age. I never really imagined that. I had thought I would get more involved as he got older, and we would play ball, and go fishing, and work on little projects around the house. You know, the typical father-and-son stuff. I think this has made me a better father and a better husband. I understand firsthand what my wife goes through. Right now she's at work, and I'm bringing home the information from school. She's bringing home the bread. What a switch!"

A woman spoke up quickly. "I wish I was in her shoes. Sometimes as soon as my husband gets home, I say 'I'm outta here,' and I'm off to the mall. He's not thrilled, but I just need a break." This kind of tag-team parenting is common as a coping strategy in many families.

A single mom with twins with hyperactivity and language delays spoke next. I wondered whether her twins were later diagnosed on the spectrum. She sounded overwhelmed and pained: "When we are all home together, I can never sit down. I can't get baby sitters. I'm almost forty; my mother is in her seventies, so she can't keep up with them even though she wants to help out. Other people just see my little boys as wild. It's so sad. That's where my frustrations are . . . it's a luxury just to sit and read the paper for ten minutes when you're a single parent. I'm worn out all the time, so I don't feel guilty sending them to school for a longer day."

The oldest woman in the room spoke up: "I thought I was done raising children, but now I'm starting all over again. My son's wife had multiple sclerosis, and when she passed away, he and my grandson came to live with us. Fortunately my husband is retired, and he's home now, so he can help out. He keeps asking me, 'Was it that hard to raise our children?' And for the most part, as I tell him each time he asks, it was. Their speech was normal, but everything else was the same."

The wisdom in this woman's experience lent a helpful perspective. Many different living situations were represented in the group, which was a microcosm of the outside world. I asked what direction the group wanted the rest of the meeting to take. The parents wanted to compile a contact list and then be able to help one another with playdates, babysitting, and just getting together informally for coffee and doughnuts. Some of the men mentioned getting together to hit golf balls or shoot a few baskets, reflecting the typically male mode of being together in an activity as opposed to just getting together to talk, a more female style.

Getting some form of respite from the daily demands can be vital. Hospitalization can occur because of the stress on the family caused by challenging behaviors associated with ASD. (In fact, 11% of children with ASD from ages 5 to 21 years have a history of psychiatric hospitalization [Mandell, 2008].) Mandell and colleagues (2012) found that increased use of respite and therapeutic services was associated with a reduced risk of psychiatric hospitalization for children, teenagers, and young adults with ASD who were enrolled in Medicaid.

These researchers at the University of Pennsylvania found an 8% drop in the odds of hospitalization for every $1,000 states had spent on respite services in the previous 60 days (Mandell et al., 2012). Unfortunately, respite care is not readily or universally available. What is interesting is that respite care is more effective than outpatient therapy, but this may be because of the quality of those services. Although families need and deserve this kind of support, parents do not have to wait helplessly for services. Some families give each other breaks, some support groups organize informal respite support, and faith congregations can help as well.

Many parents do not find their way to support groups at first. But when relatives and friends do not know what to say, other parents of children provide support that is unavailable elsewhere. It is calming to share your fears and insecurities without a lot of explaining and no worries about appearing weak or seeming to ask for pity. There is also the practical benefit of learning from one another's experience. When parents of older children share their successes, you can see that having a child with autism is not the end of your life. Parents of children even a year or two older can give a preview of what lies ahead. You can get positive but realistic ideas about what the future holds. It can also be easier to talk to a fellow parent than to a professional.

Another wonderful aspect of participating in a parent support group is being able to give as well as receive help. There are moments when you need help and moments when you may be the person with the answer or a helpful comment. A parent who can give as well as receive support is stronger and more self-confident. People used to say that the blind couldn't lead the blind, but the self-help movement has taught otherwise. Sometimes the best way to help yourself is to help someone else.

Journaling Your Way Through Stress: Finding Answers Within Yourself

"Support groups don't seem to work for me. I do get something out of them when I'm there, but day in and day out, sometimes it feels like more than I can bear. Is there anything else I can try?" This is a question I commonly hear from parents. Often parents are told to take one day at a time, and this is a helpful concept when they are trying not to be overwhelmed about the future. But what can you do when one day is just too long and too hard? Try reaching for a pen and paper. Keeping a diary, or journaling, can be an extremely effective tool for discovering your innermost thoughts and releasing tensions. Setting aside 10–15 minutes to put your thoughts into words may just help you reduce stress or get its physical symptoms under control.

Do not let journaling become a stressor in itself. Writing as a method of emotional release should be done when you feel the urge. You can do it daily, weekly, monthly, or just when you feel like it. One technique is to try writing in response to a question. Here are a few to get you started:

1.   What's been really hard about being a mother or a father today?

2.   What have I learned from this?

3.   What moment gave me pleasure or satisfaction?

4. What contributions have I made to my child and my family today?

5. How do I feel about my life in general?

Another way to approach journaling is to complete a sentence stem. Here are a few that I use:

1. The best thing about my child is . . .

2. The most challenging thing about my child is . . .

3. A feeling or thought that I am embarrassed about is . . .

4. Something that made me proud lately was when . . .

5. The most difficult thing about my spouse is . . .

6. The best thing about my spouse is . . .

7. The nicest thing someone said to me lately was . . .

8. I hope that . . .

9. I am sad about my dream that . . .

10. I dream a new dream that . . .

11. My child has taught me that . . .

12. I am becoming a better person because . . .

Try to just let it flow. What comes out may surprise you. Often in conversation the flow of the interaction will unleash thoughts you never knew you had. Writing expressively can do the same thing. Thoughts and feelings will emerge. The important thing is to look for meaning and growth. Merely writing about the same painful things over and over will not bring healing. Focus on thought as well as emotion in order to tap into your inner process. Writing about your experiences and searching for new understandings will keep you on a path of healing.

Support in Cyberspace

The Internet has exponentially increased the possibilities for connecting with other parents of children with autism. Americans unfortunately still live in a society where equal access to resources is very much an issue. Yet the Internet can be an equalizer to some extent. As computer prices have come down and more public libraries and schools provide access to the Internet, more and more people can and do take advantage of online support.

A woman I know through the local chapter of the Autism Society of America asked her Internet friends to comment on how the Internet has been helpful as a source of support. Emily wrote that the autism listservs or discussion groups have been great for her because they are available 24/7. She does not have to find a baby sitter to attend a support group because her meeting is at home. She can use precious hours when a sitter is available to go out with her husband. Another plus is that much recent information is not available in her local library but is accessible online.

Emily also felt a large part of her frustration and anger diminishing as she realized how many other people were in the same boat. As she put it, "I stopped feeling as weird, or as if I was to blame, and became empowered to try things that worked for other kids. Even if the tips don't work (they don't always work, darn it), the helpless feelings I used to be plagued by have largely gone away." She is now more self-confident because she knows more about her son's autism. She reported that she is far less depressed and has even stopped taking Prozac, replacing it with a "holistic antidepressant"—getting and giving help on the Internet.

The Internet has helped Janette, from Perth, Australia, learn about alternative therapies for children with autism that professionals in her area were reluctant to suggest or even tell her about, such as auditory training or diet. Janette also commented that the Internet "is also a place to make friends through the shared common thread of autism . . . What else are friendships made from if not common beliefs, common ideas, shared experiences."

In this vein, Tammy noted that when her child shows some improvement, she can share it with all of her friends on the Internet. These friends get really excited at the news, unlike others who may not understand seeing even the smallest steps forward by their child as a miracle.

Rosita wrote about how much brighter her son's future looks thanks to the Internet. Through the caring friends she has met she has learned everything from how to stand up to her school system to how to enjoy her child and get him to hug her. With her confidence, she has become the best advocate for her son and speaks effectively for him because he cannot do so himself.

Single moms of children with ASD have a Facebook page devoted to raising a child with autism alone. In 2012, this dynamic page has over 20,000 members. Single moms find this to be a resource they frequently consult.

Getting Help from Others

You can get the most support when you are strong enough to ask for it and when you can make the first move. Although most parents feel abandoned and isolated from others, more often than not kind people are waiting nearby for a clue as to how to help. In *The Lost Art of Listening*, Michael Nichols explores how to listen and be listened to. The heart of the problem, according to Nichols (1995), is reactive emotions that trigger hurt, anger, or fear in the listener, which in turn triggers defensiveness and blocks understanding and concern. Furthermore, when you talk to people you are close to about your upsets, they may naturally want you to feel better when you just want them to listen. An empathic, accepting response would be to say, "Tell me more about how you feel" or "What's that like for you?"

Once you understand your own grief and your child's condition, then you can explain it to others. This frequently ends the awkwardness described earlier, particularly when you are at a loss for words about your child's problem. You can often get what you want by asking for it. You can tell people, for example, that you just need to talk and need them to just listen. Likewise, you could explain that you have a problem that you need to discuss but that you are not expecting them to come up with a solution. This approach releases the listener from the responsibility of solving the problem or making the pain go away.

My friend Charley with his son Leo and Tariq

Support groups as well as professional guidance can help you learn how to reach out to others. A therapist or fellow parent is not responsible for your problems and therefore is unlikely to get defensive when told them. After you learn to listen and be listened to, you can practice these skills almost anywhere with great results. For example, you may have friends with typically developing children the same age as your child. It may be difficult to ask them how their little boy or girl is doing because it brings up your pain. Friends in turn may back off a little, worrying that hearing about their child's accomplishments may make you feel worse. Bridging these gaps whenever possible is a hurdle to get over in regaining normalcy.

After Tariq was diagnosed and when he was attending the Center for Autism, I came across old pictures of Tariq and Leo, my friend Charley's oldest son. We had drifted apart and been out of contact for about 5 years. I realized that not being able to get the word autism out of mouth was what had been holding me back from calling my friend, so I picked up the telephone, somewhat unsure of what response I would get. My ambivalence subsided when I heard Charley's voice. It was as if he had been there all along, just waiting. Resuming our friendship, we caught up on each other's lives: Tariq's diagnosis, Leo's interests, my divorce, his two other sons born in the interim, our careers, and the baby that he and Michelle had lost. Grief had divided us, and now sharing it had reunited us. When the first edition of *Special Children, Challenged Parents: The Struggles and Rewards of Raising a Child with a Disability* was released, Leo and his band played at the book release party.

Leo Dugan plays at the book launch.

My friend Dave, however, whom I had met in graduate school, did not have children, and perhaps that made it easier for me to maintain our friendship after Tariq was born. He has a wonderful ability to listen and reflect without backing off. According to a frequently repeated Zen proverb, *If you see someone crying, don't just do something, stand there.* Just being with a person in distress for a few minutes is an expression of compassion and can be very comforting. Dave's friendship did this for me.

My friend Dave was always just there when I called. When Tariq was 4, Dave helped me make a video of me working with Tariq to use as a baseline to measure progress. When he called, he was never intrusive. When his mother died unexpectedly, he sent word to me through a mutual friend. I was glad that he had remembered me in his hour of grief. I had learned by then that there was nothing better than just being there for a friend. Sharing our losses cemented the bond of our friendship. Now Dave has a grandson with autism.

The passing of time and contact with Tariq helped my family to understand what autism means for him and my immediate family. My brothers and sisters offered whatever help they could. What a reversal of roles—as the oldest, I was used to looking out for them. When Tariq entered the residential program at Devereux, my grandfather asked whether we could visit so that he could see what it was like. This was how I discovered how seeing a child's school can help relatives to understand. Pop was old and frail. We sat on a bench in the fenced-in yard behind Tariq's unit. My grandfather watched the other children intensely.

Pop turned, looked intently, and stated his conclusion: "Robert, you have had a hard life." I nodded, feeling a lump in my throat and a twitch in my eyes. From that day forward, my grandfather never talked about Tariq outgrowing his condition. He understood something that words could never have accomplished. I realized that I should take my parents to see Tariq there. When the next Family Day was held, they came to the picnic with the other families. That encounter helped them to understand in a way that they had not previously. Being able to bring my family and benefitting from the experience showed that I was getting stronger.

Autism and Faith Communities

Temples, churches, synagogues, and mosques serve as extended families for many people, and families derive considerable support from their faith communities. When this is not the case, feeling unwanted and alienated, people challenge their long-held beliefs. The diagnosis of a disability such as autism can cause a spiritual crisis for the family. There are varying interpretations of the meaning of a child with a disability.

As I mentioned earlier, it is a common belief that God is just. Some people come to the conclusion that autism may be punishment for wrongdoing or that it can be healed through prayer. I have even met people who believe that if they had only prayed enough and in the right way their child would be healed. The thought underlying these beliefs is "You did something wrong, and now you are being punished for it." I have met Jews, Christians, and Muslims who have thought this way. However, some people believe that they have been blessed and chosen to have a child with special needs or that God would not give them something they could not handle.

Regardless of how a family may interpret autism, a supportive and inclusive faith community can be a tremendous asset. Reverend Bill Gaventa at the Elizabeth M. Boggs Center on Developmental Disabilities in New Jersey has been a pioneer in this important work with congregations, families, service providers, and communities. His approach draws on the potential for supportive relationships and advocacy that already exists for many families. Bill tells a story of belonging to a community that is there for you: A family of a child with Down syndrome took their minister with them to an IEP meeting. The family reported getting everything they wanted because the school district thought he was their lawyer!

In many congregations children are not particularly welcome during worship, as people expect and may in fact need quiet to engage in prayer and meditation and to hear the sermon or teaching. Children with autism may be seen as especially disruptive if they cannot sit still quietly. If everyone is truly welcome, then accommodations are necessary. Both adult worshippers and child members have important spiritual needs that must be met. There are many possibilities for doing this. Some congregations have specific times for inclusive worship. Others have a special room into which the prayers and sermon are piped electronically. It is up to each faith community to discuss what would work best in their situation.

A growing number of resources are available to help with issues of congregational inclusion, some of which are specific to autism. *Autism and Faith: A Journey into Community* is a monograph edited by Alice Walsh, Mary Beth Walsh, and Bill Gaventa. It is available for free through the Boggs Center. In *Including People with Disabilities in Faith Communities,* Erik Carter (2007) articulates how this is necessary not just at services but on the other 6 days of the week as well. This approach honors the essential equality of all humankind and our quest to find meaning and understanding and connection between ourselves and the universe.

Children and adults such as Tariq and others with various special needs are a spiritual catalyst with much to contribute to community. They challenge and sometimes force people to look at themselves. They help people accept their own imperfections and the imperfections of others. In this sense Tariq is not damaged in the least. He is perfect as he is. Along with other children and adults with autism and other disabilities, he bears witness to the diversity of the human condition and the resilience of the collective spirit.

Connecting with Laughter

In their camaraderie, parents of children with special needs can share a special kind of laughter. It is an antidote to the pain caused by everyday events. Those who can relate to suffering can understand this laughter. Over the years many parents have told me that developing a sense of humor about their situation has been key to finding the strength to get through the hard times.

Wayne Gilpin, the father of a child with autism and the former president of the Autism Society of America, collected a volume of stories titled *Laughing and Loving with Autism*. The stories are about his son Alex as well as about many other children and adults. These accounts are based on the literal interpretations that children with autism make. Such children see things exactly as they are presented and thus highlight the humor in how seriously "normal" people often view the same words or deeds. The incidents described are simultaneously funny and touching.

The logic of a child with a developmental disability such as autism may be hard to refute. One example in Gilpin's book involves his son coming to dinner with no socks on. When asked to put on some socks before dinner, Alex responded, "But, Dad, if I drop food, I'll get my socks dirty!" (Gilpin, 1993, p. 7). Another parent describes a young boy struggling to find the right word to express himself. When his dad told him, "Spit it out, son!" the boy stopped talking and spit. Then he continued trying to find the right word.

In my own life, I have found that even a lack of speech did not stop Tariq from developing a sense of humor. Soon after he was toilet trained around age 4 he began to signal that he needed to use the bathroom by tugging at his pants and sometimes pulling them part or all the way down. I would rush him to the bathroom before he could have an accident. Sometimes while I was trying to get him to bed, he would do the same thing. But when we got to the bathroom, he did not have to go. He would laugh—deep and hearty from the belly. The joke was on me!

Often I have heard parents spontaneously sharing funny stories at meetings. One woman I know always gets a kick out of telling how she finds time to vacuum. Parents of young children cannot do this when the children are napping because it will wake them up and scare them. Her son has a hearing loss, so she runs the vacuum while he is napping. "I have the cleanest floors of any of my friends," she always likes to remark. What she seems to enjoy even more is how much other parents in similar situations understand and enjoy her sense of humor.

Another mother told me about how she was rushing one evening to get her family ready to go to the movies together. "Hurry up," she told them, "so that we can get good seats." Her 9-year-old son, who needed a wheelchair because he had cerebral palsy, spoke up, "That doesn't bother me, Mom; I'm bringing my own seat."

Laughter has a practical value. Cousins (1989) described how 10 minutes of solid belly laughter would give him 2 hours of pain-free sleep while he was suffering from severe inflammation of the spine and joints that caused great difficulty sleeping. Cousins's experience has been corroborated by medical research that shows that laughter helps the body produce endorphins and has such benefits as lower blood pressure, enhanced respiration, relaxed muscles, and an increase in disease-fighting immune cells. Cousins regarded laughter as a metaphor for the full range of positive emotions, including hope, love, determination, purpose, and a strong will to live. These emotions promote physiological well-being as much as negative inhibited emotions can damage health.

As attested by famous examples such as Christy Brown and Helen Keller, a positive outlook can help a child to develop as fully as possible. Even when a child does not accomplish as much as these role models, the quality of family life is always greatly improved through a hearty sense of the comedy in everyday life. In fact, this was one of the common characteristics I found in my doctoral study of families who had coped successfully with disability. Each and every family told me that a sense of humor had helped them to survive and even prevail through the problems they faced. As Goethe observed long ago, "A joy shared is a joy doubled."

There are many lessons on this journey for connection and support as people are drawn together by their similarities, meeting through tears and laughter. It takes courage to acknowledge the hurt of grief and loneliness and in so doing to risk being hurt again. But that risk is necessary to get beyond grief to acceptance. Whether people are related by chance or choice, they must learn to accept and honor their differences. When they do this, they can divide their sorrow, multiply their joys, and make connections to support themselves through a lifetime.

12

Adolescence

I am an old man and have known a great many troubles, but most of them never happened.

MARK TWAIN

WORRYING ABOUT ADOLESCENCE IS NOTHING NEW AND IS COMPLETELY NORMAL FOR PARENTS. Once parents have obtained a diagnosis, they have a strong need to do all they can to help their children. They search the Internet, read books, and consult professionals while trying to find answers to their questions. If they are diagnosed before preschool, by the time children have reached school age and made some progress through intervention, most parents have attained some degree of normalization. These parents have adopted a mantra of living one day at a time.

Families who have limited or unequal access to services or whose children have more severe autism may not have achieved this kind of normalization by the time their children reach adolescence. Even in families that have found a balance to life by this time, normalization often goes out the window as parents begin to face the long-term problems raised by their child's autism. There are far fewer adequate services and role models for adolescents than there are for young children. Chances are that children with autism and their families have not had much interaction with adults with autism. While reflecting on her child's dependence on her, one mother exclaimed, "I can't even die!"

A tender moment occurs as Tariq still puts his head on my shoulder. Photograph by Tommy Leonardi.

Autism affects adolescence in unique ways depending on an individual's characteristics. The most frequent worries are about surging hormones, possible abuse, bullying, vocational opportunities, and living arrangements. Fathers tend to worry more about protecting their child, whereas mothers seem to focus more on their child's relationships with others. It is a sign of their love that parents focus on these issues even early in their child's life. Fears about sexuality and relationships are well founded because people with autism are more vulnerable to physical, emotional, and sexual abuse, as well as bullying.

A New Season of Life for Both Parent and Child

As the teenage years begin, parents may find themselves experiencing some of the same strong feelings they had when their child was preschool age. In the early teenage years, children are asserting their wills. For example, a child may refuse to get ready for school and be very difficult to redirect. The parent may no longer be able to physically control that child. Or a child may refuse to take his or her medication and insist on making his or her own choice. Parents, in contrast, experience a spectrum of emotions, including sorrow, fear, and possibly nostalgia.

Remembering their own teenage years, some parents fear the worst. A mother who had a hard time talking to her own mother may hope it will be different with her and her daughter. Her daughter's communication problems, however, prevent the kind of communication the mother dreamed of. Adolescence is impossible to get ready for. Like the rest of life, it just happens at its own pace. As Galinsky (1987) pointed out, the relationship between parent and child must be redefined. The physical relationship is no exception. How much do parents and children hug, hold, cuddle, and kiss each other? Puberty changes children's bodies, and they are curious and interested about this, whether they are verbal or nonverbal. Some children with autism do not want to become teenagers because they do not want to give up cartoons and other interests that may be considered babyish.

There is an important developmental irony between parent and child during adolescence. As Steinberg (2011) pointed out, the mixed emotions that parents may feel in response to their teenagers may result from or be exacerbated by their own struggle with middle age. Parents feel more aches and pains while their child gets physically bigger and stronger. Some adults

Tariq stims just a few moments later. Photograph by Tommy Leonardi.

dwell on their aging, whereas others may deny it and say that they do not notice growing older. There may also be pressure on the relationship between the parents. A mother may feel that her child needs to be listened to, but the father thinks the child should be treated more strictly. These differences need to be resolved or accepted, but this is easier said than done.

Steinberg, who is an expert on adolescents, gives some important advice that is applicable to parents of children with ASD. He advises that it is important to have interests outside of being a parent, such as having a happy marriage, a satisfying career, good health, or an interesting hobby. It is also important to stay engaged and emotionally close to your teenage children. (Autism researchers, such as Baker, Smith, Greenberg, Seltzer, and Taylor [2011] have documented that this does indeed make a difference for children growing up with autism.) It is also important not to approach your child's adolescence as a problem for your child or for yourself. Instead of seeing your child's behavior as disrespectful, remind yourself that your child's push for independence will help him or her to become as independent as possible. Your child's push away from you is thus not a problem but actually very desirable. A close parent–child relationship can teach healthy independence to whatever extent possible.

The horror stories you may have heard about adolescence for typical teenagers as well as those with autism are stereotypical generalizations. That being said, the transition from childhood to adulthood is stormy. Mood swings are normal, and rebellion is a necessary part of growing up. However, substance abuse, irresponsible sex, and legal problems are not normal and may at times be exacerbated in those with ASD. These problems are both preventable and treatable. Steinberg (2011) noted that adolescence is not inherently more difficult than other stages of development.

However, just like other stages it may be more complicated because of autism. For example, Steinberg (2011) noted that almost all adolescents worry at one time or another that they might be homosexual. For a teenager growing up with ASD, this worry may be even harder to resolve because of the tendency for the mind to get stuck on the possibility. If teenagers are questioning their sexual orientation, it is vital that their parents confront their own biases and be able to offer unconditional support. Initially, feeling an attraction for members of the same sex may seem to further alienate an individual. In the long run, however, if that person is gay, he or she may find acceptance in a social group that is used to being treated as different. Most high schools have an organization called the Gay–Straight Alliance that offers safety and support.

Peer pressure has been characterized in a one-sided way as an evil. Yet developmental psychology has revealed that peer pressure can also be a force for good, depending on the particular group. If your teenager has a peer group with values similar to your own, he or she will be positively as opposed to adversely influenced. The majority of teenagers respect their parents and tend to have similar values, although they may have different tastes and styles. If you have a good relationship with your child, you need not fear that it will vanish during adolescence. In addition, good parent–adolescent relationships do not depend on whether parents are married, single, divorced, remarried, gay, or straight. Let's look at how these themes play out in terms of parenting a teenager with ASD.

Holding On and Letting Go

As a child gets closer to high school age, the parents' efforts to support and rally around him or her in school may begin to seem inappropriate. Parents may get a message that it is time to let go. This is especially true if a teenager has made good progress and is seen as higher functioning. He or she may be involved in groups but is unable to develop sustained friendships and is not invited to other social outings.

When to hold on, when to let go, when to push, and when to pull: These are some of the themes that every parent struggles with, with typically developing children as well as children with special needs. A parent who has a good grasp of autism and who has done a lot to meet his or her child's special needs deserves a lot of credit. The anxiety about letting go at this point in the child's education and development is not unusual or inappropriate. Consider that perhaps both holding on and letting go have some validity.

If at all possible, depending on his or her age, your child should be involved with you and the professionals in making the transition plan. A transition plan is intended to help youth with ASD or other disabilities make the transition from secondary school to adulthood. The plan includes things like postsecondary education, vocational education, integrated employment (including supported employment), adult education, adult services, independent or supported living, and community activities. What your child thinks he or she needs is important in arriving at a good plan with a chance of success. Letting go may sound too drastic, and perhaps it is. Maybe a more realistic way to look at this dilemma is to just loosen your grip and see what happens. It may be helpful to back away a bit and see how things go. If your child seems anxious about leaving school or slips backward, this may convince others that he or she needs more support than they thought. For example, a child may have a hard time getting to school on time as graduation approaches in a year, or grades may fall even in a favorite subject. If he or she is somehow able to meet the challenge, you may be pleasantly surprised. There are inevitable and unavoidable road bumps and potholes in this process. Parents cannot control them, but they can control how they respond to them.

The differences between your child and others the same age can be even more awkward during adolescence. Some of your child's best friends going forward may be other teenagers growing up with a diagnosis on the autism spectrum. Some people overlook these friendships with other children on the spectrum because they are understandably eager for their children to be accepted socially. It is not unusual that it can be hard to accept that your child will not have the kind of social network you wanted for him or her. By adolescence, you may be tired and worried. Your feelings also need to be validated. It is a long and winding road to raise a child with autism. It is hard to know at any given moment what to accept and what to work on. For example, a talkative teenager may need to work on taking turns in a conversation. A parent's job never ends—it just changes.

Also keep in mind that teenagers want their parents around when they need them but often do not want as much interaction with them as their parents want them to have. It is important to be sure that the social goals you set up for your child are based on what he or she wants, not just what you think he or she should be doing. Your child may never be the life of the party and may always be a little on the periphery, but for him or her this could be comfortable. If your child wants more help with socializing, you can help him or her learn to reach out at his or her own pace. For example, join in role-playing games at the local comic book store or find a local group for a special interest such as the movies, science fiction, or rock climbing.

Puberty

Biological change begins much earlier than most parents expect. By age 8 or 9, the average child has entered puberty. This age has fallen steadily for more than a century in countries with good nutrition and health care, especially among girls. Girls tend to show outward signs of development an average of 2 years earlier than boys do. By 11 or 12 years of age, girls of average height may tower over boys their own age. In boys the outward signs of puberty can start anywhere from age 10 to age 14 or 15. Some individuals go through puberty in less than 2 years, whereas others may take 5 or 6 years to mature. Because the biology of puberty may be out of sync with cognitive or psychological maturation, a girl may look like a woman years before she feels like one. In contrast, a boy may have matured emotionally or cognitively but still look like a child.

Important advice about puberty is available in an article by Dubie (2005) from the Indiana Institute on Disability and Community. A girl may begin menstruating as early as age 9 or as late as 17. Other physical changes make daily hygiene more important. The onset of menstruation can be extremely confusing for girls with autism. Vaginal discharge in particular may be very frightening. Parents are advised to prepare their girls by making them familiar with menstrual pads and showing them books and videos about the changes in their bodies. For girls with ID as well as autism this can be especially challenging. Barb Zimmerman wrote *Erin's Period Book* in simple language and with pictures to explain the process of menstruation to girls with these challenges as a positive development toward adulthood.

During puberty, boys begin to ejaculate semen. Because this often occurs during sleep (with dreams), some boys will think they have wet the bed and will be very upset by these nocturnal emissions. In addition, boys may have erections at awkward times. It is important that parents of boys react calmly and help them understand the changes that are happening in their bodies. Books and videos are available to help boys, even those with limited or no verbal skills, understand these changes. Whether they have a boy or a girl, it is important that parents use the proper medical terminology for body parts. The same techniques and strategies that parents use to teach other skills can and should be used to teach children about menstruation and nocturnal emissions. These strategies may include videos, books, or pictures.

Parents who are concerned about adolescence are frequently uncomfortable addressing masturbation. Dubie (2006) provided thoughtful guidance on what she calls "the M word." Masturbation is normal for both typically developing individuals and those on the spectrum, but it is different for boys and girls. Quite simply, people of all ages masturbate because it feels good. More often than not parents of typically developing adolescents do not need to address the issue because their sons and daughters understand the relevant social cues. They intuitively understand that masturbation is to be done privately and is not to be discussed in public.

Teenagers with autism, in contrast, may be unaware of the reactions of others and may continue to touch or fondle themselves or even talk about it in public despite the negative attention they may receive. *Given the wide variation in levels of functioning among children on the spectrum, there is no one-size-fits-all solution.* When the problem is understood as normal but different from typical development, uncomfortable anxiety decreases for both parent and child. When a teenager is masturbating in public, it needs to be addressed. Rules and boundaries about privacy must be taught with Social Stories, pictures, and videos. *Private* must be defined as one's bedroom only. This is important because teenagers with autism may have difficulty generalizing and may use the bathroom stalls at school to masturbate, which may expose them to ridicule from others. *Taking Care of Myself* by Mary Wrobel is a good resource that includes social stories and visual strategies that can be adapted to an individual's cognitive abilities.

Sex and Sexuality

No matter where your child falls on the spectrum, he or she can still learn, and you can still teach, as Karin Melberg Schwier and Dave Hingsburger point out in *Sexuality: Your Sons and Daughters with Intellectual Disabilities.* Everyone learns healthy ideas about human sexuality in an evolving way, step by step. Every infant, child, teenager, and adult is a sexual being, regardless of whether they have a disability. Although *sex* can refer to gender (male or female) or the physical act of sexual intercourse, *sexuality* refers to the whole person. Human sexuality thus involves one's thoughts, feelings, attitudes, and behavior toward oneself and the others with whom one interacts. The ability to go beyond sex and into sexuality is highly individual and depends on the severity of one's autism.

Men and women alike see their children through the lens of their own life experiences. They know firsthand, for example, that adolescence can be extremely turbulent, as the emotional highs and lows of teenagers are not far apart. Strong feelings are often stirred up in parents, who have difficulty seeing their children as sexual beings. As their child's body changes with the dawn of emerging sexuality, parents have to rethink their authority with their developing child. Limits and guidance are still needed but must be based on the child's needs. Most important, your child needs education about sex and sexuality at home and at school. The purpose of this training is to give your child a language he or she can use about his or her body. With this skill, your child can tell you or someone else if anything is bothering him or her or if anything abusive happens.

More than anything parents must understand the deep passions that are evoked in this stage. Particularly challenging is accepting the child as a sexual being. As a teenager establishes his or her own identity, parents review their own struggles to understand their thoughts and feelings about their own bodies as well as their wishes about how their adolescence should, or could, have been handled by their parents. As the teenager forms a separate identity, this separation brings feelings of envy, fear, anger, pride, and regret for the parents. Parents of children with autism and other special needs must once again confront the reality of how different their child may be from the norm and may have special fears about their child being taken advantage of in the world. Through it all, the image of the child as an adult looms on the horizon.

The less severe a child's disability, the more likely it will be that he or she will form a sexual relationship in adulthood with a compatible partner. Likewise, the more severe the disability the less likely such a relationship will be. Nonetheless, all children, adolescents, and adults need boundaries, information, and language to remain safe and secure. You may find *Making Sense of Sex* by Sarah Attwood and *Asperger's Syndrome and Sexuality* by Isabelle Hénault to be informative and helpful guides. I also recommend the following helpful web sites:

National Dissemination Center for Children with Disabilities (www.nichcy .org)—includes information on teaching children about sexuality, the impact of disability, and relationship issues

Quality Mall (www.qualitymall.org)—person-centered services supporting people with developmental disabilities

Sexuality Information and Education Council of the United States (www.siecus .org)—provides information and education on sexuality

Accounts by adults with autism, such as *Beyond the Wall* by Stephen Shore and *Be Different* by John Elder Robison, give insight into their intimate experiences. As is often the case, children with autism can be a catalyst for the growth of their parents. Children and teenagers with ASD are sexual beings just like everyone else. There are plenty of teachable moments in everyday life. Children teach the aware parent as much or more than the parent teaches them. There is no shame in educating or reeducating yourself to be equal to the task. Respecting each child's dignity and teaching healthy attitudes and expression while maintaining safety is the job of all parents—as well as teachers and health care professionals—whether a child has autism or not.

Research Findings

Seltzer, Krauss, Orsmond, and Vestal (2001) described the issues facing families of adolescents and adults as uncharted territory. Although ASD is a lifelong condition, the overwhelming majority of research on ASD ends after childhood. The trajectories of developmental changes from childhood to adolescence to adulthood have not yet been adequately described. It is clear that autism poses significant difficulties for the well-being of the whole family. Many families become socially isolated and wary of public events, and the challenges posed by autism are a lifelong strain on the family.

Studies reviewed by Seltzer and colleagues (2001) have consistently shown that mothers and fathers of children with autism have higher levels of stress and less marital intimacy than mothers and fathers of children with other disabilities. Mothers of children with autism had greater symptoms of depression than other groups, but this was not true of fathers who had similar levels of depression. Mothers of children with ASD reported limited feelings of attachment and closeness with their children, although child responsiveness to the mother increased with age. This review also noted that although children with autism were less likely to make eye contact and smile, they appeared to be as attached to their mothers as children in the other disability groups. Overall, parents of children with ASD experienced increased and intensified distress after their child reached adolescence.

Seltzer and colleagues (2001) found a pattern of change from childhood to adolescence and adulthood in several studies in the core symptoms of autism such as communication, social interaction, and repetitive behaviors. They concluded that the symptoms of autism lessen in severity over time and that the best outcomes occur for individuals with higher IQs and more language ability. There is cause for optimism if this pattern can be supported by adequate services in adolescence and adulthood.

On the issue of regression there is reason for concern but not panic. Based upon a longitudinal study, Billstedt, Gillberg, and Gillberg (2005) reported that 17% of the 108 individuals studied had a clear setback in puberty as measured by their Global Assessment of Functioning (GAF). Half of these recovered from that regression in GAF, a numeric scale (0 through 100) used by mental health professionals to rate social, occupational, and psychological functioning. Moreover, 38% of the 108 had "a remarkably problem-free adolescent period" (p. 357) according to parents' recollections. In addition, this study confirmed previous research indicating that childhood IQ level and language development are positively correlated with a better outcome in adulthood. The individuals in the study were diagnosed in the 1970s and 1980s. About half of the study participants had a medical problem needing regular attention; 40% had experienced epilepsy in the past or at the time of the study. The participants in this study were considered typical of individuals with autism 30–40 years ago and are not necessarily representative of individuals currently diagnosed with ASD. Therefore, the results of this study cannot be generalized to individuals in the upper ranges of the autism spectrum.

Orsmond, Seltzer, Greenberg, and Krauss (2006) studied mother–child relationship quality among adolescents and adults with autism. Previous research had shown that young children with autism do indeed become attached to their mothers and have positive interactions. Mothers, however, tend to experience the relationship as quite different from the relationships they have with their typically developing children. Mothers of children with ASD were historically seen as lacking in warmth; they were even called "refrigerator mothers" by Bettleheim (1967) and blamed for causing their child's disability. Today experts understand that the social impairments of autism may have a negative effect on the mother–child relationship and may result in less apparent warmth between mother and child, though mothers of children with autism are not less warm than other mothers. The nature of the autism affects both the mother and child and thus the relationship.

Orsmond and colleague's (2006) study focused on three aspects of the mother–child relationship: positive affect, expressed emotion, and warmth. These researchers found that mothers had relatively positive relationships with their sons or daughters as measured by their own report as well as by independent ratings. For example, 90% of the 210 mothers studied reported high levels of affection for their child. These mothers felt significantly more positive affect toward their son or daughter than they perceived from him or her. The social impairments characteristic of autism may be the reason for this. Overall mothers expressed moderate to high levels of warmth and relatively low levels of criticism and overinvolvement. This quality of the mother–child relationship was an important factor resulting in lower levels of caregiving strain and higher levels of caregiving satisfaction. It is not surprising that more significant health and language limitations were associated with greater levels of maternal overinvolvement. More severe challenging behaviors were associated with less positive affect, greater criticism, and greater caregiving strain. Overall the quality of the mother–child relationship is critical for the well-being of the family and the development of the individual with autism.

Baker, Seltzer, and Greenberg (2011) studied how a family's ability to adapt to ASD affects behavior problems and maternal depression. Research up to this point on families of individuals with developmental problems had focused on how families are affected by the stress of raising children with these challenges. Baker, Seltzer, and Greenberg's study looked at how parents maintain positive mental health and reorganize their behavior to meet the special needs of their children. *Family adaptability* refers to a family's ability to change in the face of developmental stress. An adaptable family is able to remain flexible and solve problems as well as compromise and shift roles and responsibilities. A lack of adaptability, in contrast, often results in caregivers becoming depressed.

Baker, Seltzer, and Greenberg (2011) found that children with autism, like typically developing children, both influence and respond to their family environment. Family adaptability predictably lessened maternal depression, even though behavior problems may not have been reduced. The researchers were surprised to find that mother–child relationship quality was not related to lessened maternal depression or lessened behavior problems. This study provided evidence that a family's adaptability may promote resilience in parents as well as children with autism.

Social Skills: A Hidden Curriculum

The *hidden curriculum* includes social information that is not directly taught but that people assume everyone knows. Learning this curriculum is a lifelong process. Some of the rules are gender specific. For example, women talk and socialize in the restroom, but men do not. If an adult man talks or makes eye contact in the men's room, he will most likely be perceived as homosexual and as trying to initiate sexual contact. Individuals with ASD experience social skills as a hidden curriculum. Myles, Trautman, and Schelvan (2004) used concrete examples from numerous environments to teach the hidden rules of social interactions at home, in school, and in the community. Here are some sample hidden curriculum items that you may take for granted but that people with autism may not intuitively understand:

- Not all people who are unfamiliar are strangers you can't trust. For example, your bus driver and a police officer are people who help you.

- People do not always want to know the honest truth when they ask.

- People are not always supposed to say what they are thinking.

- Treat all authority figures, such as police officers and teachers, with respect.

For teenagers on the spectrum, learning the adolescent hidden curriculum is at least as important as learning academic skills. It is vital that this instruction be included in students' IEPs. They must be taught through direct instruction, because they will not automatically learn these things. Books, one-a-day calendars, Social Stories, and even iPhone applications are available to help teach these rules to children of all ages. Many youngsters love the book *Freaks, Geeks and Asperger Syndrome: A User Guide to Adolescence* by Luke Jackson, a teenager with Asperger syndrome. Parents and siblings as well will get a few good laughs along with poignant insight on growing up and dealing with differences. Much attention has been given to dealing with autism when children are young, but all children inevitably grow up and face new and varied challenges.

Teenagers in general have a hard time admitting difference as they struggle to find out and come to terms with who they really are. Fitting in is one of the primary goals of a typical teenager during this phase of development. It may be helpful to leave books around that talk about being different or about typical teenage problems. Your daughter or son may be able to learn about what other teenagers think and do by reading about it and learn about himself or herself and some of his or her differences at the same time.

Although the process can be slow, it is also often possible to teach and to learn the art of small talk. There are several ways to try to make this happen and to help teenagers like yours to become more adept at the teenage scene. Being around other teenagers in safe settings is often helpful. Books such as *Social Skills Training* by Jed Baker and *Social Skills Success for Students with Autism/Asperger's* by Fred Frankel and Jeffrey Wood can help you to coach your child in small talk and other social skills. If your child has friends you can continue to encourage interaction while teaching the social nuances that are so difficult for so many teenagers to master. Remember, though, that your child may not feel loneliness the way you do, and ultimately it will be up to him or her to deal with aloneness and potential loneliness. If your child is motivated to reach out and interact with others, with your help he or she will learn to be more social in his or her own time.

The best basis for friendship, as recommended by numerous people with ASD as well as by professionals, is a solid base of common interests and values. These friendships can be pursued through after-school and community activities. Another tip that I always pass along is that lots of teenagers and adults, both male and female, share many of the interests that people with ASD have, such as computers, gaming, history, and science, to name a few. The Internet also offers some promising possibilities for social interaction. For example, you can find or start a group at www.meetup.com. In addition, www.wrongplanet.net is a web community of more than 60,000 teenagers and adults on the spectrum. Wrong Planet, which was founded by Alex Plank, a young man with autism, includes videos, blogs, and discussion forums on many topics of interest.

Societal pressure to begin dating and find a relationship can place undue stress and anxiety on teenagers with ASD and their families. I recommend building friendships as groundwork. Because happily coupled typically developing people in long-term relationships, both gay and straight, often report that they are best friends, developing a friendship can form a foundation for a possible long-term romantic relationship. Teenagers on the spectrum are more likely to date and have relationships with people who do not fit the norm. As Jerry Newport, an adult and author with autism, frequently comments in his lectures, "You don't have to be normal to be happy."

Hygiene

For many individuals with ASD, learning social skills includes personal hygiene. This can be confusing and even painful because of sensory processing issues that are common in individuals with ASD. For example, even something simple such as brushing your teeth can cause discomfort. The odors from some soaps and shampoos may be unbearable. This means that along with social skills, your child will likely struggle with hygiene and self-help skills. Therefore, these skills need direct teaching through visual supports such as Social Stories, flashcards, visual schedules, and so forth. Accommodations, such as odorless soaps, may also need to be used.

For example, Harry is 14 and going through puberty. Now when he sweats, he has an unpleasant odor. His lack of personal hygiene has become noticeable to his peers. For Harry personal hygiene is not an issue. He is unaware of how others are reacting to him, but he is becoming distressed by his social isolation, as his peers have been avoiding him because he smells bad. Harry is unable to understand and read other people's body language and nonverbal communication. He can benefit from the teaching of hygiene skills using Social Stories, which show the skill in detail as well as what happens to people who do not have the skill.

In *Be Different,* John Elder Robison related how when he learned to present himself properly, other people chose to connect with him. In his words,

> Take regular showers, wear clean clothes, brush your hair, and mind those manners. Listen more and talk less. All that may seem like a waste of time, but I assure you, the results are worth it. Let the friendships begin. (2011, p. 162)

Bullying

Bullying is a major problem for children on the spectrum because their social impairments make them especially vulnerable targets. According to a 2009 survey conducted by Massachusetts Advocates for Children, 88% of 400 children with autism had been bullied at school, as reported by their parents. This rate is approximately twice that of the general population. In more than half of these cases the bullying was physical and included being hit, kicked, or chased. Bullying involves a power imbalance and the intent to harm. Bullying can occur on the playground, in the classroom, in the cafeteria, or through text messaging or cyberbullying. Children with ASD may also be harassed when a bully purposely triggers a meltdown. Bullying can have serious behavioral and emotional consequences for bullies as well as victims.

Take Philip, an 11th grader, who has a meltdown in the hallway after class. He starts screaming and throws his backpack; fortunately it does not hit anyone. His aide is able to take him aside and calm him. Because of the zero-tolerance policy at his school, he receives an in-school suspension. When his parents meet with the IEP team, Philip tells everyone about being teased in the class that just ended before the incident. Because his behavior was related to his special needs, he does not have to serve the suspension. The question here is how to prevent incidents such as this from occurring in the first place.

Gould and Pratt (2008) reported that schools that have schoolwide positive behavioral supports have fewer discipline problems and less bullying because they take a systematic approach to creating a school culture that is responsive to students' needs. These supports aim to prevent problems and involve three levels: the school, the group, and the individual. For example, if bullying is more likely to occur in hallways after class, then more staff are placed there to monitor. In addition, a schoolwide antibullying program can help establish an inclusive and compassionate school culture. Bystanders often find it disturbing to witness bullying, and they need strategies and encouragement to respond and intervene.

Students with ASD can also be supported in small groups and individually and can learn alternative behaviors to deal with bullying. The National Bullying Prevention Center (www.pacer.org/bullying) is an excellent resource.

Poor emotion regulation makes children and teenagers with autism easy targets for bullies. Bullies tend to pick on kids they think they can get a rise out of. When those kids react dramatically, they just tend to get picked on more. Learning how to regulate emotion in order to prevent those outbursts is an important goal. Van Roekel, Scholte, and Didden (2010) discussed two reasons why children and teenagers with special needs are at higher risk for bullying: They are less socially competent, and they have fewer friendships. In addition, they have difficulty understanding the behavior of others, are eager to please, and can be easily set up. In the first-ever study of adolescents with ASD attending special education classes, these researchers found that adolescents with ASD often have increased levels of aggressive behavior and may bully others.

Van Roekel and colleagues found that adolescents with ASD made very few mistakes identifying bullying on video fragments and their perceptions did not differ significantly from the general population. Because bullying is so widespread, the more that teenagers with ASD in this study were bullied, the more they misinterpreted neutral or positive situations as bullying; therefore, these researchers recommended new kind of interventions that focus on improving perceptions of bullying and victimization among adolescents with ASD.

How Girls Differ in Adolescence

Girls growing up on the spectrum are in general more able than boys to verbalize their emotions. Because their peer group is made up of girls, they are more likely than boys to be supported and included by other girls. Boys, in contrast, are far less tolerant than girls on average. Much like Liane Holliday-Willey, who wrote about her experiences growing up in *Pretending to Be Normal,* girls tend to be better than boys at using imitation and modeling to hide their difficulties in social settings. Although girls with ASD can be interested in science and computers just like boys, they often have special interests such as animals and classical literature. Much like boys, these girls may see no value in being fashionable. They tend to wear plain, practical clothing and avoid makeup and deodorants. As they enter the preteenage and teenage years, both boys and girls with ASD tend to become even more conspicuous among their peers.

The transition to middle school can be difficult because same-age peers have formed cliques and crowds. The phrase "two's company and three's a crowd" certainly fits this dilemma, as Attwood (2007) has pointed out. It may be difficult for both boys and girls to cope with the social interaction of several people. One-to-one conversations work the best. Likewise, individual sports such as swimming, running, tennis, and golf provide the best opportunities for friendship for teenagers who enjoy sports. Teenagers with ASD also have success serving as managers or stat keepers for basketball, baseball, and football teams.

The onset of puberty complicates the social world for teenagers on the spectrum. After they experience physical changes, teenage girls may find themselves flattered by the attention of boys. They usually do not realize that boys' interest is sexual as opposed to a friendly overture. In general, girls' fantasies tend to be romantic in nature, whereas boys' fantasies tend to be sexually explicit. These desires and fantasies are normal and common but hard for teenagers on the spectrum to understand. This is even more true for girls on the spectrum who have flown beneath the radar and been diagnosed later than their male counterparts.

In *Aspergirls,* Rudy Simone (2010) shares her personal experiences about every aspect of life. This landmark book is part memoir, part research review, and part mentoring guide for girls growing up with ASD. Many personal vignettes are included to illustrate the varied experiences of this subculture within a subculture. Simone notes that people on the spectrum share a kind of androgyny that appears in males as gentleness and in females as a tendency to be independent. The differences are rather subtle within the spectrum but are more marked between an Aspergirl and a typically developing female.

Although their goals may be similar to those of the Aspergirl, typical girls have a wider social circle. The Aspergirl, according to Simone (2010), devotes more time to her inner life and goals but may be less likely to reach them because she does not have the requisite social skills to climb the ladder. The pressure to be social is even greater for girls on the spectrum than for boys. It is important to teach these skills to help girls reach their potential. Likewise, it is important for the typical population to understand that girls on the spectrum have much to offer in terms of their depths and talents.

In *Asperger's and Girls* (2006), Jennifer McIlwee Myers contributes an insightful essay titled "Aspie Do's and Don'ts: Dating, Relationships and Marriage." In it she dispels several unwritten myths for girls on the spectrum—and any other girl, for that matter—such as

- The best way to be happy is to have a long-term monogamous relationship.
- You should begin dating as a teenager and eventually marry.
- Any relationship is better than no relationship.

Her refreshing insights about growing up female on the spectrum are particularly helpful to parents who may feel at a loss guiding their daughters.

For a comprehensive discussion of the difficult issues facing girls with ASD, *Girls Growing Up on the Autism Spectrum* by Nichols, Moravcik, and Tetenbaum (2009) is a valuable resource. These authors cover a wide range of the spectrum, providing comprehensive resources in the form of books, videos, web sites, and teaching strategies appropriate for individuals with a wide range of abilities. Reading about puberty, sexuality, hygiene, and other adolescent issues may be uncomfortable. Talking about these issues in the family may be awkward as well, but facing them honestly is the only way to raise healthy young women as well as men.

Depression and Anxiety

"I must have seasonal depression," Eric, an 18-year-old, told me. "Right after Thanksgiving every year, I go into a funk. I can't get to sleep at night, and then I oversleep. Then I start playing the video games I've been trying to avoid. It's like I am back in middle school obsessed with gaming. I swore I wouldn't become a hardcore gamer, but now here I am doing it again. At least I don't think about my problems while I am playing, but now my grades have become a problem."

Eric's depression was not unlike that of other adolescents and young adults I have treated. This bright, friendly youth was diagnosed with Asperger syndrome in ninth grade. Although many people liked him, others teased and bullied him, and he had problems keeping friends. He helped others with math problems but was rarely invited to parties, and if he was invited he would wind up leaving early because he could not keep a conversation going. Each September he would start school full of energy and hope that things would be different. Now in his senior year, he hung out and had had a few lunch dates with a girl he had a crush on. When he asked her if they had become "boyfriend and girlfriend," he felt rejected to find out that they were "just friends." This happened shortly after the first of November and was another rejection in a seemingly seasonal pattern that started a depressive episode.

Besides having problems sleeping and maintaining concentration, Eric was skipping meals, isolating himself, and eating lots of junk food and gaining weight. He blamed himself for "screwing up another opportunity." His symptoms fit his broken heart, but understanding his social difficulties as part of ASD was vital. Even with treatment, his depression may have continued to recur. When individuals with ASD come to me feeling depressed, I first just listen to their experience: their thoughts, feelings, impulses, physical sensations, memories, dreams, and disappointments. If they are not suicidal or in crisis, I will want to see how they will respond to therapy. If the symptoms do not lessen, then I recommend a psychiatric evaluation to determine if medication could help.

Often a person with ASD will feel rejected or ostracized because of his or her differences. Both chronic suffering and longing to be typical may lead to giving up on ever being more social. Eric had not given up, but he did feel devastated. My general approach with people such as Eric is to help them let go of the hope of being typical and facilitate an acceptance of their differences. While often a natural tendency, there is substantial evidence that experiential avoidance or trying to block or stop painful thoughts, feelings, memories, or physical sensations only works in the short term. As Dena Gassner, an adult with autism, states in her presentations, "Being autistic never disabled me but trying to be normal did." She explains how she was first misdiagnosed under a mental health model. Later with accurate diagnosis under a developmental model, the goal shifted to learning to live well with autism instead of recovering.

My approach to living as a parent of a child with ASD is drawn from my struggle to accept my own hardships as well as my professional training and experience. Acceptance for parents, family members, and individuals with ASD is not about giving up or resigning oneself to rejection, social awkwardness, or a broken heart. Acceptance is a willingness to have these feelings and

Tariq learns prevocational skills in a Devereux workshop.

go on living life in ways that really matter. All feelings and experiences are a part of life's journey. Although it sounds counterintuitive, attempts to push these thoughts and feelings away actually get people stuck in the story that goes with them. Looking gently and flexibly instead often takes the rough edge off. It then becomes possible to look at choices and move in the direction of specific goals.

Social development is often the best medicine to alleviate depression and social anxiety in teenagers with ASD. The therapeutic relationship can be a vehicle to developing more relationship skills. I also recommend group therapy and instruction to develop these skills. It is sometimes helpful to read personal accounts written by people with Asperger syndrome who serve as role models and beacons of hope. The most important advice I would impart to a parent or teenager with ASD struggling with depression and social anxiety is to find a good psychotherapist. Seeing a professional experienced with Asperger syndrome can be an advantage, but it is not essential. A therapist with good skills and the willingness to learn and listen compassionately and provide patient guidance can do the job.

Planning for Life After High School

Focusing on the special interests and talents that many children with autism possess is the best way to prepare them for life after high school. Temple Grandin emphasizes in her lectures and writing that developing these interests can form the basis of skills that will make a person with ASD employable. It can be a big mistake to focus on discouraging a child's special interest even if at first it might seem odd or useless. Grandin (2008) related how her fixation on cattle squeeze chutes led to a career as a designer of livestock facilities. One of her teachers used this interest to motivate her to study science and sensory perception. Studying science helped her to stop talking endlessly about cattle chutes, and then she stopped boring people.

The important strategy illustrated here is taking a fixation and broadening it into something potentially constructive. Sometimes parents and teachers put too much emphasis on making a teenager more social and "normal" while neglecting the special interests that might actually help him or her socially. Social interactions can often be developed in a more natural way through shared interests. These interests and talents can evolve into ways of relating to others and even careers, so finding ways to develop and nurture these interests needs to become an important focus in the overall development of a teenager with autism.

According to Grandin (2008), visual thinkers may be good at things such as design, graphics, photography, architecture, or auto mechanics. Those who think in patterns are often good at music, engineering, computer science, and statistics. Verbal thinkers are often good at jobs such as library science, legal research, journalism, and other jobs that require good record keeping. Some individuals do not fit neatly into one of these three categories, and this is part of the wide variation of the autism spectrum. What is most important is finding and focusing on strengths.

This same principle applies to individuals on the lower end of the spectrum. Teenagers who are nonverbal may be taught the skills needed to stock shelves, sort items, garden, landscape, or work in repetitive factory jobs. Society needs all kinds of workers at all levels, and people with autism can be contributive and be productive. From the mentally gifted to the mentally challenged on the spectrum, multitasking is difficult if not impossible. So being a cashier in a busy store that would involve making change and talking to people at the same time would not be a good match for many individuals with autism.

More than anything else, developing skills is wonderful for improving self-esteem. Those skills and a positive attitude can lead to employment and connections with other people. Because much of one's adult life is spent working, it makes sense that a person with employable skills will generally do better and be happier than one without such skills. Likewise, special interests that do not become careers can still be valuable hobbies that can bring enjoyment and connections with others. Finally, parents and educators should keep in mind that the trajectory for teenagers on the spectrum is different from that for typically developing teens. In general, adolescence now extends even further into the early and later 20s. Keeping this in mind, it is more possible to remain patient and supportive in helping young people with autism to develop meaningful adult lives.

13

Adulthood

Development delayed is not development denied.

Don White, Father of a Young Man with Autism

From the earliest days of life parents think about their baby growing up and leaving home. These images form and re-form as the child grows and develops. Parents of typically developing children experience mixed feelings, including pride, sadness, relief, and pleasure. For parents in general this phase of life involves taking stock of the overall experience of parenthood. For the parents of a child with autism, there is often a hope that time will stop, for the future of how and under what terms their child will leave home is unimaginable. But time moves on at the speed of life.

Fears about adulthood can seem unmanageable. This is especially true if the child with autism is an only child or if there is little or no extended family to act as a support system. For the single parent of an only child with ASD, these worries can become consuming. Parents of children with autism, like all parents, want an image that their grown child will be settled in life. This usually means having a satisfying life with meaningful work and a loving family of his or her own. These images or dreams do not always come true, but being able to have them seems a luxury to parents who are raising a child with ASD.

As I write this chapter, these concerns are looming as children diagnosed in the early 1990s are leaving their special education programs. This chapter looks at the frightening realities as well as the hopes and possibilities that lie ahead for them. Although autism has been a part of the human condition for centuries, it has only recently been documented to affect 1% of the adult population (Brugha et al., 2007). It is said that there is strength in numbers, and for the sake of a humane society as well as the autism community it is essential that we use our strength to secure a meaningful future for our families as well as our children with autism. Although the social and emotional development of young people with ASD may be delayed, there is strong scientific evidence that it continues in adulthood. With support, it is reasonable to expect continued slow, steady progress.

At the 2010 national conference of the Autism Society of America I met Don White, a Baptist pastor, who spoke on a panel about fatherhood and firmly believed that development delayed is not development denied. Don and Serrita White's son, DJ, was diagnosed with ASD at an early age. DJ progressed through special education classes and graduated from public high school in 2008. He continued this education at a community college, studying developmental and physical education courses, and received services through his local vocational rehabilitation office, yet his parents still wondered if he would ever get a job and have a full life. In July 2012, DJ was hired by Price Waterhouse Coopers and receives supportive services from a job coach. For his parents and his sister, Danielle, who started medical school in September 2012, this was a fulfilled hope and answered prayer.

The White Family: Don, Danielle, Serrita, and DJ

Tariq in Adulthood

On a recent winter day as we walked arm in arm, my son Tariq and I silently enjoyed the walk along the bike trail that wound through the woods. Then a couple approached from the opposite direction. They looked with a question in their gaze. I am used to it. My 33-year-old relates to me like a little boy. He was looking up at me in the way a toddler adores his father. It is normal between me and my son but an odd sight to others. The couple smiled and said, "Good morning." I know that they knew he's different, and it's okay. The chip on my shoulder is long gone.

Since the summer of 1988, Tariq has not lived with our family. He resided and went to school at the Kanner Center of the Devereux Foundation until 2003. Since then he has lived in a group home for people with developmental disabilities run by an agency called KenCrest and gone to a day program called Helping Hands. Because of his level of disability, he has required around-the-clock care. If only he did not have autism. If only he could speak and read and write. If only he understood danger. If only he slept safely through the night. If only he was not a constant threat to run away. I still cannot help at times but wonder what might have been.

In November of 1999, when Tariq was 20, we had a big party for him. Just a few months before I had woken up and said to my wife Cindy, his stepmother, "It's his 20th birthday. Let's have a party." Cindy threw him a great party attended by family and friends as well as several of his teachers and therapists, past and present. He had not had a party since he was a little boy, something of which I am not proud. But there were so many milestones unmet and so many disappointments to absorb. It took time, and we all just did our best—Tariq included.

Most striking in retrospect is how at first I was so passionately determined to change Tariq and make him the boy I wanted him to be. Yet the book I eventually wrote became the story of how I was forced to change myself and embrace him as he is. It is a book I wish I had had when he was young. Tariq's gifts to me were not in packages, but they continue to unfold over time. Tariq has taught me the meaning of unconditional love.

I have learned to honor his sacred right to be loved for who he is. My attachment to his achievements dissolved over time. This was hard to let go of. He is now able to sit still and focus for long enough to be productive with routine tasks such as sorting things. Over these years, I have learned to accept the best he can do and celebrate that achievement. Around the time of his 21st birthday, when I took him to the bathroom, I noticed that he had learned to button the fly on his pants. He did not need me to do that anymore. My eyes glazed over with joy. I have learned to appreciate every step he learns to take in his continued development. What a priceless lesson he has taught me without words!

The inevitable juxtaposition of my son with healthy, typical children used to be so painful. I used to wince every time my friends' kids and my nieces and nephews passed a milestone that Tariq would never achieve—such as riding a bicycle; learning to swim; graduating from grade school, high school, or college; or getting a job. Now I can enjoy witnessing their progress, and that is a wonderful gift that has grown out of moments of serenity.

What Tariq has taught me besides accepting him is to accept myself. I think the challenges in children radiate inwardly to parents' own sense of being flawed. What all people face as parents, siblings, friends, and professionals is some balance of hope and reality. With typically developing children as well as those with autism, parents have to give up their expectations in order to love their child in the moment. You cannot enjoy your life if you do not love in the moment. Some dreams are deferred, and some dreams are remade. Tariq and I do run together, and that is something I imagined doing with my son. We canoe together, something else I imagined. We walk through the woods. In those moments there is nothing wrong with him or me.

Another gift has been learning not to hide differences. For years I would only keep or put into books the pictures of my son looking

I still wonder what he thinks and wants to tell me.

normal. I have finally gotten to the point of realizing that images of him flapping his hands and looking normal are both okay. He is just as lovable either way. I learned this because photographer Tommy Leonardi thought he was a great subject—and he was. How wonderful a revelation! A certain degree of shame was shed.

Tariq continues to teach me to live for myself. He needs me and he counts on me to do that. He cannot help me when I become old and frail. Rather, I must ensure that his needs are met when I am gone. When I understood that my feelings were my own, I could see reality more clearly. He was and is happy most of the time. I am grateful for the opportunity to tell my story in these pages, hopefully in a way that can help others. This is a charmed part of my existence, for so many people in every corner of the globe endure tragedy with no apparent redemption.

Telling your story is a vehicle for knowing yourself by revealing heartfelt sentiments to others and building bonds that endure. The act of telling your story can be an antidote to the alienation that often characterizes life in the modern world. People's stories help them make sense of what has happened to them. The story is a way of telling time, which stops for many people on finding out about their child's autism. It becomes the pathway to finding meaning in life. So this is not just a story about me and my son; everyone can benefit from finding links to the events in their own lives and putting them together with coherence, logic, and emotion.

In the opening lines of *David Copperfield,* Charles Dickens wrote, "Whether I am to be the hero of my own life, or whether that station will be held by anybody else, these pages must show" (p. 3). At the moment of my son's birth, I had imagined him to be the hero of my life. In the way that my writings describe, he has helped me to find the hero within me, and for that I am grateful.

Tariq is a man now. I still wonder what his voice would sound like and what he would want to tell me. Tariq is still my boy. He still puts his head on my shoulder. He has brought so many kindhearted people into my life. These experiences have made me a better person.

Research Findings

Although much of the territory remains uncharted, there is important evidence of what to expect as children with autism grow into adulthood. The rapid rise in the number of children diagnosed with ASD began in the early 1990s, and those children are now beginning to leave their school systems. Taylor and Seltzer (2010a) studied 242 of these young people over a 10-year period. They found an overall improvement over that time span in symptoms of autism and in internalized behaviors which direct feelings and emotions inward such as depression, anxiety, physical complaints, or eating too much or too little. Unfortunately, their rates of improvement slowed after leaving school. Those who did not have an ID had the greatest decrease in improvement, as did those with lower family income.

These findings were based on both parents' reports and professional observation, especially for repetitive behaviors and stereotyped interests as well as social reciprocity and verbal communication. It is significant to note that relatively few adolescents and adults with ASD had worsening symptoms over time. There were also decreases in the prevalence of maladaptive behaviors such as self-injury, aggression, and uncooperative behaviors. There were few differences between males and females with the exception that females had better quality social interactions (Taylor & Seltzer, 2010a). These findings are consistent with the generalization that autism is lifelong but that it continues to change with development.

Taylor and Seltzer (2010a) concluded that leaving high school disrupted developmental progress for youth with ASD primarily because of a lack of disability-related services, especially for young adults who did not have ID. In contrast, those who did not have ID improved more in high school than those with ID. After high school, 74% of young adults with ASD and ID were receiving adult day services compared to only 6% of those who did not have ID. Although model programs, both public and private, include services for youth who have ASD without ID, these programs are inaccessible to the majority of the population.

In another paper, Taylor and Seltzer (2010b) reported low rates of employment for 66 young adults with the majority (56%) working in sheltered workshops or day activity centers. Young adults with ASD who did not have ID were 3 times more likely to have no daytime activities than those adults who had ID. The limited previous research on post–high school activities for adults with ASD paints a bleak and pessimistic picture. Even those individuals who were able to find competitive employment tended to have part-time menial jobs. Overall only 18% of young adults without ID were getting some sort of employment or vocational services compared with 86% of young adults with ID.

The obvious conclusion is that more autism-focused adult services are needed to help people with ASD without ID achieve maximum levels of independence and sustainable careers. There appears to be a group of people whose symptoms are not severe enough for them to receive adult day services but are too severe to enable them to function independently. On a more upbeat note, Taylor and Seltzer (2010b) found that nearly 50% of youths with ASD without ID were pursuing postsecondary education, so this appears to be a viable option for those individuals. There is still insufficient evidence to determine whether those degrees translate into sustainable careers.

Taylor and Seltzer (2011) also broke new ground by studying changes in the mother–child relationship over a 7-year period during the transition to adulthood for 170 mothers of young people with ASD who had recently left the school system. This was part of a longer longitudinal study with data collected over 7 years. Their results indicated improvement in the mother–child relationship during the high school years but not so much improvement after high school. Mothers of youth with ASD without ID had more stress because of unmet needs for services. This group had the least relationship improvement after high school. It is not surprising that this study provides further evidence that the years after high school have increased risks, especially for individuals with ASD without ID and those whose families have less income. As is frequently the case, the father–child relationship was not studied.

Barker and colleagues (2010) studied the emotional well-being of 397 mothers of adolescents and adults with ASD in terms of symptoms of depression and anxiety over a 10-year period. The overall results indicated resilience or positive adjustment as indicated by improved emotional well-being in response to the challenges of parenting a child with ASD. However, when challenging behavior was more severe, symptoms of maternal depression and anxiety were greater. When the adult child no longer lived in the family home, maternal anxiety was lower. It is important to note that anxiety was greater when there was less social support and during stressful life events.

Mothers of grown children with ASD continue to have elevated stress and compromised well-being compared with parents of individuals with other developmental disabilities, such as Down syndrome. They spend more time caregiving and fewer hours in leisure activities than mothers of typically developing adolescents and adults. Although Barker and colleagues (2010) broke new ground, most of the mothers were Euro-American, and fathers were not included. Nonetheless, it is clear that parents of adult children with ASD need support in midlife and beyond.

Kring, Greenberg, and Seltzer (2010) studied the impact of health problems on behavior problems in adolescence and adulthood and the implications for mothers. Kring and colleagues reviewed recent research which has highlighted the fact that the risk for health problems in individuals with ASD increases with age. Because of impairments in communication and social interaction, it is difficult for individuals with ASD to cope with their physical health problems and associated pain; this often leads to behavioral outbursts. This affects the well-being of their caregivers—especially their mothers, who are often the primary caregivers. For example, there is evidence of higher rates of sudden aggression in children with ASD who have gastrointestinal problems than those with ASD who do not have gastrointestinal problems. Kring and colleagues highlighted the importance of targeting health problems. Despite study participants' elevated levels of health problems, the researchers still found improvement in behavior over time.

There has been very limited research on the impact of autism on the family as well as the impact of the family environment on the development of a child with autism. This may be because of the history of blaming families of children with autism, but nonetheless it makes good sense to study how family interactions affect both parents and children with autism. Greenberg, Seltzer, Hong, and Orsmond (2006) studied how high levels of expressed emotion affect behavior problems and other symptoms in adolescents and adults with ASD. This is a complex problem because children with ASD have difficulty communicating their needs, and parents' frustration and criticism are quite understandable. In addition, mothers of children with more severe behavior problems need to be more involved in their care, and this may lead to higher levels of apparent criticism as the mothers try to teach their children important social behaviors.

Greenberg and colleagues (2006) found that high levels of maternal expressed emotion in the form of criticism had detrimental effects on the well-being of individuals with ASD. Overall, the researchers found a pattern of family strengths and effective coping in most families that suggested a positive influence of the family environment on the development of individuals with ASD. Another interesting finding is that mothers had overall higher levels of expressed emotion and overinvolvement with daughters than with sons. Generally speaking, increases in parental criticism toward the child impedes improvement in behavior, and decreased criticism decreases behavior problems. This study highlights the importance of positive behavioral supports for adolescents and adults with ASD and their families, who face increasing levels of stress, especially in the absence of suitable services.

Little is known about the complex issue of caregiving by parents of adults with autism. Krauss, Seltzer, and Jacobson (2005) studied 133 mothers' perceptions of coresidence versus supported out-of-family living. There were positive and negative aspects to both arrangements. Families whose adult child lived with supports away from home attributed most of the positive benefits to the adult child as opposed to the family or the mother. The positive benefits included personal growth, the development of new skills, social benefits, and structured programs. As the primary caregiver, the mother missed her child but reported more free time and less fatigue. However, these mothers had more worries about their adult child's future. Families with a son or daughter at home reported fewer benefits, which focused on security and peace of mind rather than growth and development.

It is important to note that there was a high level of contact and involvement by mothers even after their adult child with ASD was placed in a residential facility. The vast majority of mothers reported at least monthly visits and frequent communication with the residential staff. This is an important consideration for families and service providers when making transition plans. The stereotypes of the bygone era of institutionalization can be laid to rest. The child has not been put away. Family involvement is not contingent on where the adult child lives. This underscores the importance of families taking a life-span perspective on residential options for adults with ASD.

Learning from Role Models with Autism

It is natural for families and everyone who knows and loves people with autism to wish for an outcome such as Temple Grandin who has high-functioning autism. She has a doctorate in animal science, and she is a professor at Colorado State University, bestselling author, and consultant to the livestock industry on animal behavior. Dr. Grandin was listed in the *Time* 100 list of the 100 most influential people in the world. Although it is impossible to predict the destiny of individual children, for the overwhelming majority of people affected by autism, Grandin's reality will not be theirs. This makes it vital for people in the autism community to hear from people such as Grandin and many others. Hearing from people who live with the signs and symptoms of the autism spectrum provides essential information that is available from no other source.

What is it like to live with sensory issues? Or to experience the world and think in a distinctly different way? People who live on the spectrum spend a lifetime struggling to understand the rules of conventional society. It seems overdue for society to understand the culture of people who were born and remain different. These men and women have the same heartaches and the same needs and desires as people who are not diagnosed on the spectrum. They say so clearly, "Love and accept me as I am." They help everyone else understand that autism is not just something that a person has but rather is a way of being.

Jim Sinclair is an autism rights activist who formed Autism Network International (ANI) in 1992 along with Kathy Lissner Grant and Donna Williams. Sinclair did not speak until age 12. Sinclair wrote "Don't Mourn for Us," an essay with an anticure perspective on autism. Sinclair was featured in the book *Somebody Somewhere* by Donna Williams, which discusses the founding of ANI. In the mid-1990s autism conferences rarely featured speakers with autism and rarely paid them for their work; Sinclair was among the first international self-advocates in the autism field. "Don't Mourn for Us" is a classic essay and highly recommended reading. In it he says,

> Some amount of grief is natural as parents adjust to the fact that an event and a relationship they've been looking forward to isn't going to materialize. But this grief over a fantasized normal child needs to be separated from the parents' perceptions of the child they do have: the autistic child who needs the support of adult caretakers and who can form very meaningful relationships with those caretakers if given the opportunity. Continuing focus on the child's autism as a source of grief is damaging for both the parents and the child, and precludes the development of an accepting and authentic relationship between them. For their own sake and for the sake of their children, I urge parents to make radical changes in their perceptions of what autism means. (Sinclair, 1993)

As a child, Donna Williams was thought to be deaf, psychotic, and emotionally disturbed, and fortunately she was finally diagnosed with autism in adulthood. She became an international bestselling author with eight published books, including her autobiography *Nobody Nowhere*. Donna has been the subject of three international television documentaries and is a consultant to professionals, families, and people with autism. She lives in Australia with her husband Chris. In *Voices from the Spectrum,* Donna proposed a middle ground in which the perspectives of both autism rights advocates (culturists) and those seeking a cure can be respected:

> The "culturalists" rightly argue that many people on the Autism Spectrum have one or more parents with features of an Autism Spectrum Condition and that often

the condition is at least partially genetic but that this does not necessarily make it an illness. On the other side, those who seek a "cure" or eradication of autism from the planet are often traumatised by feeling deeply for the frustration and distress of some of the most severely affected individuals diagnosed with autism, some of whom actually suffer from (sometimes treatable) severe medical conditions including gut and immune disorders, and/or mood, anxiety and compulsive disorders to such severe degrees these severely limit the expression, comfort and capacity of those individuals. (Williams, 2006, p. 205)

Donna herself would not be who she is without all that she has been through and the help she has received. Temple Grandin frequently comments that she too would not have become who she is without the help of antidepressant medications. So it is not sufficient to say that the suffering of those diagnosed with autism merely comes down to society not understanding or accommodating them. Likewise, it is narrow-minded to aim to cure people who do not need or want it and who are functioning independently—albeit often differently from social norms.

Beth Adler described her experience by saying,

The loneliest thing in the world is having nobody understand you. I'd tried for years to explain . . . I'd like to start out by telling my neighbors that I'm really not crazy. I know how it must have looked when I started screaming my lungs out just outside my house, but you really didn't have to call the cops. It was just a fly. An ordinary insect. The feel and sound of it buzzing in my ear so suddenly felt like an atomic bomb exploding. (2006, p. 164)

Not diagnosed until age 45, she also shared that

Just because I don't talk to you doesn't mean I don't want to. People mistakenly think I'm anti-social and want to be left alone (sometimes I do). But being ignored because I can't initiate a conversation only increases my isolation. (p. 166)

Earlier diagnosis and the availability of good services can improve life for those growing up with ASD today.

Transition Planning

The transition from school to adult life is a pivotal time in the lives of young people, especially those with ASD. Federal law in the form of the IDEA 1990 (PL 101-476) requires the development of a transition plan for students with special needs beginning at age 16. Experts generally recommend that this begin much sooner and no later than age 14. It should be an integral part of the IEP because the goal is to facilitate an individual's development from school to the world of work and adult living. Section 504 of the Vocational Rehabilitation Act of 1918 (PL 65-178) and the Americans with Disabilities Act of 1990 (PL 101-336) promote equal access to activities and services for individuals with ASD, but these are not entitlements or guarantees like those that people receive under IDEA.

For many families there is a rude awakening as the federal mandates for special education expire when a child graduates high school or reaches his or her

22nd birthday, whichever comes first. There is no mandate or automatic entitlement for postsecondary education or training. The purpose of planning is for parents, students who are able to participate, and the local school system to plan for the road to graduation and beyond. If a student is not able to participate fully, his or her interests and needs should still be taken into account. It is important to begin thinking as early as possible about the connections between what your child is good at and interested in and the implications for what your child can do in the future. Planning should include

- Vocational training

- On-the-job training, volunteering, or internships

- Employment goals

- Residential goals

- Community participation goals for social and leisure activities

- Personal care/life skills goals

- Postsecondary education (college) goals when appropriate

- Coordination with state and private agencies and service providers

Like earlier transitions, the transition to adulthood may evoke anxiety for parents and children. Your job as a parent is to be your child's primary advocate as the process begins and to transition as much of that role as possible to your child. Some school districts do a good job with transition planning, whereas others just seem to go through the motions. Your job as a parent is to make sure that the planning is meaningful, practical, and useful. Too often students graduate with nowhere to go and nothing to do. Like everywhere else along the road to adulthood, young people with active involved parents tend to get better services that lead to maximizing outcomes.

Self-Advocacy

The process of planning for your adult child's future provides an opportunity, to whatever extent possible, for him or her to be a part of the team creating a useful plan for life after graduation. If your child cannot participate in this process, then other steps should be made to make sure that his or her needs and preferences are taken into account. For example, photographs or videos can be used to assess the interest of nonverbal learners by observing individual reactions. Community and vocational options can be explored through experience, and again interest and reactions can be observed.

People on the autism spectrum range from those who are nonverbal to brilliant scientists and professors. Many individuals in the middle are verbal but have rigid speech or repetitive behaviors that pose special challenges. Others have sensory problems that may be so severe that they cannot function in a typical work environment without modifications to noise levels or lighting. In technical fields, many people with autism perform well in their job functions but have difficulties in their personal lives or with interpersonal skills at work. How to advocate and how much to disclose varies with the severity of the person's condition. There is no distinct dividing line, for example, between a nerd or a geek and someone with Asperger syndrome.

In *Ask and Tell,* Stephen Shore (2004) relates his experiences making the transition from being advocated for to advocating for himself. He explains the link between self-advocacy and disclosure. Self-awareness is critical; a person must first be aware of his or her needs before he or she can communicate these needs to others. Self-advocacy is necessary when a person's needs are not being met, and part of self-advocacy involves educating others about these needs. Discussing needs usually includes the reasons why accommodations might be necessary and necessitates disclosure about one's condition. For example, a college student with ASD may need extra time for a written assignment, or an employee may need to communicate primarily by e-mail or text due to challenges with social interaction. Doing this while in public school builds skills that are necessary for a lifetime. Empowering students to speak up as active participants in the IEP process requires collaboration by parents, teachers, therapists, and school administrators. This may take longer than doing it for the student, but the end result is worth it.

Employment and Self-Employment

For typical people, being out of work with no meaningful activities may lead to depression. The same is true for people living on the spectrum. Having a job that is satisfying and valued by others is a foundation for a meaningful life. Having a purpose and structure for the day provides a reason for living, especially for people with ASD. Yet finding and keeping a job is more difficult for people with autism than for typical people with the same qualifications because of the social challenges of autism. Beginning to explore possibilities for meaningful work while in high school can lead to a successful transition. Volunteering, internship programs, and summer jobs can provide on-the-job learning experiences for a broad range of individuals on the spectrum. Employment options are many and varied and range from least to most supportive.

Competitive employment implies a full-time or part-time job with wages at the going rate in the open labor market. These jobs do not include long-term support to help an individual learn or keep the job. The majority of jobs are considered competitive employment. For example, Shirley, who has autism, is paid $12 per hour, and her pay and medical, vacation, and retirement benefits are the same as those of all new employees at ABC Company. Shirley interacts with typical individuals to the same extent as a typical person performing similar work. Competitive employment is an optimal outcome but may take more time for individuals with ASD to achieve.

Supported employment is a mainstream job in a work setting that includes people who do not have special needs or disabilities. An agency provides ongoing support and training. The level of support may be reduced as the individual becomes able to do the job more independently. Supported employment can be funded through state departments of developmental disabilities or vocational rehabilitation agencies. Supported employment is intended for people with significant disabilities and provides a built-in safety net. It has been well documented that individuals with ASD can work given proper support and training and a job that matches their characteristics and strengths (Grandin & Duffy, 2008).

Secured or segregated employment for individuals with disabilities provides work in a self-contained unit. This type of work situation does not involve integration with workers who do not have disabilities. Typical tasks include collating, assembling, packaging, and so forth. Compensation is minimal, but behavioral supports are in place as necessary. Although these programs are generally available, critics contend that they foster dependence as opposed to independence in the community. This type of work occurs in a setting known as a sheltered workshop, and having visited several, I have seen people with severe disabilities enjoying their work with dignity and purpose.

Self-employment is another possibility for people on the spectrum. Griffin and Hammis (2003) described a person-centered approach that brings together people who know and understand the person with the disability to plan a business based on what interests and excites that individual. Like most businesses, seed money is required, along with support for planning the endeavor. Self-employment can provide an opportunity for long-term success, although it may take creative thinking on the part of service systems and families. Griffin and Hammis suggested that self-employment for people with disabilities be seen in the context of microenterprise, which is challenging mainstream economic theory and thought.

Muhammad Yunus is a Bangladeshi economist and founder of the Grameen Bank, which provides microcredit in the form of small loans to poor people. These people are thus enabled to establish credit and financial self-sufficiency despite having no collateral. In 2006 Yunus and Grameen received the Nobel Peace Prize. This recognition has helped to spawn thousands of similar enterprises in Bangladesh and around the world. This movement has provided a foundation of hope and possibilities that Griffin and Hammis (2003) have drawn on in their work. People with disabilities and people in developing countries face similar circumstances and challenges, such as poverty, limited choices, health care challenges, and prejudice.

In the United States alone, the unemployment rate among people with disabilities (including autism) is approximately 75%. Small business ownership or self-employment can be a sensible strategic option to counter poverty, isolation, and dependence. Although the community of families, professionals, and people on the spectrum continues to advocate for services for adults, they cannot afford to just wait. In the areas of employment and housing, people with the resources to do so are taking matters into their own hands. They are creating models that have the potential to be adopted on a broad scale. For example, I know of a small group of families of modest means who are pooling their resources to buy a proven business franchise for their young adults with ASD. Their plan includes having a typical sibling or friend with an interest in business to manage the enterprise.

Housing

Finding and settling on a place to live is a worry that consumes many families. Just like every other issue, there is a range of possibilities and options based on the strengths and challenges of the individual with autism. Some adults with autism might require housing that limits light or noise because of their sensory issues. Some might need shared housing to accommodate live-in aides or require easy access to public transportation or medical care. There is a range of options from least to most restrictive. Some adults with autism are able to live on their own in the community. They may purchase their own home or may have homes purchased for them by family members, whereas others will choose rental options.

Next on the continuum is supported living in an apartment or home that allows the individual with autism to choose agencies or change service providers while remaining in the same residence, if desired. A number of different scenarios are possible here, such as living alone with in-home supports or having one or more roommates. If the roommates also need supports, there may be different service providers.

The supervised community is a model in which adults receive less intensive support than in a family or group home setting. Services are provided by the agency that runs the community, which can be a number of supervised apartments or homes in urban or suburban communities or even a farmstead.

Group homes are typically run by an agency. The caregivers are employees of the service provider or agency. Choosing the service provider in the group home is not usually an option. Although some group homes focus specifically on adults with autism, most serve a variety of people with developmental and intellectual disabilities. Many states are now capping the number of residents a group home may serve, with three to four being the typical number. Providers are reimbursed for their services through state agencies, and an individual's Supplemental Security Income (SSI) payments are also used to support this service.

Cindy, Tariq, and I take a break while walking. Photograph by Zoë Naseef.

Living with parents or other family members is the most common living situation, with existing data indicating that more than 50% of adults with autism continue to live with parents or other family members. Support in this setting can come strictly from family or can be augmented with in-home services from state or federal programs. A person's choices in support services depend on how those services are funded.

Institutional settings are the most restrictive living arrangements, and fortunately the nationwide process of deinstitutionalization has resulted in fewer and fewer adults with autism receiving such placements. In addition, because states are closing many, if not all, of their facilities, adults who are living in institutional settings are making the transition back into the community through group homes. Adults with autism who also have mental illness may still receive short- or long-term treatment in psychiatric hospitals when necessary.

You can find a comprehensive discussion of housing issues as well as a Housing and Residential Supports Tool Kit at Autism Speaks (see www.autismspeaks.org/family-services/housing). The Pennsylvania Bureau of Autism Services has also produced an extensive report on housing options that is available at www.bastraining.tiu11.org.

Postsecondary Education

Going to college is an option for many young people with ASD growing up today. Because their diagnosis no longer guarantees services, the choice of whether to go to college and which one to attend needs careful planning. Those who are qualified to attend college need different levels of structure and support. Fortunately, support programs, both public and private, are springing up around the country. The individual's specific needs in terms of cognitive, social, and emotional development need to be carefully considered. The autobiographies of adults with ASD and books such as *Developing College Skills in Students with Autism and Asperger's Syndrome* by Sarita Freedman can be extremely helpful in this process.

It is not unusual for some students to be reluctant to inform a college of their diagnosis. They are tired of being considered different from others. They feel good about getting this far, and they may be unwilling to ask for accommodations. So the issues of self-advocacy and disclosure must be treated with sensitivity. Despite the anxiety that it may cause for their parents, some young adults may need to exercise their autonomy and find out on their own what kind of help they need through trial and error. In this new phase of development, it is important for parents to be available for support as opposed to imposing their will on their adolescent child. Some individuals may not need as much help as their parents and teachers assume; some may need more.

The transition to college can be daunting even for typical students with exceptional academic skills. It is even more complex for those with ASD. Without the supports and structure they have been accustomed to through high school, the stress of college life may lead to anxiety or depression. Newfound freedoms and social difficulties fitting in can intensify problems and even lead to withdrawal from college and "failure to launch" successfully. Even typical students can run into unexpected problems and need to take a leave of absence or transfer, so parental worries are normal. Although there are no data on graduation rates for college students with ASD, Koegel and LaZebnik (2009) reported that the percentage of young people with disabilities who flunk out is about the same as the percentage of typical students who flunk out.

There are distinct advantages for students with ASD to live at home, at least in the beginning of their college careers, so that parents can provide support in terms of the self-care and organizational skills required to be successful. Just as in earlier phases of development, what often works best is taking small steps based on the individual's unique profile. Vocational schools, community colleges, technical institutes, state colleges, or small liberal arts colleges are all options worth considering. Visiting schools and observing classes is the best way to consider and narrow down the options. Getting information and looking at possibilities tends to ease anxiety.

Shore and Rastelli (2006) suggested considering the benefits of attending a community college in order to ease the transition. Shore has observed a greater number of people with learning differences at the community college level, and he suggested that given this diversity people with autism are more likely to be accepted at a community college. There is also less academic pressure and expense, which makes it possible to explore areas of interest. Many typical students as well as those with learning differences use the community college experience in order to make the transition to a 4-year college. Shore and Rastelli also suggested taking fewer classes or even just one class per semester to avoid crashing and burning. Those planning to live on campus may find a single dorm room to be beneficial as an accommodation. Shore also suggested that if higher education seems intimidating, consider postponing postsecondary education to a later time. Individual differences need to be assessed; the typical trajectory for adolescence may need to be postponed to accommodate your child's unique learning curve.

Parents on the Spectrum

Previously undiagnosed adults often find out that they are on the spectrum when they have a child diagnosed with autism. I see this frequently in my psychology practice in Philadelphia. It usually occurs first through an informal process that I refer to as *self- or spousal diagnosis.* Given the genetic roots of the autism spectrum, it makes sense that one or both parents may have some of the symptoms or even enough characteristics to warrant a formal diagnosis. Parents who embrace and accept their own issues, whether or not they are formally diagnosed, become exemplary role models and can give excellent guidance to their children.

Liane Holliday-Willey's autobiography *Pretending to Be Normal* resonates strongly with people who slipped under the radar and were diagnosed in adulthood. She herself was diagnosed after one of her daughters was. She is able to tell the story of growing up and living with Asperger syndrome as well as give a mother's account of struggling with her child's ASD. As she humbly explains, "My children provide me with just about as much role modeling as I provide them" (Holliday-Willey, 1999, p. 94). Just like a typical parent, her children have forced her to grow both literally and figuratively, but with the added twist of Asperger syndrome. Understanding the autism spectrum has helped her not to be so hard or critical on herself. By talking to other parents she has discovered that "it is possible to adore our children without adoring everything that goes hand-in-hand with childhood" (p. 95).

Elizabeth Lipp first connected autism to herself after her son's diagnosis when she heard Temple Grandin speak at a conference. She also connected traits to her father and maternal grandmother. As she put it, "The pieces of the puzzle that is my son started to fall into place" (Lipp, 2006, p. 62). Her biggest problem was "imposing my own Aspie baggage on my son" (p. 62). She recounted being furious and outraged when another little boy called her son "queer" at the playground. Her son just shrugged it off and went back to what he was doing. As a result of this incident, Elizabeth realized that she could not protect her son from everything and that his reactions were not hers. Unless there is danger, she has learned to just watch and not interfere so that he can figure out for himself how the world and other people work.

Todd Schmidt, another contributor to *Voices from the Spectrum,* is another parent who was diagnosed after his son. He described himself growing up as an underachiever who was oversensitive and gullible. He was bullied, and he considered himself a failure. Somehow he managed to fall in love, get married, and become a father. After the birth, however, he had anxiety attacks because he could not control the baby. More than ever, he was convinced that something was wrong with him. He found the answer through his son Jordan.

Jordan's tantrums, difficulty with transitions, scripted language, and social difficulties eventually resulted in a diagnosis on the spectrum. While learning about autism in order to help his son, Todd came across information about Asperger syndrome and realized,

> This was who I was! There is a reason for this! There are other people like this! This is nothing I did, this is not my fault, I am not lazy, or crazy, or wrong—this is the way I came! (Schmidt, 2006, p. 197)

Todd's diagnosis helped him become a better father and a better partner to his wife Debbie. All three of the Schmidts are well known in their community as spokespeople and ambassadors for autism.

Loving Someone with Autism

Many men and women with ASD have the potential to develop intimate relationships and become long-term partners. Parents of course hope that this will be the case for their child with ASD. As the definition of autism has expanded, previously undiagnosed individuals already in relationships are seeking out counseling for relationship problems just as typical couples are apt to do. Their issues are both similar to and different from the issues of average couples.

Attwood (2007) observed from his extensive experience that men with ASD tend to seek a partner from the other end of the social continuum who can help them compensate for their difficulties in everyday life. Women, in contrast, tend to seek a partner who is similar to them, who does not have a busy social life, and who may not desire frequent physical intimacy. When the expectations are compatible, the relationship, whether different sex or same sex, can flourish. In the beginning of the relationship, the partner with autism may be extremely attentive while experiencing the romantic relationship as a new special interest. Another possibility is that sometimes two people on the spectrum, whether diagnosed or not, wind up together because they share similar interests and values. Parents can help their adolescent and adult children by teaching social skills and helping them to find other people who share their special interests. But finding a personal relationship must ultimately be left to the individual, who will pair up or not depending on his or her own need, desire, and abilities.

Harmon (2011) reported on the romantic relationship between Jack Robison and Kirsten Lindsmith. From childhood, Jack thought of himself as "not like other humans" (Harmon, 2011, p. 1). He always told Kirsten what he meant even if it was not what she wanted to hear. Although Kirsten did not know it when they met, she too would be subsequently diagnosed with autism. Their physical relationship had to be negotiated taking their sensory differences into account. For example, Kirsten liked only deep pressure, whereas Jack pulled away from it, did not like kissing, and preferred a light touch. That their story appeared on the front page of the *New York Times* in 2011 is a reflection of the increase in awareness about autism. Like other young adults with autism that I know, Jack and Kirsten longed for someone to love them back. It is a myth that people with autism shun human contact. On the contrary, many crave it, but in a different way.

People with ASD tend to be very loyal and honest, and this can make them attractive to others, but over time their partners may wind up feeling lonely and rejected when a special interest seems more important than the relationship. You can help your child learn about this and other hidden curriculum issues to help improve his or her chances of meeting and relating intimately to someone. Typical partners may experience embarrassment in social situations, such as when their partners with ASD go on and on about a topic when others are not interested. The partner with ASD is often very content being alone for long periods of time. Early on in the relationship the typical partner may be optimistic that his or her partner will gradually change and develop and become more social. Communication difficulties are one of the defining characteristics of ASD, so couples in which one partner is on the spectrum are especially challenged in this aspect of sharing life together. Conversation tends to mostly involve exchanging information rather than sharing experiences and opinions.

Having an intimate long-term relationship requires communicating one's emotional life more than other more casual relationships. In *Alone Together: Making an Asperger Marriage Work,* Katrin Bentley shares the struggle of her and her husband to save their marriage. They learned to accept each other's different approaches and found ways to get past misunderstandings. As they demonstrate,

Tariq still likes to give a high five. Photograph by Zoë Naseef.

there is hope for improvement. This book and others like it by people in relationships with partners on the spectrum, as well as by professionals, such as *Loving Someone with Asperger's Syndrome* by Cindy Ariel, offer couples hope and strategies for making progress in their relationships.

Children growing up today are being diagnosed with ASD earlier than those whose lives form the basis of the professional literature about adults with autism. So there is hope that more and more people with ASD will be able to learn enough social skills to live in intimate partnerships. That being said, some people on the spectrum choose to stay single or celibate for a variety of reasons. Temple Grandin, for example, finds meaning in her work and is happy with her lifestyle. In my opinion, remaining single should be viewed as a valid lifestyle choice. It is a mistake to pressure any adolescent or young adult into looking for a romantic relationship. Some who are not interested may turn out to be late bloomers and surprise their families at a later point. Others can find great life satisfaction in other ways, such as through a meaningful career or special interest.

Facing the Future and Financial Planning

Almost from the moment of the diagnosis, parents worry about what will happen to their child after they die. As they themselves age along with their child, this worry becomes more troubling. Whereas a typical child will be a support as parents age and need help, an adult child with a disability may be left with no one to serve as an advocate. If you believe your child will need assistance, whether financially or practically, after you are gone, it is important that you make a transition plan for his or her future. If you are anything like me, you may have avoided this topic because it is difficult to face your own mortality. However, facing these issues can give you peace of mind.

You can start by gathering information from disability organizations, books, and web sites. The more you understand, the better you can utilize an attorney to help address your child's special needs. Autism Speaks has a comprehensive guide available for download (see www.autismspeaks.org/family-services/tool-kits/

transition-tool-kit/legal-matters). *Managing a Special Needs Trust: A Guide for Trustees* (Jackins, Blank, Shulman, & Onello, 2010) is highly recommended and includes comprehensive information. The authors, who are attorneys, explain in clear and easy-to-understand language how to meet the financial needs of a person with a disability and comply with the rules of government benefit programs. The topics covered include public benefit programs such as SSI, Social Security Disability Insurance, Medicare, and Medicaid; taxes and special needs trusts; payment of recreation, transportation, and medical costs; housing subsidies; and trustee duties.

Having a plan in place for an adult child on the spectrum is also important for the peace of mind of typical siblings. Planning for a child's future after the parents' death is the last topic to consider in a life-span view of raising a child with autism while taking care of the needs of everyone in the family. In the concluding chapter, I discuss how to find peace and happiness along the way.

14

Reflections on Peace of Mind and Happiness

Although the world is full of suffering, it is also full of overcoming it.

HELEN KELLER, *THE WORLD I LIVE IN AND OPTIMISM: A COLLECTION OF ESSAYS*

THERE ARE STILL SOME TIMES WHEN TEARS COME TO MY EYES WHEN I WONDER AND LONG FOR WHAT MIGHT HAVE BEEN. One of those times was just after the 2008 presidential election. I was speaking to a support group of parents of residential students at Devereux's Kanner Center. Without warning, my eyes watered and words stuck in my throat as I showed them a PowerPoint slide (see "Learning to Cope" PowerPoint screenshot with the picture of a puzzle piece and Tariq as a child).

I took a few slow breaths and checked in with myself. My tears spoke to me. A young man of mixed race, Tariq has a complexion much like that of Barack Obama. In that moment, I realized that if my son had been typical, I would have been talking with him that week about this historic moment and how much our country has changed since the day he was born. For at that time, it had seemed inconceivable that there would be an African American president in our lifetime.

After gaining this clarity of thought and emotion, I shared my reflections with this diverse group of mothers and fathers. It was a poignant moment for all of us. Intense feelings come and go like the weather. People have no control over this, but just as after a storm, the sky clears and the sun does come out again. In this book I have tried to put together how I understand autism throughout the life cycle and what parents can and cannot do about it while taking care of the family. I believe that with support and services fulfillment of everyone's needs is within

Learning to Cope: Is your child a puzzle to be solved or a child to be embraced and loved as she is?

This dichotomy is unavoidable. It often obsesses the family. The answer is that it is both– and that the balance is found through struggle and reflection.

our power. This is the balance that I hope for everyone who loves and cares for people with autism—parents, family members, and professionals alike.

Although Tariq and I could not have a conversation about this moment in history, there were things I could do. I have continued to share experiences such as this with my family and others to teach that people do not have to turn away from their pain in order to have a full life. I have included this very emotional experience here in order to illustrate how our deepest experiences are always a part of people's inner lives.

Psychologist Daniel Gilbert (2006) pointed out that it is extremely difficult for people to consider experiences they have not had. For example, the average person tends to overestimate the happiness of people who live in warm, sunny California and underestimate the happiness of people who live and cope with chronic illnesses or disabilities. Moreover, sighted people tend to overlook the many things that people without sight can do and instead focus on what they cannot do. Thus, people who are sighted often overlook how satisfied a person without sight might actually be and how much happiness can be experienced without sight.

Likewise, able-bodied people tend to focus on what they could not do if they were paralyzed in an accident—as Dan Gottlieb was more than 30 years ago (see Chapter 11)—even though he and others with spinal cord injuries lead happy, fulfilling lives. This phenomenon to focus on the negative is all too common and keeps people from stumbling on happiness in the moments of their daily lives. This is not to imply that quadriplegia or autism is easy, but a hard life can still be a good one. Dan has suffered through bouts of depression and ongoing medical issues which he has shared, but he has thrived as a psychologist, radio talk show host, newspaper columnist, and author of several books. People from all walks of life in every corner of the globe struggle heroically and are amazingly resilient.

Parents of children with autism make monumental efforts to raise their children to be all they can be but also report that their lives are enhanced in the process and that they become better people. Gilbert (2006) pointed out that negative events affect people but generally not for as long or as intensely as they might predict. Adults and children with autism often rate their lives as fulfilling, whereas many others who are healthy or who have typical children might think their fate to be one of deep and unending depression. I want to wrap up this book with my thoughts about how autism can stimulate, perplex, and guide you toward a life that is happier—perhaps more than you imagined it could be.

Whether you are a birth or an adoptive parent, holding and touching your infant for the first time can be one of life's most powerful experiences. Feeling the infant's soft skin and tiny body nestled against you is an unforgettable experience that lives inside you. From those early days parents discover what pleases and displeases the infant. Parents learn to pay attention to the infant's needs to sleep, to eat, or to be changed. The infant teaches the parents to be in the moment in order to notice and respond to these cues. This is a skill that has to be learned and relearned throughout the stages of parenthood, as things rarely go as imagined. As Galinsky (1987) noted about parenting in general, "Our dreams are in a constant tug-of-war with realities" (p. 317).

The process of sorting out the struggle between dreams and reality is also at war with Western culture, which states that with hard work people can achieve anything. But how do people handle things such as autism that they cannot, or even in some cases should not, fix or cure? When Tariq was diagnosed with autism, I believed that with hard work he would talk again and that all my dreams for him would come true. Good services and hard work do help tremendously, but classic autism can be relentless. I worked so hard to change him, but I reiterate that he has changed me. I can see now that this is the journey of parenthood.

Tariq has taught me that hard work is not everything. That grief comes and goes. That anxiety and sadness come and go. That it takes time to heal a broken heart. That happiness and meaning can abound with acceptance. That accepting does not mean giving up but rather learning to live mindfully in the present. When people are honest with themselves and their loved ones, there is great joy in being alive and together.

Since the mid-1970s mindfulness meditation has increasingly become a part of the Western cultural landscape. Meditation is secular in nature, and although it originated in an Eastern culture, it is congruent with all major faith traditions. There is an art in facing the difficulties of life and solving as many problems as possible while finding some measure of inner peace. As Kabat-Zinn (2005) pointed out, people accept that no one controls the weather. He used the metaphor of sailing to point out that good sailors will avoid storms, if possible. But if the storm cannot be avoided, good sailors batten down the hatches and ride things out, controlling what is controllable and letting go of what is not.

From the perspective of mindfulness, acceptance means seeing things as they actually are. For example, if you are having trouble going to sleep, you accept your difficulty. If you are overweight, you accept this as a description of your body in the present moment. Acceptance requires a willingness to see things as they actually are. This frame of mind then makes it more likely that you will be able to figure out what can be done and what needs to be let go of. You may have to go through intense emotions, such as denial, anger, shame, or depression, to come to terms with what really is in your life.

Brach (2003) described this willingness of people to experience themselves and their lives as "radical acceptance" and a moment of genuine freedom. The root of suffering in life is longing for things to be different from the way they really are. Seeing this clearly frees people to begin seeing their choices for what is possible. Radical acceptance is a quality of awareness when physical or emotional pain arises. As opposed to trying to push it away, people may recognize fear, for example, and notice that their thoughts are racing, that their breathing is speeding up, and that they want to run away. Accepting does not mean liking this fear but rather being kind and loving to oneself in the moment-to-moment experience. Although this way of thinking comes from Buddhist thought, psychologist Carl Rogers had a similar insight when he stated, "The curious paradox is that when I accept myself just as I am, then I can change" (1961, p. 17).

This does not mean that people can get rid of anxiety any more than they can get rid of autism. What it does mean is that they can have these feelings and experiences and go on living a life full of meaning and purpose. As Wilson and Dufrene (2010) noted, it is precisely the willingness to learn how to sit with the ambiguity of what may or may not happen that actually begins to liberate people from anxiety. Chasing answers to questions that may not be answerable is like being stuck in quicksand and actually heightens anxiety. From my point of view, living with autism includes many unanswerable questions. In this sense there is no exit from autism.

If this makes sense to you, it can be a pivotal realization. As Gilbert (2006) explained, people are much more likely to find a positive view of things that they see as unmovable than things they think they can change. So when people cannot change their experience they are apt to look for ways to change their view of or relationship to that experience. In Gilbert's words, "We just can't make the best of a fate until it's inescapably, inevitably, and irrevocably ours" (p. 183).

You may be wondering how this could possibly apply to how unmanageable your life seems at times. I do not mean to imply that life is without troubles or to encourage blind optimism. Loving and caring for a child or adult with autism compounds the stressors of daily living with a huge set of potentially overwhelming problems, so let's look at how these concepts derived from mindfulness might apply to your family life. I assume your deeply held values include being a loving and caring parent to your children, being a faithful and loving partner, and being a kind and compassionate person in the world you inhabit with all living things.

Loving the person you are with starts with paying attention. When I ask parents what they are learning from their children with autism, they frequently report that they are learning patience to be with a child who is so different than they imagined. Because of their different way of being, children with autism teach parents to notice moments of connection, and in this way parents build the relationship they can have. This is the essence of mindful parenting—focusing on what happens in the moment as it unfolds. How do you do this in the midst of the challenges that autism presents? The steps are simple:

- Take a mindful breath or two.

- Notice your thoughts, feelings, and sensations without judging or criticizing. What are you telling yourself about what is happening?

- Observe what is going on with your child and between you and your child. What is right or wrong with what is happening?

- Pause and just be there in the present moment without acting.

- Accept your experience as either good, bad, or in between.

- If there is a problem, consider it in terms of specific behaviors. Is there an action to take or not to take? Try to be aware of any judgmental language you may be using with yourself, such as wanting your child to be more "respectful" or behave more "appropriately."

- Continue in this way relating to what is happening as each moment unfolds while choosing whether and how to act.

Kaplan (2010) applied these concepts to parenting by suggesting that parents observe what draws a child's attention. It is important to take a mindful breath and practice acceptance whenever a child is doing something you do not want him or her to do. (This principle actually applies to anyone in your life.) Chances are you are getting stressed or angry because you may want your child to stop self-stimulating, for example, and be more "normal." Dreams conflict with reality over and over again. Tuning in to this moment with an open mind and heart and remembering that a child with autism is still a child, think about what kind of parent you want to be. Chances are your values are to be kind and loving as opposed to critical and judgmental. If you can keep these values in mind, you have a much better chance of guiding your child to the best of your ability.

If you are finding that you have to go through this over and over again, it is just because you are human. It is like *Groundhog Day* for everyone, not just because you are dealing with autism. As Sharon Salzberg (2011) teaches in *Real Happiness,* not paying attention keeps people in an endless struggle for things to be different from how they really are. As opposed to struggling or straining, she suggests engaging in relaxed perseverance as the path to tranquility and balance. People cannot stop the activity going on constantly in their minds—the thoughts, feelings, sensations, and memories. But they can pause, notice, and decide how to respond. When they practice this way of relating as parents, people can notice not just the bitter problems but the sweet moments of connection with their loved one with autism.

Being mindful does not mean eliminating unpleasant or painful thoughts and feelings but rather being aware of what you are thinking and feeling. Too much focusing on what is wrong and too much trying to change someone with ASD blocks you from experiencing happiness in your life. You need to make a conscious effort to include the positive as a focus of attention. This does not mean denying real problems or lying to yourself about the pain you may be experiencing. It just means paying attention to the moments you might otherwise overlook or ignore, such as your child running to you when you get home even though the house may be a mess. So make a practice of paying attention to the experiences that bring pleasure in life as a whole and as a parent.

If you are not already doing this, here is a simple way to begin. Spend time with your son or daughter without trying to make anything different. If possible, find something that is mutually enjoyable and join together in this activity regularly. As preferences change, notice this and find new ways to

connect through mutually pleasurable activities. Whether I meet
parents once in a large group at a
workshop or conference or regularly in my office, I promote this
concept. It is extremely powerful
and potentially life altering.

When parents are present
with the bitter and the sweet, hope
does live in their relationships. I
did not invent or discover this,
but I have learned it in large part
because I have a son with autism. I
have learned to be more comfortable with my thoughts and feelings
about my life as it really is, not as I
wish it would be.

Thoughts and feelings about
autism and the daily challenges it
presents come and go, but autism
remains as an international public
health issue. Autism affects people

We still enjoy long walks together. Photograph by Zoë Naseef.

equally, approximately 1 in 100 around the globe across racial and class divi-
sions. There is equal opportunity to be challenged but an uneven distribution
of services. It is not a level playing field once a child is diagnosed. Poverty and
racism compound the struggle. We have a moral imperative as a society to level
that playing field by bringing support and services to all.

The infant I held for the first time did not grow to be the man I imagined.
However, I have come to know that Tariq's life does make a difference in the
world. This book is the product so far of how his autism speaks through me.
I am thankful to Tariq for being a good son, and I thank you for reading this and
listening to my voice.

References

Adler, B. (2006). No! You don't understand. In C. Ariel & R. Naseef (Eds.), *Voices from the spectrum: Parents, grandparents, siblings, people with autism, and professionals share their wisdom* (pp. 162–165). London, England: Jessica Kingsley Publishers.

Alberti, R., & Emmons, M. (1982). *Your perfect right.* San Luis Obispo, CA: Impact.

American Academy of Pediatrics. (2009). *When is the right time to start toilet training?* Retrieved from http://www2.aap.org/publiced/BR_ToiletTrain.htm

American Psychiatric Association. (2000). *Diagnostic and statistical manual of mental disorders* (4th ed., text rev.). Washington, DC: Author.

American Psychiatric Association. (In press). *Diagnostic and statistical manual of mental disorders* (5th ed.). Washington, D.C.: Author.

Americans with Disabilities Act of 1990, PL 101-336, 42 U.S.C. §§ 12101 *et seq.*

Asperger, H. (1991). Autistic psychopathy in childhood. In U. Frith (Ed.), *Autism and Asperger syndrome* (pp. 37–92). New York, NY: Cambridge University Press.

Attwood, S. (2008). *Making sense of sex: A forthright guide to puberty, sex and relationships for people with Asperger's syndrome.* London, England: Jessica Kingsley Publishers.

Attwood, T. (2007). *The complete guide to Asperger's syndrome.* London, England: Jessica Kingsley Publishers.

Attwood, T., Grandin, T., Bolick, T., Faherty, C., Iland, L., Myers, J. . . . Wrobel, M. (2006). *Asperger's and girls.* Arlington, TX: Future Horizons.

Baio, J. (2012). Prevalence of autism spectrum disorders: Autism and developmental disabilities monitoring network, 14 Sites, United States, 2008. *Surveillance Summaries. 61,* 3, 1–19. Retrieved August 2012 from http://www.cdc.gov/mmwr/preview/mmwr html/ss6103a1.htm?s_cid=ss6103a1_w

Baker, J. (2008). *No more meltdowns: Positive strategies for managing and preventing out-of-control behavior.* Arlington, TX: Future Horizons.

Baker, J.E. (2003). *Social skills training: For children and adolescents with Asperger syndrome and social-communication problems.* Shawnee Mission, KS: Autism Asperger Publishing Company.

Baker, J.K., Seltzer, M.M., & Greenberg, J.S. (2011). Longitudinal effects of adaptability on behavior problems and maternal depression in families of adolescents with autism. *Journal of Family Psychology, 25,* 601–609. doi:10.1037/a0024409

Baker, J.K., Smith, L.E., Greenberg, J.S., Seltzer, M.M., & Taylor, J.L. (2011). Change in maternal criticism and behavior problems in adolescents and adults with autism across a 7-year period. *Journal of Abnormal Psychology, 120,* 465–475. doi:10.1037/a0021900

Bank, S.P., & Kahn, M. (1982). *The sibling bond.* New York, NY: Basic Books.

Barker, E.T., Hartley, S.L., Seltzer, M.M., Floyd, F.J., Greenberg, J.S., & Orsmond, G.I. (2010). Trajectories of emotional well-being in mothers of adolescents and adults with autism. *Developmental Psychology, 47,* 551–561. PubMed #211717753

Batshaw, M.L., Pellegrino, L., & Roizen, N.J. (Eds.). (2007). *Children with disabilities* (6th ed.). Baltimore, MD: Paul H. Brookes Publishing Co.

Bettelheim, B. (1967). *The empty fortress: Infantile autism and the birth of the self.* New York, NY: Free Press.

Billstedt, E., Gillberg, C.I., & Gillberg, C. (2005). Autism after adolescence: Population-based 13- to 22-year follow-up study of 120 individuals with autism diagnosed in childhood. *Journal of Autism and Developmental Disorders, 35,* 351–360.

Bittner, K. (2006). An unexpected blessing. In C. Ariel & R. Naseef (Eds.), *Voices from the spectrum: Parents, grandparents, siblings, people with autism, and professionals share their wisdom* (pp. 141–144). London, England: Jessica Kingsley Publishers.

Blackledge, J.T., & Hayes, S.C. (2006). Using acceptance and commitment training in the support of parents of children diagnosed with autism. *Child & Family Behavior Therapy, 28*(1), 1–18.

Brach, T. (2003). *Radical acceptance: Embracing your life with the heart of the Buddha.* New York, NY: Bantam.

Brazelton, T.B. (1992). *Touchpoints: Your child's emotional and behavioral development.* Reading, MA: Addison Wesley.

Brazelton, T.B., & Cramer, B.G. (1990). *The earliest relationship: Parents, infants, and the drama of early attachment.* New York, NY: Addison Wesley.

Bristol, M.M., & Schopler, E. (1984). A developmental perspective on stress and coping in families of autistic children. In J. Blacher (Ed.), *Severely handicapped young children and their families* (pp. 91–141). New York, NY: Academic Press.

Brugha, T., McManus, S., Meltzer, H., Smith, J., Scott, F.J., Purdon, S., Harris, J., & Bankart, J. (2007). *Autism spectrum disorders in adults living in households throughout England: Report from the Adult Psychiatric Morbidity Survey 2007.* London, England: National Centre for Social Research.

Buie, T., Campbell, D.B., Fuchs, G.J., III, Furuta, G.T., Levy, J., Vandewater, J., . . . Winter, H. (2010). Evaluation, diagnosis, and treatment of gastrointestinal disorders in individuals with ASDs: A consensus report. *Pediatrics, 125*(Suppl. 1), S1–S18.

Carter, E.W. (2007). *Including people with disabilities in faith communities: A guide for service providers, families, and congregations.* Baltimore, MD: Paul H. Brookes Publishing Co.

Cassel, T.D., Messinger, D.S., Ibanez, L.V., Haltigan, J.D., Acosta, S.I., & Buchman, A.C. (2006). Early social and emotional communication in the infant siblings of children with autism spectrum disorders: An examination of the broad phenotype. *Journal of Autism and Developmental Disorders, 37,* 122–132. doi:10.1007/s10803-006-0337-1

Chakrabarti, S., & Fombonne, E. (2001). Pervasive developmental disorders in preschool children. *JAMA, 285*(24), 3093–3099.

Cheslack-Postava, K., Kayuet, L., & Bearman, P. (2011). Closely spaced pregnancies are associated with increased odds of autism in California sibling births. *Pediatrics, 127,* 246–253.

Coffin, C.M. (1994). *The complete poetry and selected prose of John Donne.* New York, NY: Random House.

Coplan, J. (2010). *Making sense of autistic spectrum disorders: Create the brightest future possible for your child with the best treatment options.* New York, NY: Bantam.

Cousins, N. (1989). *Head first: The biology of hope.* New York, NY: Dutton.

Cowley, G. (2003). The biggest prize of all: For men, the challenge is to take better care of themselves. Now science is showing them how. A NEWSWEEK special report. Newsweek. Harmon Newsweek LLC. 2003. *HighBeam Research.* 10 Jul. 2012. Retrieved from http://www.highbeam.com/doc/1G1-103227980.html.3w

Craik, D.M.M. (1859). *A life for a life.* London, England: Hurst and Blackett.

Cutler, B.C., & Pratt, S. (2010). *You, your child, and "special" education: A guide to dealing with the system* (Rev. ed.). Baltimore, MD: Paul H. Brookes Publishing Co.

Dickens, C. (2011). *David Copperfield.* New York, NY: Simon and Brown.

Dingfelder, S. (2011). Must babies always breed marital discontent? *Monitor on Psychology, 42*(9), 51–52.

Dubie, M. (2005). Puberty. *The Reporter, 10*(3), 3–4, 20.

Dubie, M. (2006). The "M" word. *The Reporter, 11*(1), 12–14.

Durand, V.M. (1998). *Sleep better! A guide to improving sleep for children with special needs.* Baltimore, MD: Paul H. Brookes Publishing Co.

Durand, V.M. (2011). *Optimistic parenting: Hope and help for you and your challenging child.* Baltimore, MD: Paul H. Brookes Publishing Co.

Education for All Handicapped Children Act of 1975, PL 94-142, 20 U.S.C. §§ 1400 *et seq.*

Education of the Handicapped Act Amendments of 1986, PL 99-457, 20 U.S.C. §§ 1400 *et seq.*

Eifert, G.H., McKay, M., & Forsyth, J.P. (2006). *ACT on life not on anger: The new acceptance and commitment therapy guide to problem anger.* Oakland, CA: New Harbinger Publications.

Emond, A., Emmett, P., Steer, C., & Golding, J. (2010). Feeding symptoms, dietary patterns, and growth in young children with autism spectrum disorders. *Pediatrics, 126,* e337. Originally published online July 19, 2010.

Ernsperger, L., & Stegen-Hanson, T. (2004). *Just take a bite: Easy, effective answers to food aversions and eating challenges!* Arlington, TX: Future Horizons.

Faber, A., & Mazlish, E. (1987). *Siblings without rivalry: How to help your children live together.* New York, NY: W.W. Norton.

Featherstone, H. (1980). *A difference in the family: Life with a disabled child.* New York, NY: Basic Books.

Fein, D. (2011, October). *Optimal outcomes in children with a history of ASD.* Presentation at the Children's Hospital of Philadelphia, PA.

Fialka, J., Feldman, A.K., & Mikus, K.C. (2012). *Parents and professionals partnering for children with disabilities: A dance that matters.* Thousand Oaks, CA: Corwin.

Flaschen, K. (2006). Living life. In C. Ariel & R. Naseef (Eds.), *Voices from the spectrum: Parents, grandparents, siblings, people with autism, and professionals share their wisdom* (pp. 149–152). London, England: Jessica Kingsley Publishers.

Flippin, M., & Crais, E.R. (2011). The need for more effective father involvement in early autism intervention: A systematic review and recommendations. *Journal of Early Intervention, 33,* 24–50.

Folstein, S., & Rutter, M. (1977). Infantile autism: A genetic study of 21 twin pairs. *Journal of Child Psychology and Psychiatry, 18*(4), 297–321.

Frankel, F., & Wood, J.J. (2011). *Social skills success for students with autism/Asperger's: How to teach conversation skills, prevent meltdowns, and help kids fit in.* San Francisco, CA: Jossey-Bass.

Freedman, B., Kalb, L., Zablotsky, B., & Stuart, E. (2011). Relationship status among parents of children with autism spectrum disorders. *Journal of Autism and Developmental Disorders, 42,* 539–548.

Freedman, S. (2010). *Developing college skills in students with autism and Asperger's syndrome.* London, England: Jessica Kingsley Publishers.

Galinsky, E. (1987). *The six stages of parenthood.* New York, NY: Addison Wesley.

Gallagher, P.A., Powell, T.H., & Rhodes, C.A. (2006). *Brothers and sisters: A special part of exceptional families* (3rd ed.). Baltimore, MD: Paul H. Brookes Publishing Co.

Gaul, G.M. (1993). *Giant steps: The story of one boy's struggle to walk.* New York, NY: St. Martin's Press.

Gilbert, D. (2006). *Stumbling on happiness.* New York, NY: Alfred A. Knopf.

Gillberg, C., Steffenberg, S., & Schaumann, H. (1991). Is autism more common now than 10 years ago? *The British Journal of Psychiatry, 158,* 403–409.

Gilligan, C. (1982). *In a different voice: Psychological theory and women's development.* Cambridge, MA: Harvard University Press.

Gilpin, R.W. (1993). *Laughing and loving with autism—A collection of "real life" warm and humorous stories.* Arlington, TX: Future Horizons.

Girardi, D. (2007). Til autism do we part: After all the doctors and therapy appointments, parents struggle to keep their marriage intact. *Spectrum Magazine.* Retrieved from http://www.davegerardi.com/works/divorceautism.php

Glasburg, B.A. (2006). *Functional behavior assessment for people with autism: Making sense of seemingly senseless behavior.* Bethesda, MD: Woodbine House.

Goldberg, W., Jarvis, K., Osann, K., Laulhere, T., Straub, C., Thomas, E. . . . Spence, M.A. (2005). Brief report: Early social communication behaviors in the younger siblings of children with autism. *Journal of Autism and Developmental Disabilities, 35,* 657–664.

Goleman, D. (1995). *Emotional intelligence: Why it can matter more than IQ.* New York, NY: Bantam.

Gottman, J.M. (1999). *The seven principles for making marriage work.* New York, NY: Random House.

Gottman, J.M., & Gottman, J.S. (2008). *And baby bakes three: The six-step plan for preserving marital intimacy and rekindling romance after baby arrives.* New York, NY: Three Rivers Press.

Gould, K., & Pratt, C. (2008, May/June). Schoolwide discipline and individual supports for students with autism spectrum disorder. *Principal,* 38–41.

Grandin, T. (2008). *The way I see it: A personal look at autism and Asperger's.* Arlington, TX: Future Horizons.

Grandin, T., & Duffy, K. (2008). *Developing talents: Careers for individuals with Asperger's syndrome and high functioning autism.* Arlington, TX: New Horizons.

Gray, C. (2000). *The new Social Story book: Illustrated edition.* Arlington, TX: Future Horizons.

Gray, C.A. (2010). *The new Social Story book, revised and expanded 10th anniversary edition: Over 150 Social Stories that teach everyday social skills to children with autism or Asperger's syndrome, and their peers.* Arlington, TX: New Horizons.

Greenberg, J.S., Seltzer, M.M., Hong, J., & Orsmond, G.I. (2006). Bidirectional effects of expressed emotion and behavior problems and symptoms in adolescents and adults with autism. *American Journal of Mental Retardation, 111,* 229–249.

Greene, R.W. (2010). *The explosive child: A new approach for understanding and parenting easily frustrated, chronically inflexible children.* New York, NY: Harper.

Greenfeld, J. (1970). *A child called Noah.* New York, NY: Washington Square.

Greenfeld, K. (2009). *Boy alone: A brother's memoir.* Hammersmith, England: HarperCollins.

Greenspan, S.I., & Wieder, S. (2006). *Engaging autism: Using the Floortime approach to help children relate, communicate, and think.* Cambridge, MA: Perseus Books Group.

Griffin, C., & Hammis, D. (2003). *Making self-employment work for people with disabilities.* Baltimore, MD: Paul H. Brookes Publishing Co.

Groopman, J. (2005). *The anatomy of hope: How people prevail in the face of illness.* New York, NY: Random House.

Grossman, F.K. (1972). *Brothers and sisters of retarded children.* Syracuse, NY: Syracuse University Press.

Gupta, V.B. (2007). Comparison of parenting stress in different developmental disabilities. *Journal of Developmental and Physical Disabilities, 19,* 417–425.

Hall, K. (2001). *Asperger's syndrome, the universe and everything: Kenneth's book.* London, England: Jessica Kingsley Publishers.

Harmon, A. (2011, December 26). Navigating love and autism. *The New York Times,* 1.

Harris Interactive. (2008). *Easter Seals' living with autism study.* Retrieved from http://www.easterseals.com/site/PageServer?pagename=ntlc8_living_with_autism_study_home

Hartley, S., Barker, E., Seltzer, M., Floyd, F., Greenberg, J., Orsmond, G., . . . Bolt, D. (2010). The relative risk and timing of divorce in families of children with an autism spectrum disorder. *Journal of Family Psychology, 24,* 449–457.

Hastings, R.P. (2003). Behavioral adjustment of siblings of children with autism engaged in applied behavior analysis early intervention programs: The moderating role of social support. *Journal of Autism and Developmental Disorders, 33*(2), 141–150.

Heller, T., Kaiser, A., Meyer, D., Fish, T., Kramer, J., & Dufresne, D. (2008). *The sibling leadership network: Recommendations for research, advocacy, and supports relating to siblings of people with developmental disabilities.* Retrieved July 9, 2011 from https://docs.google .com/viewer?url=http%3A%2F%2Fwww.communitywebs.org%2Fsiblingsaustralia% 2Fassets%2Fresources%2Fsln_white_paper_final-2-1-.pdf

Hénault, I. (2006). *Asperger's syndrome and sexuality: From adolescence through adulthood.* London, England: Jessica Kingsley Publishers.

Herbert, J.D., & Brandsma, L.L. (2002). Applied behavior analysis for childhood autism: Does the emperor have clothes? *The Behavior Analyst Today, 3*(1), 45–50.

Herman, J. (1992). *Trauma and recovery: The aftermath of violence—From domestic abuse to political terror.* New York, NY: Basic Books.

Holliday-Willey, L. (1999). *Pretending to be normal: Living with Asperger's syndrome.* London, England: Jessica Kingsley Publishers.

Hoopmann, K. (2006). *All cats have Asperger syndrome.* London, England: Jessica Kingsley Publishers.

Individuals with Disabilities Education Act of 1990, PL 101-476, 20 U.S.C. §§ 1400 *et seq.*

Interactive Autism Network. (2011). *New data shows half of all children with autism wander and bolt from safe places* [Press Release]. Retrieved from https://docs.google.com/ viewer?url=http%3A%2F%2Fwww.iancommunity.org%2Fgalleries%2Fpdf_gallery%2 FIAN%2520Elopement%2520Survey%2520Results_FINAL_4%252020%252011.pdf

Jackins, B.D., Blank, R.S., Shulman, K.W., & Onello, H.H. (2010). *Managing a special needs trust: A guide for trustees.* Brookline, MA: DisABILITIES Books.

Jackson, L. (2002). *Freaks, geeks and Asperger syndrome: A user guide to adolescence.* London, England: Jessica Kingsley Publishers.

Kabat-Zinn, J. (2005). *Full catastrophe living: Using the wisdom of your body and mind to face stress, pain, and illness* (15th anniversary ed.). New York, NY: Bantam Dell.

Kabat-Zinn, M., & Kabat-Zinn, J. (1997). *Everyday blessings: The inner work of mindful parenting.* New York, NY: Hyperion.

Kanner, L. (1943). Autistic disturbances of affective contact. *Nervous Child, 2,* 217–250.

Kanner, L. (1971). Follow-up study of eleven autistic children originally reported in 1943. *Journal of Autism and Childhood Schizophrenia, 2,* 119–145.

Kaplan, J.S. (2010). *Urban mindfulness: Cultivating peace, presence and purpose in the middle of it all.* Oakland, CA: New Harbinger Publications.

Keller, H. (2010). *The world I live in and optimism: A collection of essays.* Mineola, NY: Dover Publications.

Klagsbrun, F. (1992). *Mixed feelings: Love, hate, rivalry, and reconciliation among brothers and sisters.* New York, NY: Bantam.

Klein, K.C., & Diehl, E.B. (2004). Relationship between MMR vaccine and autism. *The Annals of Pharmacotherapy, 38,* 1297–1300.

Klin, A., Warren, J., Schultz, R., Volkmar, F., & Cohen, D. (2002). Visual fixation patterns during viewing of naturalistic social situations as predictors of social competence in individuals with autism. *Archives of General Psychiatry, 59*(9), 809–816. doi:10.1001/ archpsyc.59.9.809

Kluth, P. (2011). *You're going to love this kid!. A professional development package for teaching students with autism in the inclusive classroom.* Baltimore, MD: Paul H. Brookes Publishing Co.

Kluth, P., & Schwarz, P. (2008). *"Just give him the whale!" 20 ways to use fascinations, areas of expertise, and strengths to support students with autism.* Baltimore, MD: Paul H. Brookes Publishing Co.

Koegel, L.K., Koegel, R.L., & Dunlap, G. (1996). *Positive behavioral support: Including people with difficult behavior in the community.* Baltimore, MD: Paul H. Brookes Publishing Co.

Koegel, L.K., & LaZebnik, C. (2009). *Growing up on the spectrum: A guide to life, love, and learning for teens and young adults with autism and Asperger's.* New York, NY: Viking.

Kranowitz, C.S. (1998). *The out-of-sync child: Recognizing and coping with sensory integration dysfunction.* New York, NY: Berkley.

Kranowitz, C.S. (2003). *The out-of-sync child has fun: Activities for kids with sensory processing disorder.* New York, NY: Penguin Books.

Krauss, M.W., Seltzer, M.M., & Jacobson, H.T. (2005). Adults with autism living at home or in non-family settings: Positive and negative aspects of residential status. *Journal of Intellectual Disability Research, 49,* 111–124.

Kring, S.R., Greenberg, J.S., & Seltzer, M.M. (2010). The impact of health problems on behavior problems in adolescents and adults with ASD: Implications for maternal burden. *Social Work in Mental Health, 8*(1), 54–71.

Kübler-Ross, E. (1969). *On death and dying: What the dying have to teach doctors, nurses, clergy, and their own families.* New York, NY: Collier Books.

Kupfer, F. (1998). *Before and after Zachariah: A family story about a different kind of courage.* Chicago, IL: Academy Chicago.

Kushner, H. (1981). *When bad things happen to good people.* New York, NY: Avon.

Lamb, M.E. (Ed.). (1997). *The role of the father in child development* (3rd ed.). New York, NY: Wiley.

Levant, R.F., & Pollack, W.S. (1998). Desperately seeking language: Understanding, assessing, and treating normative male alexithymia. In R.F. Levant & W.S. Pollock (Eds.), *New psychotherapy for men* (pp. 35–56). Hoboken, NJ: John Wiley & Sons.

Levy, S.E., & Hyman, S.L. (2005). Novel treatments for autistic spectrum disorders. *Mental Retardation and Developmental Disabilities Research Reviews, 11,* 131–142.

Levy, S.E., Mandell, D.S., Merhar, S., Ittenbach, R.F., & Pinto-Martin, J.A. (2003). Use of complementary and alternative medicine among children recently diagnosed with autistic spectrum disorder. *Journal of Developmental and Behavioral Pediatrics, 24*(6), 418–423.

Liang, L. (2006). Why am I so resentful? In C. Ariel & R. Naseef (Eds.), *Voices from the spectrum: Parents, grandparents, siblings, people with autism, and professionals share their wisdom* (pp. 156–157). London, England: Jessica Kingsley Publishers.

Lipp, E. (2006). Our lives at the edge of the spectrum. In C. Ariel & R. Naseef (Eds.), *Voices from the spectrum: Parents, grandparents, siblings, people with autism, and professionals share their wisdom* (pp. 60–63). London, England: Jessica Kingsley Publishers.

Lord, C., Rutter, M., & Le Couteur, A. (1994). Autism diagnostic interview-revised: A revised version of a diagnostic interview for caregivers of individuals with possible pervasive developmental disorders. *Journal of Autism and Developmental Disorders, 24*(5), 659–685.

Lovaas, I.O. (1987). Behavioral treatment and normal educational and intellectual functioning in young autistic children. *Journal of Consulting and Clinical Psychology, 55,* 3–9.

Lovaas, I.O. (2008). The early years: Pioneering the first studies of ABA for children with autism. *Autism Advocate, 50*(4), 12–14.

Mackey, W.C. (1985). *Fathering behaviors: The dynamics of the man-child bond.* New York, NY: Plenum.

Madsen, K.M., Hviid, A., Vestergaard, M., Schendel, D., Wohlfahrt, J., Thorsen, P., . . . Melbye, M. (2002). A population-based study of measles, mumps, and rubella vaccination and autism. *New England Journal of Medicine, 347,* 1477–1482.

Mahoney, G., & Perales, F. (2005). Relationship-focused early intervention with children with pervasive developmental disorders and other disabilities: A comparative study. *Developmental and Behavioral Pediatrics, 26,* 77–85.

Mandela, N. (2000). *Long walk to freedom: With connections.* New York, NY: Holt Rinehart & Winston.

Mandell, D.S. (2008). Psychiatric hospitalization among children with autism spectrum disorders. *Journal of Autism and Developmental Disorders, 38*(66), 1059–1065.

Mandell, D.S., Ittenbach, R.S., Levy, S.E., & Pinto-Martin, J.A. (2007). Disparities in diagnoses received prior to a diagnosis of autism spectrum disorder. *Journal of Autism and Developmental Disorders, 37*(9), 1795–1802.

Mandell, D., & Salzer, M. (2007). Who joins support groups among parents of children with autism? *Autism, 11*(2), 111–122.

Mandell, D.S., Wiggins, L.D., Carpenter, L.A., Daniels, J., DiGuiseppi, C., Durkin, M.S., . . . Kirby, R.S. (2009). Racial/ethnic disparities in the identification of children with autism spectrum disorders. *American Journal of Public Health, 99,* 493–498.

Mandell, D.S., Xie, M., Morales, K.H., Lawer, L., McCarthy, M., & Marcus, S.C. (2012). The interplay of outpatient services and psychiatric hospitalization among Medicaid-enrolled children with autism spectrum disorders. *Archives of Pediatrics and Adolescent Medicine, 166,* 68–73. doi:10.1001/archpediatrics.2011.714

Marshak, L.E., & Prezant, F. (2007). *Married with special-needs children: A couples' guide to keeping connected.* Bethesda, MD: Woodbine House.

Marshall, L.G. (2006). Stump the cook. In C. Ariel & R. Naseef (Eds.), *Voices from the spectrum: Parents, grandparents, siblings, people with autism, and professionals share their wisdom* (pp. 73–77). London, England: Jessica Kingsley Publishers.

Massachusetts Advocates for Children. (2009). *Targeted, taunted, tormented: The bullying of children with autism spectrum disorder.* Retrieved July 5, 2012 from http://www.massadvocates.org/documents/Bullying-Report_000.pdf

Matson, J.L., Dempsey, T., LoVullo, S.V., & Wilkins, J. (2008). The effects of intellectual functioning on the range of core symptoms of autism spectrum disorders. *Research in Developmental Disabilities, 29*(4), 341–350.

May, J. (1991). *Fathers of children with special needs: New horizons.* Bethesda, MD: Association for the Care of Children's Health.

McGarry, L. (2011a, June 20). Study shows "a diagnosis of autism is not a diagnosis of divorce" [Web log post]. Retrieved from http://www.alternativechoicespa.blogspot.com/2011/06/study-shows-diagnosis-of-autism-is-not.html

McGarry, L. (2011b, August 1). The window [Web log post]. Retrieved from http://www.alternativechoicespa.blogspot.com/2011/08/window.html

McHugh, M. (1999). *Special siblings: Growing up with someone with a disability.* New York, NY: Hyperion.

Meyer, D. (Ed.). (1995). *Uncommon fathers: Reflections on raising a child with a disability.* Bethesda, MD: Woodbine House.

Meyer, D. (Ed.). (2005). *The sibling slam book: What it's really like to have a brother or sister with special needs.* Bethesda, MD: Woodbine House.

Meyer, D. (Ed.). (2009). *Thicker than water: Essays by adult siblings of people with disabilities.* Bethesda, MD: Woodbine House.

Meyer, D., & Vadasy, P. (2008). *Sibshops: Workshops for siblings of children with special needs* (Rev. ed.). Baltimore, MD: Paul H. Brookes Publishing Co.

Miller, N.B., & Sammons, C.C. (1999). *Everybody's different: Understanding and changing our reactions to disabilities.* Baltimore, MD: Paul H. Brookes Publishing Co.

Miller, S. (1983). *Men and friendship.* San Leandro, CA: Gateway Books.

Miller, S. (1990). *Family pictures.* New York, NY: Harper & Row.

Montanaro, D. (2007). *Uncle Greg, our latest trader.* [Web log post]. Retrieved from http://community.tradeking.com/members/bigdog/blogs/258-uncle-greg-our-latest-trader

Morgan, S.P., Lye, D.N., & Condran, G.A. (1998). Sons, daughters, and the risk of marital disruption. *American Journal of Sociology, 94*(1), 110–129.

Moses, K.L. (1985). *Not me! Not my child! Dealing with parental denial and anxiety* [Audio tapes]. Chicago, IL: Resource Networks.

Myles, B., Trautman, M., & Schelvan, R. (2004). *The hidden curriculum: Practical solutions for understanding unstated rules in social situations.* Shawnee Mission, KS: Autism Asperger Publishing Company.

Naseef, R. (1991). Lost dreams, new hopes. *Journal of Counseling & Development, 70,* 354–355.

Naseef, Z. (2006). My brother . . . Ahhhhhhhh! In C. Ariel & R. Naseef (Eds.), *Voices from the spectrum: Parents, grandparents, siblings, people with autism, and professionals share their wisdom* (pp. 158–160). London, England: Jessica Kingsley Publishers.

National Institute of Mental Health. (2009). *Depression in men.* Retrieved from http://www.nimh.nih.gov/health/topics/depression/men-and-depression/depression-in-men.shtml

National Research Council. (2001). *Educating children with autism.* Washington, DC: National Academies Press.

Newport, G. (2001). *Life is not a label: A guide to living fully with autism and Asperger's syndrome.* Arlington, TX: New Horizons.

Nichols, M. (1995). *The lost art of listening.* New York, NY: Guilford Press.

Nichols, S., Moravcik, G.M., & Tetenbaum, S.P. (2009). *Girls growing up on the autism spectrum: What parents and professionals should know about the preteen and teenage years.* London, England: Jessica Kingsley Publishers.

Notbohm, E. (2005). *Ten things every child with autism wishes you knew.* Arlington, TX: Future Horizons.

Orsmond, G.I., & Seltzer, M.M. (2009). Adolescent siblings of individuals with an autism spectrum disorder: Testing a diathesis-stress model of sibling well-being. *Journal of Autism and Developmental Disorders, 39,* 1053–1065.

Orsmond, G.I., Seltzer, M.M., Greenberg, J.S., & Krauss, M.W. (2006). Mother-child relationship quality among adolescents and adults with autism. *American Journal of Mental Retardation, 111,* 121–137.

Osherson, S. (1986). *Finding our fathers: The unfinished business of manhood.* New York, NY: Free Press.

Oswald, D.P., & Sonenklar, N.A. (2007). Medication use among children with autism spectrum disorders. *Journal of Child and Adolescent Psychopharmacology, 17*(3), 348–355. doi:10.1089/cap.2006.17303

Ozonoff, S., Young, G.S., Carter, A., Messinger, D., Yirmiya, N., Zwaigenbaum, L., . . . Stone, W.L. (2011). Recurrence risk for autism spectrum disorders: A baby siblings research consortium study. *Pediatrics*; originally published online August 15, 2011; doi: 10.1542/peds.2010-2825

PBS. (n.d.) *Infant mortality and life expectancy.* Retrieved July 10, 2012 from http://www.pbs.org/fmc/timeline/dmortality.htm

Pennebaker, J.W. (1990). *Opening up: The healing power of confiding in others.* New York, NY: Avon.

Pollack, W.S. (1998). *Real boys: Rescuing our sons from the myths of boyhood.* New York, NY: Random House.

Prizant, B. (2008, Summer). On recovery. *Autism Spectrum Quarterly,* pp. 39–42.

Prizant, B. (2009, Spring). Treatment options and parent choice: Is ABA the only way? *Autism Spectrum Quarterly,* pp. 28–32.

Prizant, B., & Laurent, A. (2011). Behavior is not the issue: An emotional regulation perspective on problem behavior, part 1. *Autism Spectrum Quarterly,* pp. 28–30.

Real, T. (1998). *I don't want to talk about it: Overcoming the secret legacy of male depression.* New York, NY: Scribner.

Remen, R.N. (1996). *Kitchen table wisdom: Stories that heal.* New York, NY: Berkley.

Rimland, B. (1964). *Infantile autism: The syndrome and its implications for a neural theory of behavior.* New York, NY: Appleton-Century-Crofts.

Robertson, L. (1995). The hardest lesson: Learning to accept. In D. Meyer (Ed.), *Uncommon fathers: Reflections on raising a child with a disability* (pp. 29–40). Bethesda, MD: Woodbine House.

Robison, J.E. (2011). *Be different: Adventures of a free-range Aspergian with practical advice for Aspergians, misfits, families and teachers.* New York, NY: Random House.

Rogers, C.R. (1961). *On becoming a person: A therapist's view of psychotherapy*. New York, NY: Houghton Mifflin Company.

Rudy, L.J. (2010). *Get out, explore, and have fun: How families of children with autism or Asperger syndrome can get the most out of community activities*. London, England: Jessica Kingsley Publishers.

Salzberg, S. (2011). *Real happiness: The power of meditation*. New York, NY: Workman.

Schieve, L.A., Blumberg, S.J., Rice, C., Visser, S.N., & Boyle, C. (2007). The relationship between autism and parenting stress. *Pediatrics, 119,* S114–S121. doi:10.1542/peds.2006-2089Q

Schiff, H.S. (1978). *The bereaved parent*. New York, NY: Penguin.

Schmidt, T.J. (2006). Jordan's gift. In C. Ariel & R. Naseef (Eds.), *Voices from the spectrum: Parents, grandparents, siblings, people with autism, and professionals share their wisdom* (pp. 193–197). London, England: Jessica Kingsley Publishers.

Schwier, K.M., & Hingsburger, D. (2000). *Sexuality: Your sons and daughters with intellectual disabilities*. Baltimore, MD: Paul H. Brookes Publishing Co.

Seligman, M. (1985). Handicapped children and their families. *Journal of Counseling & Development, 64,* 274–277.

Seligman, M., & Darling, R.D. (2007). *Ordinary families, special children: A systems approach to childhood disability* (3rd ed.). New York, NY: Guilford Press.

Seltzer, M.M., Krauss, M.W., Orsmond, G.I., & Vestal, C. (2001). Families of adolescents and adults with autism: Uncharted territory. *International Review of Research on Mental Retardation, 23,* 267–294.

Seltzer, M.M., Orsmond, G.I., & Esbensen, A.J. (2009). Siblings of individuals with autism spectrum disorder: Sibling relationships and well-being in adolescence and adulthood. *Autism, 13*(1), 59–80.

Shakespeare, W. (1992). *Hamlet*. New York, NY: Dover.

Shore, S. (2003). *Beyond the wall: Personal experiences with autism and Asperger syndrome*. Shawnee Mission, KS: Autism Asperger Publishing Company.

Shore, S. (2004). *Ask and tell: Self-advocacy and disclosure for people on the autism spectrum*. Shawnee Mission, KS: Autism Asperger Publishing Company.

Shore, S. (2010). Should you tell your child about his/her autism diagnosis? [Video file]. Retrieved from http://www.youtube.com/watch?v=MmrR4UgKFyA

Shore, S.M., & Rastelli, L.G. (2006). *Understanding autism for dummies*. Hoboken, NJ: Wiley.

Siegel, B. (1996). *The world of the autistic child: Understanding and treating autistic spectrum disorders*. New York, NY: Oxford University Press.

Simone, R. (2010). *Aspergirls: Empowering females with Asperger's syndrome*. London, England: Jessica Kingsley Publishers.

Sinclair, J. (1993). *Don't mourn for us*. Retrieved from http://www.autreat.com/dont_mourn.html

Skinner, B.F. (1976). *Walden two*. New York, NY: Macmillan.

Steinberg, L. (2011). *You and your adolescent: The essential guide for ages 10-25*. New York, NY: Simon & Schuster.

Stern, D.N., Bruschweiler-Stern, N., & Freeland, A. (1998). *The birth of a mother: How the motherhood experience changes you forever*. New York, NY: Basic Books.

Styron, W. (2007). *Darkness visible: A memoir of madness*. New York, NY: Modern Library.

Tannen, D. (1990). *You just don't understand: Women and men in conversation*. New York, NY: Ballantine.

Taylor, J.L., & Seltzer, M.M. (2010a). Changes in the autism behavioral phenotype during the transition to adulthood. *Journal of Autism and Developmental Disorders, 40,* 1431–1446.

Taylor, J.L., & Seltzer, M.M. (2010b). Employment and post-secondary educational activities for young adults with autism spectrum disorders during the transition to adulthood. *Journal of Autism and Developmental Disorders, 41,* 566–574.

Taylor, J.L., & Seltzer, M.M. (2011). Changes in the mother-child relationship during the transition to adulthood for youth with autism spectrum disorder. *Journal of Autism and Developmental Disorders, 41,* 1397–1410.

Thompson, T. (2008). *Dr. Thompson's straight talk on autism.* Baltimore, MD: Paul H. Brookes Publishing Co.

Thompson, T. (2011). *Individualized autism intervention for young children: Blending discrete trial and naturalistic strategies.* Baltimore, MD: Paul H. Brookes Publishing Co.

Thoreau, H.D. (2012). *Walden.* Madison, NC: Empire Publishing.

Tolstoy, L. (2012). *Childhood, Boyhood, Youth.* New York, NY: Penguin Classics.

Turnbull, H.R., III, & Turnbull, A.P. (Eds.). (1985). *Parents speak out: Then and now.* Columbus, OH: Charles E. Merrill.

U.S. Census Bureau. (2009). *New census disability statistics released: One in five Americans have a disability* [Press release]. Retrieved from http://jfactivist.typepad.com/jfactivist/2009/01/new-census-disability-statistics-released-one-in-five-americans-have-a-disability.html

van der Kolk, B.A., McFarlane, A.C., & Weisaeth, L. (Eds.). (1996). *Traumatic stress: The effects of overwhelming experience on mind, body, and society.* New York, NY: Guilford Press.

van Roekel, E., Scholte, R.H.J., & Didden, R. (2010). Bullying among adolescents with autism spectrum disorders: Prevalence and perception. *Journal of Autism and Developmental Disorders, 40,* 63–73.

Viorst, J. (2003). *Grown-up marriage: What we know, wish we had known, and still need to know about being married.* New York, NY: Simon & Schuster.

Vocational Rehabilitation Act of 1918, PL 65-178, 17 U.S.C. §§ 486A *et seq.*

Wakefield, A.J., Murch, S.H., Anthony, A., Linnell, J., Casson, D.M., Malik, M., . . . Walker-Smith, J.A. (1998). Ileal-lymphoid-nodular hyperplasia, non-specific colitis, and pervasive developmental disorder in children. *The Lancet, 351,* 637–641.

Walsh, A., Walsh, M.B., & Gaventa, B. (2007). *Autism and faith: A journey into community.* New Brunswick, NJ: Elizabeth M. Boggs Center.

Wexler, D.B. (2009). *Men in therapy: New approaches for effective treatment.* New York, NY: W.W. Norton.

Wheeler, M. (2007). *Toilet training for individuals with autism or other developmental issues* (2nd ed.). Arlington, TX: Future Horizons.

Williams, D. (2006). Culture, conditions and personhood: A response to the cure debate on autism. In C. Ariel & R. Naseef (Eds.), *Voices from the spectrum: Parents, grandparents, siblings, people with autism, and professionals share their wisdom* (pp. 204–207). London, England: Jessica Kingsley Publishers.

Wilson, K.G., & Dufrene, T. (2010). *Things might go terribly, horribly wrong: A guide to life liberated from anxiety.* Oakland, CA: New Harbinger Publications.

Wiltshire, M. (2011). *Understanding the HighScope approach: Early years education in practice.* New York, NY: Routledge.

Winnicott, D.W. (1993). *Talking to parents.* New York, NY: Addison Wesley.

Wrobel, M. (2003). *Taking care of myself: A healthy hygiene, puberty and personal curriculum for young people with autism.* Arlington, TX: Future Horizons.

Yaffe, L. (2006). Katie's question. In C. Ariel & R. Naseef (Eds.), *Voices from the spectrum: Parents, grandparents, siblings, people with autism, and professionals share their wisdom* (pp. 116–118). London, England: Jessica Kingsley Publishers.

Yeargin-Allsopp, M., Rice, C., Karapurkar, T., Doernberg, N., Boyle, C., & Murphy, C. (2003). Prevalence of autism in a US metropolitan area. *Journal of the American Medical Association, 289,* 49–55.

Zimmerman, B. (2010). *Erin's period book.* Bloomington, IN: AuthorHouse.

Resources

Autism and Special Needs References

Ariel, C. (2012). *Loving someone with Asperger's syndrome: Understanding and connecting with your partner.* Oakland, CA: New Harbinger Publications.

Ariel, C., & Naseef, R. (Eds.). (2006). *Voices from the spectrum: Parents, grandparents, siblings, people with autism, and professionals share their wisdom.* London, England: Jessica Kingsley Publishers.

Attwood, S. (2008). *Making sense of sex: A forthright guide to puberty, sex, and relationships for people with Asperger's syndrome.* London, England: Jessica Kingsley Publishers.

Attwood, T. (1997). *Asperger syndrome: A guide for parents and professionals.* London, England: Jessica Kingsley Publishers.

Attwood, T. (2006). *The complete guide to Asperger's syndrome.* London, England: Jessica Kingsley Publishers.

Attwood, T., Grandin, T., Bolick, T., Faherty, C., Iland, L., McIlwee Myers, J., . . . Mary Wrobel, M. (2006). *Asperger's and girls.* Arlington, TX: Future Horizons.

Baker, J. (2003). *Social skills training for children and adolescents with Asperger syndrome and social-communications problems.* Shawnee Mission, KS: Autism Asperger Publishing Company.

Baker, J. (2008). *No more meltdowns: Positive strategies for managing and preventing out-of-control behavior.* Arlington, TX: Future Horizons.

Batshaw, M.L., Roizen, N.J., & Lotrecchiano, G.R. (Eds.). (2013). *Children with disabilities* (7th ed.). Baltimore, MD: Paul H. Brookes Publishing Co.

Bentley, K. (2007). *Alone together: Making an Asperger marriage work.* London, England: Jessica Kingsley Publishers.

Bolick, T. (2004). *Asperger's syndrome and adolescents: Helping preteens and teens get ready for the real world.* Beverly, MA: Fair Winds Press.

Brazelton, T.B., & Cramer, B.G. (1990). *The earliest relationship: Parents, infants, and the drama of early attachment.* New York, NY: Addison Wesley.

Brooks, R., & Goldstein, S. (2012). *Raising resilient children with autism spectrum disorders: Strategies for maximizing their strengths, coping with adversity, and developing a social mindset.* New York, NY: McGraw Hill.

Carter, E.W. (2007). *Including people with disabilities in faith communities: A guide for service providers, families, and congregations.* Baltimore, MD: Paul H. Brookes Publishing Co.

Coplan, J. (2010). *Making sense of autistic spectrum disorders: Create the brightest future possible for your child with the best treatment options.* New York, NY: Bantam.

Cutler, B.C., & Pratt, S. (2010). *You, your child, and "special" education: A guide to dealing with the system* (Rev. ed.). Baltimore, MD: Paul H. Brookes Publishing Co.

Darling, R.B. (1983). "Parent-professional interaction: The roots of misunderstanding." In M. Seligman (Ed.), *The family with a handicapped child: Understanding and treatment* (pp. 106–114). New York, NY: Grune & Stratton.

Durand, V.M. (1998). *Sleep better! A guide to improving sleep for children with special needs.* Baltimore, MD: Paul H. Brookes Publishing Co.

Durand, V.M. (2011). *Optimistic parenting: Hope and help for you and your challenging child.* Baltimore, MD: Paul H. Brookes Publishing Co.

Ernsperger, L., & Stegen-Hanson, T. (2004). *Just take a bite: Easy, effective answers to food aversions and eating challenges!* Arlington, TX: Future Horizons.

Fialka, J., Feldman, A.K., & Mikus, K.C. (2012). *Parents and professionals partnering for children with disabilities: A dance that matters.* Thousand Oaks, CA: Corwin Press.

Freedman, S. (2010). *Developing college skills in students with autism and Asperger's syndrome.* London, England: Jessica Kingsley Publishers.

Gallagher, P.A., Powell, T.H., & Rhodes, C.A. (2006). *Brothers and sisters: A special part of exceptional families* (3rd ed.). Baltimore, MD: Paul H. Brookes Publishing Co.

Gaus, V. (2011). *Living well on the spectrum: How to use your strengths to meet the challenges of Asperger's syndrome/high-functioning autism.* New York, NY: Guilford Press.

Glasburg, B.A. (2006). *Functional behavior assessment for people with autism: Making sense of seemingly senseless behavior.* Bethesda, MD: Woodbine House.

Grandin, T., & Duffy, K. (2008). *Developing talents: Careers for individuals with Asperger's syndrome and high functioning autism.* Arlington, TX: New Horizons.

Gray, C. (2000). *The new Social Story book: Illustrated edition.* Arlington, TX: Future Horizons.

Greene, R.W. (2010). *The explosive child: A new approach for understanding and parenting easily frustrated, chronically inflexible children.* New York, NY: Harper.

Greenspan, S., & Weider, S. (1997). *The child with special needs: Encouraging intellectual and emotional growth.* New York, NY: Addison Wesley.

Greenspan, S.I., & Wieder, S. (2003). *Engaging autism: The Floortime approach to helping children relate, communicate and think.* New York, NY: Perseus Books Group.

Griffin, C., & Hammis, D. (2003). *Making self-employment work for people with disabilities.* Baltimore, MD: Paul H. Brookes Publishing Co.

Grossman, F.K. (1972). *Brothers and sisters of retarded children.* Syracuse, NY: Syracuse University Press.

Gutstein, S. (2001). *Autism/Aspergers: Solving the relationship puzzle.* Arlington, TX: Future Horizons.

Jackins, B.D., Blank, R.S., Shulman, K.W., & Onello, H.H. (2010). *Managing a special needs trust: A guide for trustees.* Brookline, MA: DisABILITIES Books.

Johnson, J., & Van Rensselaer, A. (2008). *Families of adults with autism: Stories and advice for the next generation.* London, England: Jessica Kingsley Publishers.

Klein, S., & Schleifer, M. (1993). *It ISN'T fair: Siblings of children with disabilities.* Westport, CT: Bergin & Garvey.

Kluth, P. (2011). *You're going to love this kid! A professional development package for teaching students with autism in the inclusive classroom.* Baltimore, MD: Paul H. Brookes Publishing Co.

Kluth, P., & Schwarz, P. (2008). *"Just give him the whale!" 20 ways to use fascinations, areas of expertise, and strengths to support students with autism.* Baltimore, MD: Paul H. Brookes Publishing Co.

Koegel, L.K., Koegel, R.L., & Dunlap, G. (1996). *Positive behavioral support: Including people with difficult behavior in the community.* Baltimore, MD: Paul H. Brookes Publishing Co.

Koegel, L.K., & LaZebnik, C. (2009). *Growing up on the spectrum: A guide to life, love, and learning for teens and young adults with autism and Asperger's.* New York, NY: Viking.

Koegel, R.L., & Koegel, L.K. (2006). *Pivotal response treatments for autism: Communication, social, and academic development.* Baltimore, MD: Paul H. Brookes Publishing Co.

Kranowitz, C.S. (1998). *The out-of-sync child: Recognizing and coping with sensory integration dysfunction.* New York, NY: Berkley.

Kranowitz, C.S. (2003). *The out-of-sync child has fun: Activities for kids with sensory processing disorder.* New York, NY: Penguin Books.

Levine, J., Murphy, D.T., & Wilson, S. (1993). *Getting men involved: Strategies for early childhood programs.* New York, NY: Scholastic.

Marshak, L.E., & Prezant, F. (2007). *Married with special needs children: A couples' guide to keeping connected.* Bethesda, MD: Woodbine House.

May, J. (1991). *Fathers of children with special needs: New horizons.* Bethesda, MD: Association for the Care of Children's Health.

McHugh, M. (1999). *Special siblings: Growing up with someone with a disability.* New York, NY: Hyperion.

Meyer, D., & Vadasy, P. (2008). *Sibshops: Workshops for siblings of children with special needs* (Rev. ed.). Baltimore, MD: Paul H. Brookes Publishing Co.

Miller, N.B., & Sammons, C.C. (1999). *Everybody's different: Understanding and changing our reactions to disabilities.* Baltimore, MD: Paul H. Brookes Publishing Co.

Miller, S. (1990). *Family pictures.* New York, NY: Harper & Row.

Moses, K.L. (1985). *Not me! Not my child! Dealing with parental denial and anxiety* [Audio tapes]. Chicago, IL: Resource Networks.

Myles, B., Trautman, M., & Schelvan, R. (2004). *The hidden curriculum: Practical solutions for understanding unstated rules in social situations.* Shawnee Mission, KS: Autism Asperger Publishing Company.

National Research Council. (2001). *Educating children with autism.* Washington, DC: National Academies Press.

Nichols, S., Moravik, G.M., & Tetenbaum, S.P. (2009). *Girls growing up on the autism spectrum: What parents and professionals should know about the preteen and teenage years.* London, England: Jessica Kingsley Publishers.

Oberleitner, R., Ball, J., Gillete, D., Naseef, R., & Hudnall Stamm, B. (2006). Technologies to lessen the distress of autism. In J. Garrick & M.B. Williams (Eds.), *Trauma treatment techniques: Innovative trends* (pp. 221–242). Binghamton, NY: Haworth Press.

Pollack, W. (1998). *Realboys: Rescuing our sons from the myths of boyhood.* New York, NY, Random House.

Prizant, B.M., Wetherby, A.M., Rubin, E., Laurent, A.C., & Rydell, P.J. (2006). *The SCERTS® model: A comprehensive educational approach for children with autism spectrum disorders.* Baltimore, MD: Paul H. Brookes Publishing Co.

Quill, K.A. (2000). *Do-watch-listen-say: Social and communication intervention for children with autism.* Baltimore, MD: Paul H. Brookes Publishing Co.

Rimland, B. (1964). *Infantile autism: The syndrome and its implications for a neural theory of behavior.* New York, NY: Appleton-Century-Crofts.

Rudy, L.J. (2010). *Get out, explore, and have fun: How families of children with autism or Asperger syndrome can get the most out of community activities.* London, England: Jessica Kingsley Publishers.

Schneider, C. (2007). *Acting antics: A theatrical approach to teaching social understanding to kids and teens with Asperger syndrome.* London, England: Jessica Kingsley Publishers.

Schwier, K.M., & Hingsburger, D. (2000). *Sexuality: Your sons and daughters with intellectual disabilities.* Baltimore, MD: Paul H. Brookes Publishing Co.

Seligman, M., & Darling, R.B. (2006). *Ordinary families, special children: A systems approach to childhood disability* (3rd ed.). New York, NY: Guilford Press.

Shore, S.M., & Rastelli, L.G. (2006). *Understanding autism for dummies.* New York, NY: Wiley.

Siegel, B. (1998). *The world of the autistic child: Understanding and treating autistic spectrum disorders.* London, England: Oxford University Press.

Simone, R. (2010). *Aspergirls: Empowering females with Asperger's syndrome.* London, England: Jessica Kingsley Publishers.

Smith-Myles, B., Cook, K., Miller, N., Rinner, L., & Robbins, L. (2000). *Asperger syndrome and sensory issues: Practical solutions for making sense of the world.* Shawnee Mission, KS: Autism Asperger Publishing Company.

Stanford, A. (2011). *Business for Aspies: 42 best practices for using Asperger's syndrome traits at work successfully.* London, England: Jessica Kingsley Publishers.

Stern, D.N., Bruschweiler-Stern, N., & Freeland, A. (1998). *The birth of a mother: How the motherhood experience changes you forever.* New York, NY: Basic Books.

Thompson, T. (2008). *Dr. Thompson's straight talk on autism.* Baltimore, MD: Paul H. Brookes Publishing Co.

Thompson, T. (2011). *Individualized autism intervention for young children: Blending discrete trial and naturalistic strategies.* Baltimore, MD: Paul H. Brookes Publishing Co.

Walsh, A., Walsh, M.B., & Gaventa, B. (2007). *Autism and faith: A journey into community.* New Brunswick, NJ: Elizabeth M. Boggs Center.

Wheeler, M. (1998). *Toilet training for individuals with autism and related disorders.* Arlington, TX: Future Horizons.

General References

Alberti, R., & Emmons, M. (1982). *Your perfect right.* San Luis Obispo, CA: Impact.

American Psychiatric Association. (2000). *Diagnostic and statistical manual of mental disorders* (4th ed., text rev.). Washington, DC: Author.

Bank, S.P., & Kahn, M. (1982). *The sibling bond.* New York, NY: Basic Books.

Brach, T. (2003). *Radical acceptance: Embracing your life with the heart of the Buddha.* New York, NY: Bantam.

Brazelton, T.B. (1992). *Touchpoints: Your child's emotional and behavioral development.* Reading, MA: Addison Wesley.

Cousins, N. (1989). *Head first: The biology of hope.* New York, NY: Dutton.

Coyne, L.W., & Murrell, A.R. (2009). *The joy of parenting: An acceptance and commitment therapy guide to effective parenting in the early years.* Oakland, CA: New Harbinger Publications.

Eifert, G.H., McKay, M., & Forsyth, J.P. (2006). *ACT on life not on anger: The new acceptance and commitment therapy guide to problem anger.* Oakland, CA: New Harbinger Publications.

Faber, A., & Mazlish, E. (1987). *Siblings without rivalry: How to help your children live together.* New York, NY: W.W. Norton.

Galinsky, E. (1987). *The six stages of parenthood.* New York, NY: Addison Wesley.

Gaul, G.M. (1993). *Giant steps: The story of one boy's struggle to walk.* New York, NY: St. Martin's Press.

Gilbert, D. (2006). *Stumbling on happiness.* New York, NY: Alfred A. Knopf.

Gilligan, C. (1982). *In a different voice: Psychological theory and women's development.* Cambridge, MA: Harvard University Press.

Goleman, D. (1995). *Emotional intelligence: Why it can matter more than IQ.* New York, NY: Bantam.

Gottman, J.M. (1999). *The seven principles for making marriage work.* New York, NY: Random House.

Groopman, J. (2005). *The anatomy of hope: How people prevail in the face of illness.* New York, NY: Random House.

Hayes, S., & Smith, S. (2005). *Get out of your mind and into your life: The new acceptance and commitment therapy.* Oakland, CA: New Harbinger Publications.

Hendrix, H. (1988). *Getting the love you want: The guide for couples.* New York, NY: Harper & Row.

Herman, J. (1992). *Trauma and recovery: The aftermath of violence—From domestic abuse to political terror.* New York, NY: Basic Books.

Kabat-Zinn, J. (2005). *Full catastrophe living: Using the wisdom of your body and mind to face stress, pain, and illness* (15th anniversary ed.). New York, NY: Bantam Dell.

Kabat-Zinn, M., & Kabat-Zinn, J. (1997). *Everyday blessings: The inner work of mindful parenting.* New York, NY: Hyperion.

Kaplan, J.S. (2010). *Urban mindfulness: Cultivating peace, presence and purpose in the middle of it all.* Oakland, CA: New Harbinger Publications.

Klagsburn, F. (1992). *Mixed feelings: Love, hate, rivalry, and reconciliation among brothers and sisters.* New York, NY: Bantam.

Kübler-Ross, E. (1969). *On death and dying: What the dying have to teach doctors, nurses, clergy, and their own families.* New York, NY: Collier Books.

Kushner, H.S. (1981). *When bad things happen to good people.* New York, NY: Avon.

Lamb, M.E. (Ed.). (1997). *The role of the father in child development* (3rd ed.). New York, NY: Wiley.

Levine, J., Murphy, D.T., & Wilson, S. (1993). *Getting men involved: Strategies for early childhood programs.* New York, NY: Scholastic.

Mackey, W.C. (1985). *Fathering behaviors: The dynamics of the man-child bond.* New York, NY: Plenum.

Miller, N., & Sammons, C. (1999). *Everybody's different: Understanding and changing our reactions to disabilities.* Baltimore, MD: Paul H. Brookes Publishing Co.

Miller, S. (1983). *Men and friendship.* San Leandro, CA: Gateway Books.

Moyers, B. (1993). *Healing and the mind.* New York, NY: Doubleday.

Nichols, M. (1995). *The lost art of listening.* New York, NY: Guilford Press.

Osherson, S. (1986). *Finding our fathers: The unfinished business of manhood.* New York, NY: Free Press.

Pennebaker, J.W. (1990). *Opening up: The healing power of confiding in others.* New York, NY: Avon.

Pollack, W.S. (1998). *Real boys: Rescuing our sons from the myths of boyhood.* New York, NY: Random House.

Real, T. (1997). *I don't want to talk about it: Overcoming the secret legacy of male depression.* New York, NY: Scribner.

Remen, R.N. (1996). *Kitchen table wisdom: Stories that heal.* New York, NY: Berkley Publishing.

Salzberg, S. (2011). *Real happiness: The power of meditation.* New York, NY: Workman.

Schiff, H.S. (1977). *The bereaved parent.* New York, NY: Crown.

Steinberg, L. (2011). *You and your adolescent: The essential guide for ages 10-25.* New York, NY: Simon & Schuster.

Stern, D.N. (1990). *Diary of a baby.* New York, NY: Basic Books.

Tannen, D. (1990). *You just don't understand: Women and men in conversation.* New York, NY: Ballantine.

van der Kolk, B.A., McFarlane, A.C., & Weisaeth, L. (Eds.). (1996). *Traumatic stress: The effects of overwhelming experience on mind, body, and society.* New York, NY: Guilford Press.

Viorst, J. (2003). *Grown-up marriage: What we know, wish we had known, and still need to know about being married.* New York, NY: Simon & Schuster.

Wexler, D.B. (2009). *Men in therapy: New approaches for effective treatment.* New York, NY: Norton.

Wilson, K.G., & Dufrene, T. (2010). *Things might go terribly, horribly wrong: A guide to life liberated from anxiety.* Oakland, CA: New Harbinger Publications.

Winnicott, D.W. (1993). *Talking to parents.* New York, NY: Addison Wesley.

Personal Accounts by Family Members and People with Autism and Special Needs

Brown, C. (1954). *My left foot*. London, England: Mandarin Paperbacks.

Buck, P. (1992). *The child who never grew*. Rockville, MD: Woodbine House.

Carley, M.J. (2008). *Asperger's from the inside out*. New York, NY: Penguin Group.

Featherstone, H. (1980). *A difference in the family: Life with a disabled child*. New York, NY: Basic Books.

Finch, D. (2012). *The journal of best practices: A memoir of marriage, Asperger syndrome, and one man's quest to be a better husband*. New York, NY: Scribner.

Fling, E.R. (2000). *Eating an artichoke: A mother's perspective on Asperger syndrome*. London, England: Jessica Kingsley Publishers.

Gaul, G.M. (1993). *Giant steps: The story of one boy's struggle to walk*. New York, NY: St. Martin's Press.

Gilpin, R.W. (1993). *Laughing and loving with autism—A collection of "real life" warm and humorous stories*. Arlington, TX: Future Horizons.

Gottlieb, D. (2008). *Letters to Sam: A grandfather's lessons on love, loss, and the gifts of life*. New York, NY: Sterling.

Gottlieb, D. (2010). *The wisdom of Sam: Observations on life from an uncommon child*. New York, NY: Hay House.

Grandin, T. (1995). *Thinking in pictures*. New York, NY: Vintage Books.

Grandin, T. (2008). *The way I see it: A personal look at autism and Asperger's*. Arlington, TX: Future Horizons.

Grandin, T., & Scariano, M. (1996). *Emergence: Labeled autistic*. New York, NY: Warner Books.

Greenfeld, K. (2009). *Boy alone: A brother's memoir*. Hammersmith, England: HarperCollins.

Greenfield, J. (1970). *A child called Noah*. New York, NY: Washington Square.

Hénault, I. (2006). *Asperger's syndrome and sexuality: From adolescence through adulthood*. London, England: Jessica Kingsley Publishers.

Jackson, L. (2002). *Freaks, geeks and Asperger syndrome: A user guide to adolescence*. London, England: Jessica Kingsley Publishers.

Johnson, J., & Van Rensselaer, A. (2008). *Families of adults with autism: Stories and advice for the next generation*. London, England: Jessica Kingsley Publishers.

Kupfer, F. (1998). *Before and after Zachariah: A family story about a different kind of courage*. Chicago, IL: Academy Chicago Publishers.

Lawson, W. (1998). *Life behind glass: A personal account of autism spectrum disorder*. London, England: Jessica Kingsley Publishers.

Meyer, D. (Ed.). (1995). *Uncommon fathers: Reflections on raising a child with a disability*. Bethesda, MD: Woodbine House.

Meyer, D. (Ed.). (1997). *Views from our shoes: Growing up with a brother or a sister with special needs*. Bethesda, MD: Woodbine House.

Meyer, D. (Ed.). (2005). *The sibling slam book: What it's really like to have a brother or sister with special needs*. Bethesda, MD: Woodbine House.

Meyer, D. (Ed.). (2009). *Thicker than water: Essays by adult siblings of people with disabilities*. Bethesda, MD: Woodbine House.

Mont, D. (2001). *A different kind of boy: A father's memoir about raising a gifted child with autism*. London, England: Jessica Kingsley Publishers.

Newport, J. (2001). *Your life is not a label: Living fully with autism and Asperger syndrome*. Arlington, TX: Future Horizons.

Notbohm, E. (2005). *Ten things every child with autism wishes you knew*. Arlington, TX: Future Horizons.

Oe, K. (1970). *A personal matter*. New York, NY: Grove Press.

Paradiz, V. (2007). *Elijah's cup: A family's journey into the community of autism and Asperger syndrome.* New York, NY: Free Press.

Peete, R. (2010). *Not my boy!: A father, a son, and one family's journey with autism.* New York, NY: Hyperion.

Robison, J.E. (2007). *Look me in the eye: My life with Asperger's.* New York, NY: Three Rivers Press.

Robison, J.E. (2011). *Be different: Adventures of a free-range Aspergian with practical advice for Aspergians, misfits, families and teachers.* New York, NY: Random House.

Shore, S.M. (2003). *Beyond the wall: Personal experiences with autism and Asperger syndrome* (2nd ed.). Shawnee Mission, KS: Autism Asperger Publishing Company.

Shore, S. (2004). *Ask and tell: Self-advocacy and disclosure for people on the autism spectrum.* Shawnee Mission, KS: Autism Asperger Publishing Company.

Tammet, D. (2007). *Born on a blue day: Inside the extraordinary mind of an autistic savant.* New York, NY: Free Press.

Turnbull, H.R., III, & Turnbull, A.P. (1985). *Parents speak out: Then and now.* Columbus, OH: Charles E. Merrill.

Willey, H.L. (1999). *Pretending to be normal.* London, England: Jessica Kingsley Publishers.

Williams, D. (1994). *Nobody nowhere: The extraordinary autobiography of an autistic.* New York, NY: Harper Paperbacks.

Children's Books

Al Ghani, A.J. (2008). *Red beast: Controlling anger in children with Asperger's syndrome.* London, England: Jessica Kingsley Publishers.

Altman, A. (2008). *Waiting for Benjamin.* Morton Grove, IL: Albert Whitman.

Amenda, C. (1992). *Russell is extra special.* New York, NY: Bruner Mazel.

Band, E. (2001). *Autism through a sister's eyes.* Arlington, TX: Future Horizons.

Bishop, B. (2003). *My friend with autism.* Arlington, TX: Future Horizons.

Bleach, F. (2001). *Everybody is different: A book for young people who have brothers or sisters with autism.* Shawnee Mission, KS: Autism Asperger Publishing Company.

Buron, K.D., & Myles, B.S. (2004). *When my autism gets too big! A relaxation book for children with autism spectrum disorder.* Shawnee Mission, KS: Autism Asperger Publishing Company.

Cain, B. (1990). *Double-dip feelings: Stories to help children understand emotions.* New York, NY: Magination Press.

Crissey, P., & Crissey, N. (2005). *Personal hygiene? What's that got to do with me?* London, England: Jessica Kingsley Publishers.

Elder, J. (2005). *Different like me: My book of autism heroes.* London, England: Jessica Kingsley Publishers.

Fox Luchsinger, D. (2007). *Playing by the rules: A story about autism.* Bethesda, MD: Woodbine House.

Gehret, J. (1990). *Eagle eyes: A child's guide to paying attention.* Fairport, NY: Verbal Images Press.

Gray, C. (2002). *Sixth sense II.* Arlington, TX: Future Horizons.

Hall, K. (2001). *Asperger's syndrome, the universe and everything: Kenneth's book.* London, England: Jessica Kingsley Publishers.

Hoopmann, K. (2006). *All cats have Asperger syndrome.* London, England: Jessica Kingsley Publishers.

Lears, L. (1998). *Ian's walk: A story about autism.* Morton Grove, IL: Albert Whitman.

Lobby, T. (1990). *Jessica and the wolf: A story for children who have bad dreams.* New York, NY: Magination Press.

Lord, C. (2008). *Rules.* New York, NY: Scholastic.

Marcus, I., & Marcus, P. (1990). *Scary night visitors: A story for children with bedtime fears.* New York, NY: Magination Press.

Meyer, D. (Ed.). (1997). *Views from our shoes: Growing up with a brother or a sister with special needs.* Bethesda, MD: Woodbine House.

Meyer, D., Vadasy, P., & Fewell, R. (1985). *Living with a brother or sister with special needs: A book for sibs.* Seattle: University of Washington Press.

Myles, H.M., & McAfee, J. (2002). *Practical solutions to everyday challenges for children with Asperger syndrome.* Shawnee Mission, KS: Autism Asperger Publishing Company.

Ogaz, N. (2003). *Wishing on the midnight star: My Asperger brother.* London, England: Jessica Kingsley Publishers.

Reiner, A. (1991). *The potty chronicles: A story to help children adjust to toilet training.* New York, NY: Magination Press.

Thompson, T. (1996). *Andy and his yellow frisbee.* Bethesda, MD: Woodbine House.

Vermullen, P. (2000). *I am special: Introducing children and young people to their autistic spectrum disorder.* London, England: Jessica Kingsley Publishers.

Wrobel, M. (2003). *Taking care of myself: A healthy hygiene, puberty and personal curriculum for young people with autism.* Arlington, TX: Future Horizons.

Zimmerman, B. (2010). *Erin's period book.* Bloomington, IN: AuthorHouse.

Internet Resources

American Academy of Pediatric Dentistry
www.aapd.org
Asperger Syndrome Education Network
www.aspennj.org
Asperger Syndrome Partners and Individuals Resources, Encouragement and Support (for spouses and family members of adults with autism spectrum disorder)
www.aspires-relationships.com
Association for Behavior Analysis International
www.ABAinternational.org
Autism and PDD Support Network
www.autism-pdd.net/autism.htm
Autism Research at the National Institute of Child Health and Human Development
www.nichd.nih.gov/autism/
Autism Research Institute
www.autism.com/ari
Autism Resources
www.autism-resources.com
Autism Society of America
www.autism-society.org
Autism Speaks
www.autismspeaks.org
Autism Speaks, Housing and Residential Supports Tool Kit
www.autismspeaks.org/family-services/housing
Autism Speaks, Legal Matters to Consider
www.autismspeaks.org/family-services/tool-kits/transition-tool-kit/legal-matters
Collaborative Problem Solving
www.explosivechild.com
Early Start Denver Model
www.autismspeaks.org/what-autism/treatment/early-start-denver-model-esdm

Easter Seals Society
www.easterseals.com
Fathers Network
www.fathersnetwork.org
Federation for Children with Special Needs
www.fcsn.org
First Signs
www.firstsigns.org
FIRST WORDS Project
firstwords.fsu.edu/
Floortime (Developmental, Individual-Difference, Relationship-Based Model)
www.Floortime.org
Interactive Autism Network
www.ianproject.org
Lekotek (for information on toys and play)
www.lekotek.org
Meetup
www.meetup.com
National Autistic Society
www.nas.org.uk
National Bullying Prevention Center
www.pacer.org/bullying/
National Dissemination Center for Children with Disabilities
www.nichcy.org
National Sleep Foundation
www.sleepfoundation.org
NeuroDiversity
www.neurodiversity.com
OASIS @ MAAP
aspergersyndrome.org/
Parents Helping Parents
www.php.com
Pennsylvania Bureau of Autism Services
bastraining.tiu11.org/
Picture Exchange Communication System
www.pecs.com
Quality Mall
www.qualitymall.org
RDIconnect
www.RDIconnect.com
Schafer Autism Report
www.sarnet.org
Sensory Integration Network
www.sensoryintegration.org.uk
Sensory Processing Disorder Foundation
www.sinetwork.org
Sexuality Information and Education Council of the United States
www.siecus.org
Sibling Support Project
www.siblingsupport.org
Siblings of Autism
www.siblingsofautism.com

Social Communication/Emotional Regulation/Transactional Support
www.SCERTS.com
The Arc
www.thearc.org
Training and Education of Autistic and Related Communication Handicapped Children
   Autism Program
www.TEACCH.com
University of California, Davis, MIND Institute
www.ucdmc.ucdavis.edu/mindinstitute
University of California, Santa Barbara, Koegel Autism Center (for information on pivotal response treatment)
www.Education.UCSB.edu/autism
World Autism Organization
www.worldautism.org/
Wrong Planet
www.wrongplanet.net

Index